Rethinking the Western Tradition

The volumes in this series
seek to address the present debate
over the Western tradition
by reprinting key works of
that tradition along with essays
that evaluate each text from
different perspectives.

On Liberty

JOHN STUART MILL

Edited by
David Bromwich and George Kateb
with essays by
Jean Bethke Elshtain
Owen Fiss
Richard A. Posner
Jeremy Waldron

Yale University Press
New Haven and London

Printed in the United States of America by Vail-Ballou Press, Binghamton, New York.

Library of Congress Cataloging-in-Publication Data
Mill, John Stuart, 1806–1873.
On liberty / John Stuart Mill ; edited by David Bromwich and George Kateb ;
with essays by Jean Bethke Elshtain . . . [et al.].
p.   cm. — (Rethinking the Western tradition)
Includes bibliographical references (p.   ).
ISBN 0-300-09608-9 (cloth) — ISBN 0-300-09610-0 (paper)
1. Liberty. I. Bromwich, David, 1951–. II. Kateb, George.
III. Title. IV. Series.
JC585 .M76 2003
323.44 — dc21
2002006676

A catalogue record for this book is available from the British Library.
The paper in this book meets the guidelines
for permanence and durability of the Committee on
Production Guidelines for Book Longevity of the
Council on Library Resources.

10 9 8 7 6 5 4 3 2 1

Contributors

David Bromwich is Housum Professor of English at Yale University. His books include *Hazlitt: The Mind of a Critic, Politics by Other Means,* and *Skeptical Music.* He has edited a selection of Edmund Burke's speeches and writings, *On Empire, Liberty, and Reform.*

Jean Bethke Elshtain is the Laura Spelman Rockefeller Professor of Social and Political Ethics at the University of Chicago, where she is a member of the Divinity School, the Department of Political Science, and the Committee on International Relations. Her most recent book is *Jane Addams and the Dream of American Democracy* (Basic Books, 2002).

Owen Fiss is Sterling Professor of Law at Yale University.

George Kateb is William Nelson Cromwell Professor of Politics, Princeton University, and the author most recently of *Emerson and Self-Reliance* (rev. ed., Rowman and Littlefield, 2002).

Richard A. Posner is a judge of the U.S. Court of Appeals for the Seventh Circuit and a senior lecturer at the University of Chicago Law School. His most recent book is *Public Intellectuals: A Study of Decline* (Harvard University Press, 2001).

Jeremy Waldron is Maurice and Hilda Friedman Professor of Law and director of the Center for Law and Philosophy at Columbia University. His most recent books are *Law and Disagreement* (Oxford University Press, 1999), *The Dignity of Legislation* (Cambridge University Press, 1999), and *God, Locke, and Equality* (Cambridge University Press, forthcoming).

Contents

Editorial Note

The present edition of *On Liberty* makes available again the text of the first edition (London: John W. Parker and Son, 1859); and it is the integrity and importance of Mill's book itself that we would stress. Readers new to *On Liberty* are encouraged to read it and allow the argument to sink in before they turn to the introduction or the supplementary essays. From the passage of time, there are references or allusions that now need clarifying. Our rule has been to supply a note wherever a modern reader might reasonably stop for an explanation Mill does not give; but the local sense of his words commonly explains itself, or is soon explained by the argumentative context. Mill wrote an English that has not faded much in a century and a half. Few works by his contemporaries have lasted so well with so little need to account for changing usage.

A biographical essay by David Bromwich and an interpretative essay by George Kateb together make up the introduction. The aim has been at once to meditate on the intricate design of *On Liberty* and to show its coherence with the preoccupations of a long career of thought. Mill wrote this book in a spirit of contest, and it has attracted controversy ever since: a tradition we seek to continue. The four scholars invited to contribute the additional essays here — Owen Fiss, Richard Posner, Jean Bethke Elshtain, and Jeremy Waldron — were encouraged to connect Mill's historical concerns, as much as they wished, with the discussion of liberty today in such fields as law, ethics, and politics. Apart from that suggestion, no attempt was made to enforce or elicit uniformity.

In a generous survey, Owen Fiss brings out the relevance to American constitutional law of Mill's definitions of personal and political liberty, and the resource the book still offers in debates on the shifting boundary between freedom of speech and freedom of expression. Richard Posner finds a persuasive analogy between economic individualism, with its antipaternal reliance on free markets, and moral individuality, with its rejection of social meddling in the lives of persons. Jean Bethke Elshtain criticizes the Mill of *On Liberty* and other writings for a failure to take stock of instincts that are prior to rights, and a consequent failure to admit, alongside the principle of liberty, a rival and complementary principle of authority. Finally, Jeremy Waldron explores an abiding tension in Mill's argument between the freedom of one person to act unconventionally and the freedom of another to criticize and rally influence against unconventional behavior.

These essays approach *On Liberty* with varying degrees of formality, and from remarkably disparate motives. They draw their incitement from elements so discrete and emphatic as to call attention once more to the range of the book: the moral premise that extends liberty to every action short of harm to others; the intuition that personal liberty unconditionally but exclusively belongs to people who can be responsible for themselves; the idea that an absorbing care for equality may render individuality a good achieved by few and despised by many; the hope that respect for individuality nevertheless may fortify a sense of human dignity that applies to all human beings. The contributors scarcely agree on a right method for pursuing any or all of these intimations. They agree that Mill's thinking on liberty is a provocation to further thought.

A Note on the Life and Thought of John Stuart Mill

DAVID BROMWICH

John Stuart Mill said in his *Autobiography* that his father, James Mill, was "the last of the eighteenth century." He intended a deep homage to the man who had educated him to carry on the work of social amelioration and enlightenment — an homage a little touched by irony, since James Mill did in fact live most of his life in the nineteenth century. But the description of his father also implies a judgment by John Stuart Mill of himself. What accomplishments of the earlier epoch did he look back on with so mingled a sense of loyalty and reserve? The philosophers of the Enlightenment believed that progress would come from clearing away the unnecessary evils of life. The worst of these was cruelty, and in the later eighteenth century one can discern, in writers as various as Johnson, Hume, Wesley, and Bentham, a new vehemence of detestation for cruelty. The milder evils were thought to derive largely from the customs of society itself, a world of inconveniences multiplied by prejudice and superstition. Yet there were eccentricities or irregularities, seemingly at home in human nature, which the Enlightenment could not pretend to reform altogether. To this category belonged madness as well as genius — including the genius of poetry, with its ardent subjection to feeling. On the whole the passions gave the Enlightenment more trouble than did virtue and vice and the definition of a happy life.

James Mill's hero and mentor, Jeremy Bentham, had declared that all poetry was misrepresentation. His son John would come to define poetry in words of earnest praise as "feeling confessing itself to itself." The difference between these sentiments tells much of the story of the development of John Stuart Mill. A transparent representation of things in words had been part of the larger Enlightenment project of "perfectibility." Yet of all the imaginable helps toward perfection, the surest was supposed to come from the adoption by society of Bentham's standard of utility, which offered a system for the exact calculation of the pleasures and pains that follow from any proposed action. The aim was to achieve the greatest good for the greatest number of persons; the index of good was pleasure, and the sum of pleasures, happiness. Though John Stuart Mill never doubted the truth in this way of thinking about morals, Bentham's formulae of pleasure and pain would come to seem to him far from satisfactory. For the late eighteenth and early nineteenth centuries had discovered other truths besides that of utility. Romanticism, in the writings of Rousseau, Goethe, Schiller, Wordsworth, and Coleridge, by the scope and freedom it gave the imagination had sought to change the very texture of human thought and feeling. The result was to turn the energies of the Enlightenment toward a fresh concern with the experience of individuality. Every thinking, feeling, reading person in the next generation felt the excitement of the new mood, and the younger Mill was among those who felt it most strongly. He started out in his teens and twenties as a utilitarian bigot, an exquisite enforcer of pure rationality. Yet he was to become the thinker of all the nineteenth century in whom romanticism and utilitarianism were most nearly joined. The consequences are visible in the pattern of his career; and they can be felt in his way of forming sentences. He exhibits at last an intelligence that is scrupulous and unavoidably hesitant. He is the most downright and yet the most corrigible of thinkers.

Born on May 20, 1806, John Stuart Mill was the first child in a family of nine brothers and sisters. They lived in a house owned by Bentham in Queen Square, and the great philosopher of law and legislation was a familiar domestic presence. James Mill designed for his son an education in science and society that aimed to prepare him for life as a radical reformer of thought. He began learning Greek when he was three years old, Latin when he was seven; the study of logic was deferred to his thirteenth year, and political economy to his fourteenth. By that time, James Mill had become the intellectual patron of the political economist David Ricardo, whose doctrine on the relation between labor and value and on the all-importance of rent would define a new school of economics. Accordingly, John, in his early teens, absorbed at once the elementary concepts of the science and the vanguard theory that was to dominate the next generation. Again, instead of a professional course of study in the law, it was arranged for him to take lessons from John Austin, a family friend later to be known as one of the great English writers on jurisprudence. Meanwhile, James Mill was working hard at the *History of British India,* which appeared in three volumes in 1817. His great work was performed, as John Stuart Mill records with wonder in his *Autobiography,* under conditions of almost constant distraction, with young John interrupting him for checks on his own tutoring of the younger children or to find out the English meanings of Greek words. John Stuart Mill in his later life was fond of the text "the night cometh when no man can work." In his childhood, he always had before him an example of indefatigable work.

Though *agnosticism* was not a word known to the generation of James Mill, he had come to the conclusion (as the *Autobiography* puts it) that "concerning the origin of things nothing whatever can be known." The children of the family were baptized, but John, at least, shared with his father a settled indifference to the Christian religion. Too powerful an institution to be always resisted overtly, it was never in any case to be relied on as an agency for reform. "I looked upon the modern," Mill recalls, "exactly as I did upon the ancient religion, as something which in no way concerned me. It did not seem to me more strange that English people should believe what I did not, than that the men I read of in Herodotus should have done so."[1] The secular virtues that his father inculcated were justice, temperance, truthfulness, perseverance; also "readiness to encounter pain and especially labour; regard for the public good; estimation of persons according to their merits, and of things according to their intrinsic usefulness; a life of exertion, in contradiction to one of self-indulgent sloth."

John found his first break from the regimen in the summer of 1820 when he commenced a long year in the south of France with the family of Sir Samuel Bentham. Even then, his energies were well employed. On that visit he learned French and immersed himself in the literature of continental liberalism. A love of the grand and heroic came to him early and never departed: his favorite book was Pope's translation of the *Iliad,* which Mill says he read twenty times. This interest now combined with his studies of French society, and on his return to England he submitted himself to a course of reading in the French Revolution, a subject that would become a lifelong fascination. He says in his *Autobiography* that he liked to imagine himself a Girondin at an English convention, ready to sacrifice himself for a liberal creed of the common good. It was about this time, in his middle teens, that, under the guidance of John Austin, he read Dumont's redaction of Bentham's *Traité de legislation.* When he laid down the final volume of the book, "I had become," says Mill, "a different being." Now like the Girondins he had a cause and a creed. It took nothing from the charm of the discovery that the creed had been his father's all along.

In 1822–23, Mill formed the plan for a Utilitarian Society. "With a boy's fondness for a name and a banner," he remembers, "I seized on the word, and for some years called myself and others by it as a sectarian appellation." The young Benthamites were provocative advocates of the useful. They were polemicists against all in society that was savage, archaic, recondite, superfluous, iniquitous, and sunk in mystification. What good is a thing, they asked, if it does not promote happiness? And in judging of happiness, what is the pride and pleasure of a few beside the wretchedness or inconvenience of millions? Their weapon was exposure, their hope was efficiency. The members of the small society, never so many as ten, went on meeting regularly into 1826. Another development of those years would carry broader consequences for Mill. In 1823 James Mill obtained for John an appointment, under himself, in the office of the Examiner of Correspondence of the East India Company. It was a position the younger Mill would occupy for the next thirty-five years, achieving, when finally he was appointed examiner, the second–most powerful office of the company. He would give credit to the sustained experience of a responsible corporate post for fixing in his mind how theories and general views must make their way in practice. The work at India House accustomed Mill "to see and hear the difficulties of every course, and the means of obviating them, stated and discussed deliberately with a view to execution."

Enlightened opinion on the political left, George Orwell observes in his essay on Kipling, is chronically weakened by a failure "to imagine what action and responsibility are like." It seems fair to extend this charge to many nineteenth-century radicals: they refused to think like people who have to sacrifice one good to achieve another. Yet the criticism does not apply to John Stuart Mill in any phase of his career. In his early youth, Mill was a sectarian fanatic with little tolerance for persons outside the Benthamite thrall, but he had a solution for every problem, he believed the only morality was the calculus of general happiness, and he expected his party to ascend to power imminently. One catches a glimpse of the confidence of the young "philosophic radical" in a letter of October 1831 to his friend John Sterling, when the popular pressure for a reform bill and the government's tardiness and insensitivity stir him to predict a seizure of power by a revolutionary assembly. The storm he thinks will not let up until "the whole of the existing institutions of society are levelled with the ground." This would be acceptable, says Mill to Sterling, so long as the destruction left "but a few dozens of persons safe (whom you and I could select) to be missionaries of the great truths in which alone there is any well-being for mankind." By contrast, the mature thinker whom one starts to see a few years later is remarkable for his patience. He is prepared to measure the obstacle posed by "the difficulties of every course" and to enter into discussion "with a view to execution." He has by then acquired a tact and a skill—to quote again from his comment on his work at India House — which have enabled him to find out "by practice the mode of putting a thought which gives it easiest admittance into minds not prepared for it by habit." At the same time he has grown more "conversant with the difficulties of moving bodies of men, the necessities of compromise, the art of sacrificing the non-essential to preserve the essential."

Public debate and public service would never amount to more than one walk of Mill's ambition. Another direction was intellectual and literary. The first issue of the *Westminster Review,* a journal founded to serve the cause of the philosophic radicals, appeared in January 1824. It contained a devastating analysis by James Mill of the ideology of the Whig *Edinburgh Review.* Far from representing the common interest of the middle class and the nation, the established journal was shown to stand for the party interest of an elite of wealthy manufacturers and landowners. The younger Mill made his debut in a sequel to his father's article that exposed the *Edinburgh* taste to the impartial measure of utility. Why, he asked, in all its praises of Shakespeare did not the *Edinburgh* utter "even a wish that the moral tendency of his plays had been more decided"? He wrote like a disciple. But by his own testimony, already in his late teens Mill realized that his political imagination had taken him beyond his father's opinions. He did not agree with James Mill that women could justifiably be excluded from the franchise on the ground that their interests were identical with those of men. Nevertheless, in his early articles for the *Westminster,* John Stuart Mill showed an overriding solidarity of purpose with the utilitarians. They shared, he says, "an almost unbounded confidence in the efficacy of two things: representative government, and complete freedom of discussion." Here they were following a long radical tradition. James Mill himself had remarked in 1813: "Grant, in any quarter of the globe, a reading people and a free press — and the prejudices on which misrule supports itself will gradually and silently disappear."[2] As early as 1793, William Godwin in *Political Justice* had argued that the truth could never be told so as to be understood and not be believed. The path, in short, from clear knowledge of the evidence, as known by an impartial spectator, to agreement on correct propositions concerning the moral and natural world was supposed by the utilitarians to be impeded only by selfishness and ignorance. The remedy for selfishness was to place the levers of power in the hands of the enlightened middle class, who alone could act for the common good. Incapacities arising from ignorance were to be solved by education.

Belief in the final triumph of progress through enlightenment seems always to have been an inseparable element of John Stuart Mill's thought. So much so that this inheritance from his father and Bentham and perhaps from Godwin too — a faith in the power of truth to ignite conviction — may account for some of the few questions that are not asked in his writings on morals and politics. The optimism anyway was broadly shared by other schools of utopian thought. Mill's sect held one of their public debates against the disciples of Robert Owen, on the merits of Owen's system of co-operative labor and employment. From every such encounter, Mill himself learned what he could and enlarged his store of tactics. And yet, with this confidence and this sense of solidarity, at the height of his youthful suc-cess — a position settled at India House, spare hours given to work for benevolent causes whose influence was growing, and an immense and useful intellectual labor completed at the age of eighteen: the editing of the five volumes of Bentham on evidence — at this pinnacle of consummated apprenticeship he felt his entire being stunned and appalled by a doubt. "In a dull state of nerves, such as everybody is occasionally liable to," he had asked himself what he would feel at the moment if all the reforms he was working for were realized. Would he be happy? He knew that he would not; and the recognition was shattering. It was as if the ground beneath him had fallen away. "The end had ceased to charm, and how could there ever again be any interest in the means? I seemed to have nothing left to live for" (1: 139). In the *Autobiography,* he blames the dejection that followed, in part, on the habit of analysis that had pervaded his conduct of life. Still, given his belief in the connection between reform and happiness, he could not but feel "that the flaw in my life, must be a flaw in life itself; that the question was, whether, if the reformers of society and government could succeed in their objects, and every person in the community were free and in a state of physical comfort, the pleasures of life, being no longer kept up by struggle and privation, would cease to be pleasures" (1: 149).

This crisis of Mill's development lasted for a single winter or for several years, depending on which biographer one trusts, and which mood of Mill's own recollections is allowed to carry authority. What is certain is that his pages about it bear a striking resemblance to William Wordsworth's de-scription of a similar crisis in the mid-1790s. Wordsworth, too, had been a convert to an ethics of utility. He had looked to political theory for an engine to effect the reforms the French Revolution had failed to accomplish in practice. As he recounts in book XI of *The Prelude,* he searched the springs of human action for help from impersonal calculations,

> till, demanding formal *proof,*
> And seeking it in every thing, I lost
> All feeling of conviction.

The result, says Wordsworth, was an "utter loss of hope itself / And things to hope for." Mill in his time of disenchantment could have known nothing of the coincidence: *The Prelude* was not yet published and the facts of the poet's early life were hidden. But it is interesting that Mill should have found encouragement in his despair by reading the poems of Wordsworth. More than any other literature, he says, they restored for him a balance between the understanding and what he calls "the internal culture of the individual" — feelings and ways of adapting to experience that are inscrutable to a social estimate of helpful or harmful consequences. The poems by Wordsworth that Mill was reading were intended to serve as reminders of an inward life. They work by an undeviating record of encounters between person and person, or between person and place, and so produce small narratives, or effusions, which tell of the accidents by which "feeling comes in aid / Of feeling, if but once we have been strong." The poems all tend to show that the mere life of a human being is a self-sufficing good. Their morality is profoundly anti-utilitarian.

In the self-examination that followed the crisis, Mill found himself reading Coleridge and Goethe and his own contemporary Thomas Carlyle, from whose early writings he would derive the doctrine of "anti-self consciousness." The unhappy self, as Carlyle diagnosed it in his essay "Characteristics" and in his grotesque and original autobiography, *Sartor Resartus,* can draw no support by refining upon ideas of happiness, or by thinking about the self that is to be happy. The only cure lies in subduing oneself to work, for an end beyond personal or collective self-interest, an end whose good is admitted to be incalculable. Mill sought conscientiously now to correct a pressure in himself toward the acceptance of half-truths — all of natural science, in the view of the thinkers he was reading, embodied a half-truth about nature — and he aspired to the Goethean ideal of "many-sidedness."

He was also studying the work of the Saint-Simonians and their theorist Auguste Comte, and taking heart from the division of progress into a dialectic of "organic" and "critical" epochs. On this scheme, the characteristic undertakings of analysis and imagination could be seen as supplementary and not antagonistic. A feature of Comte's writings certain to have repelled Mill was their insistence on the intellectual and moral inferiority of women. But he was capable of simply discarding the stray elements of a system that he found wrong-headed; and he sympathized in principle with Comte's idea for a picked body of persons charged with the keeping and renovation of knowledge. To Mill, the possibility of such an artificial class of authorized guardians was always attractive; he would be equally drawn to it, under a more theological description, in Coleridge's account of a "clerisy." In later writings he mocked the compulsive detail with which Comte elaborated the offices, the dignities and rituals, the mandatory worship by a grateful society of the secular sages of progress: an excess of speculative self-absorption of a sort that Mill could only regard with distaste. Yet the acknowledgment of an outstanding class appeared to him necessary in order to civilize democracy.

That a democratic society might be incapable of realizing any benefit from its greatest minds, was a nightmare that haunted Mill, as it did Matthew Arnold and many others of the mid-Victorian generation. A similar fear is a recurrent motive in the writings of Tocqueville; and of all the thinkers Mill read in his adult life, it was Tocqueville who had the longest-lasting and the deepest impact. Mill reviewed both volumes of *Democracy in America,* the first in 1835, the second in 1840, and these articles reveal a transition in his own thinking. Tocqueville had noticed in America a striking contrast between the plenitude of individual talents over-all and their absence from places of high visibility in the public life of the nation. Mill says in his first review of Tocqueville, responding to this evident division between power and competence, "The people ought to be the masters, but they are masters who must employ servants more skillful than themselves" (18: 72). A main task of democracy becomes therefore the education of the people for the performance of that choice.

Yet even as he sought assistance from Tocqueville on the way to assure a connection between intelligence and government, Mill had acquired a fresh interest in the relation between individual genius and the energy that enables a society to flourish rather than stagnate. Nothing could be further from Tocqueville's prudent and aristocratic sympathy with democratic progress than Carlyle's ferocious hatred of aristocracy and progress, or his account of the unconscious affinity by which a race discovers its appropriate heroes. Yet, improbably, the two British writers became friends. Mill was happy to submit himself to Carlyle for the virtues that made him the very type of the inspired social critic. "You," he wrote to Carlyle in the autumn of 1831, "I look upon as an artist, and perhaps the only genuine one now living in this country."

This was a time when Mill was struggling to introduce into reform circles "other ideas and another tone" than those of James Mill and Jeremy Bentham, "and to obtain for my own shade of opinion a fair representation." It would prove a difficult victory to carry openly — though a different tone and shading, partly traceable to Carlyle, might have been detected in the late 1830s in some of the younger Mill's essays for the *London and*

Westminster Review (which merged the new *London Review* and the old *Westminster*). Carlyle, to say it plainly, was a guru who cast an ineffable spell over some persons, and Mill, with his new and restless habit of self-questioning, seems to have traveled far on the path of subjection. Possibly he would have gone farther had he not met, and soon after fallen in love with, Harriet Taylor, whom his *Autobiography* introduces by a comparison to Carlyle: "more a poet than he, and more a thinker than I—whose mind and nature included his, and infinitely more." Mill was twenty-four years old when they met, and Mrs. Taylor was twenty-two; her husband, John Taylor, was a prosperous merchant in the city; she was an intense and accurate follower of the teachings of Shelley on love, sincerity, and free-dom—believing that the ties that conventionally bind persons in society have nothing to do with the deeper affinities between soul and soul. She loved Mill and thought of leaving Taylor, but, drawn back by their children and by residual but real feelings of friendship for Taylor, she decided on another arrangement, to which her husband eventually consented. Harriet Taylor and John Stuart Mill would dine together, spend hours together at a separate residence, and, so far as she inclined, be treated as a couple at social gatherings, while she remained married to John Taylor. It is commonly assumed that Mill's belief in the moral and political equality of women was arrived at under Mrs. Taylor's guidance. In fact he held these views before he met her, and they were a reason for her interest in him.

In the *Autobiography* and elsewhere, Mill's language about Harriet Taylor has an effusiveness of praise and a humility of self-subordination that have made some readers doubt the realism of the portrait and others wonder whether she was not the virtual author of the works whose debt to her he proclaims. It is well therefore to recall the impression of a keen observer who would not have erred by excessive tenderness. Mrs. Taylor was, thought Carlyle when he met her, "a living romance heroine, of the clearest insight, of the royalest volition, very interesting, of questionable destiny, not above five-and-twenty." Mrs. Taylor's voice of thought and the idiom of her prose were often strikingly close to Mill's. We are right to find a germ of *On Liberty* in an early essay of Mill's like "Civilization." We are right to find a germ of it, too, in an essay Mrs. Taylor wrote in her mid-twenties. She there asserted that all conformity, religious, political, moral, and social, agrees in one point, "hostility to individual character," and she added: "What is called the opinion of Society is . . . a combination of the many weak, against the few strong: an association of the mentally listless to punish any manifestation of mental independence. The remedy is, to make all strong enough to stand alone."[3] She was as inveterate as the elder Mill in her rejection of privilege, as wary as the younger in her scrutiny of conventions, and far more consistent than either in her hatred of paternalism. When John Stuart Mill, in mid-career, withdraws his defense of the secret ballot as a necessary feature of widened suffrage, to attack it as an instrument likely to foster mental dependency and listlessness, we can certainly see the impact of Harriet Taylor's thinking on his receptive intellect. Yet it is also a change consistent with the pattern of his own thought and temperament.

By 1840 Mill's views of morality and society had become pretty much what they would remain. He had begun drafting his essay on Bentham in 1833, a year after Bentham's death. In 1836, James Mill died; and at that moment, for all his sorrow John Stuart Mill must have felt that an enormous burden had been lifted. "Bentham" was published in revised form in 1838, and its companion-piece "Coleridge" in 1840. Coleridge is praised for teaching the latent reason that may inhere in ancient and apparently useless practices, while Bentham is criticized for failing to derive light from other minds. Yet it is clear in both essays that Mill considers himself — free now of actual oversight by the elders of reform — decidedly a thinker of Bentham's party. What renders his service unique is his eagerness to draw light from other minds. In his political thought and practice, Mill continued to be instructed by Tocqueville. A new field of exertion was to show how civil associations might offset the aggrandizing tendency of government. Tocqueville, however, also fortified Mill with reasons to support his belief in centralized supervision in some areas of social life, in education above all. The presiding aim of his politics, he remarks in the *Autobiography,* from now on would be to steer "carefully between the two errors" of familiar partiality for local self-government and a bureaucratic trust of central institutions.

Mill recounts his life as a story of what the nineteenth century made of the eighteenth; and one may sum up his growth in the 1840s in the light of that larger shift. He turned away from the belief in human perfectibility and toward a belief in gradual reform. He no longer looked for a cure of the irregularities of human nature but saw toleration as the means, and variety and individuality as the end, of all of human existence. As much as ever, he hoped to find a counterpoise against the errors of the majority in the talents of people exceptional for their depth of knowledge and range of experience. Of the practical wisdom of such an elite, Mill formed a highly favorable picture during his years of service at India House. This side of his politics was to emerge most plainly in 1857, the year of the Indian Mutiny, when Palmerston's ministry introduced the Act for the Better Government of

India—in effect, a measure to place control of the subcontinent under the direct authority of the Crown. Mill opposed the act in an eloquent petition that received wide circulation, and many of his suggestions were adopted when Lord Grey succeeded Palmerston as prime minister. This petition argued that the company's Home Government of India, in view of its ultimate accountability to Parliament, served as a deliberative check of the sort proper in a mixed constitutional system, and that it thereby helped British rule to exemplify a thoughtful combination of local agency and central authority.

In 1836 he had suffered a general physical collapse, which left him with weakened lungs and for many months sapped his power for sustained work. Yet it was during the long months of his recovery that he found his great theme of sociality and individuality and the necessary tension between them. Mill himself believed that his lasting fame would be associated most with *On Liberty,* which brought the theme to a brave finality of statement, but his second candidate was the *System of Logic,* which he worked on intermittently from 1837 and published in 1843. One circumstance of its publication tells us a great deal about nineteenth-century intellectual manners and the state of controversy that Mill could take for granted.

When composing the *Logic* he had looked for a guide to "spread out before me the generalities and processes of the sciences," and had found it in 1837 in William Whewell's *History of the Inductive Sciences,* whose evidence and information he gratefully diverted to his own purposes. Yet the philosophy of that formidable work "appeared open to objection": Whewell was an intuitionist, and Mill's *Logic* was written to be, as in fact it became, the canonical presentation of the rival empiricist theory which derived all thought from experience and association. While Mill was revising the *Logic,* Whewell published his *Philosophy of the Inductive Sciences,* and this provided, says Mill, "what I greatly desired, a full treatment of the subject by an antagonist," which allowed his own views to emerge the more strongly in contrast. He introduced polemical passages in the hope of eliciting a reply from Whewell — only a spirited debate could draw many readers to so long a work on so abstract a subject — and Whewell did reply, even if "not till 1850, just in time for me to answer him in the third edition." The *Logic,* like all of Mill's work, was written to advance an argument with practical consequences. The prospects for reform would be dimmer if it were supposed that the mental processes of human beings were merely natural and intuitive, instead of being acquired from experience and open to modification by changes of experience. Mill sought to press his theory against an articulate, established, and capable opponent, in the expectation that the discussion thus joined would bring the general knowledge of the subject to a more edifying stage.

His second full-scale work, the *Principles of Political Economy,* was published in 1848, a year important for other reasons. The Chartist Movement of the 1830s had already drawn Mill to recognize the future importance of organized laborers and their proposals of reform: he called the protests of that time "the revolt of nearly all the active talent, and a great part of the physical force, of the working classes, against their whole relation to society." But the revolutions of Europe in 1848 gave a shock to opinion that did not soon abate. They astonished by their intensity and by the nature of the discontents which they laid bare: nothing, it seemed, short of democratic representation and an assurance of elementary rights to workers could appease the new self-estimate of the people. The success of counter-revolution only deepened the feeling of the change. These events divided the British liberals of the day, moving some much further toward socialism than they could have thought possible before, others toward an implicit embrace of stability and a dread of disorder that gave them a common ground with the Tory party. Among Mill's circle John Austin was of the latter group, Harriet Taylor decisively of the former. She was stirred to feelings of pity for the wretched and sympathy with the struggles of working men to improve their lot. Mill came around to her view of the events, and of the necessities of reform that they indicated: he would register the change of his opinions in the third edition of the *Political Economy,* with its radical sketch of "the Probable Futurity of the Labouring Classes." When, in 1848, Mill was offered joint management of the *Morning Chronicle,* Harriet Taylor asked her husband to purchase it for him to prevent its falling into Tory hands. John Taylor thought better of the suggestion; that she could venture it shows Mrs. Taylor's confidence.

In 1849 John Taylor died. His wife had nursed him alone during the last weeks, and only after a long interval was Mill permitted to marry her. He would say in the *Autobiography* that the part her thought played in his writings could not be disentangled from his own — "all my published writings were as much her work as mine; her share in them constantly increasing as the years advanced." They were to enjoy only seven years of marriage before her death of tuberculosis at the age of fifty-six. But these years of intimacy hastened another change in Mill's life that bears a curious relation to his thought. He was a man, for those who knew him well, deeply attentive to others and naturally lovable. James Fitzjames Stephen, one of his bitterest opponents in public debate, said that "one who knew Mill only through his writings knew but half of him, and that not the best half." Yet Mill had never had a use for what is called, colloquially, "society," and with the late-found intensity of his relationship with Harriet Mill, his interest in encountering people beyond his familiar associates seems to have vanished. The *Autobiography* gives a memorable explanation:

> The sole attraction of what is called society to those who not are at the top of the tree, is the hope of being aided to climb a little higher in it; while to those who are already at the top, it is chiefly a compliance with custom, and with the supposed requirements of their station. To a person of any but a very common order in thought or feeling, such society, unless he has personal objects to serve by it, must be supremely unattractive: and most people, in the present day, of any really high class of intellect, make their contact with it so slight, and at such long intervals, as to be almost considered as retiring from it altogether. . . . Persons even of intellectual aspirations had much better, if they can, make their habitual associates of at least their equals, and as far as possible, their superiors in knowledge, intellect, and elevation of sentiment. Moreover, if the character is formed, and the mind made up, on the few cardinal points of human opinion, agreement of conviction and feeling on these has been felt in all times to be an essential requisite of anything worthy the name of friendship. (1: 235–37)

The observation makes an unexpected supplement to his testimony on the way his *Logic* was written with a deliberate view to controversy.

Mill's empiricism had pointed to the growth of the mind by association. Such growth, he argued, was an affair of experience and induction. Yet his own practice in the 1850s, which the passage above recommends for adoption by others, calls for isolation of the thinker from ordinary experiences and associations once the mind and character are settled regarding the "few central points." He gives two reasons for this: that the company of most human beings cannot excite a thinker to fresh thoughts; and that the minds of people in society require a conformity that is alien to the special conditions needed to foster discovery. An original plan of life has therefore, as one of its prerequisites, withdrawal from all society except that of one's most intelligent, frank, and uncensorious contemporaries, in whose presence open discussion is a benefit free as air. Such people can be trusted not to mistake opposition for animosity; additional explanations hardly ever have to be made to them. Yet from the perspective of Mill's broader thinking on liberty, the question may be asked, Where do *they* derive the experiences that have caused this exemplary aliveness? Not all of it can be traced to their acquaintance with each other, for they were distinctive before the acquaintance began; but Mill's argument on the stultifying effects of society presumes that any other resource is futile — the circle has been closed convincingly. The freedom of all within has been obtained by excluding most of the imaginable candidates, and those who live and think in such conditions are supposed to be gainers by the economy. Mill has touched a contradiction between the manners of an intellectual elite and its avowed intentions — a contradiction he did not invent, and which remains a puzzle in the commercial democracies today. The observation, like so much else in the *Autobiography,* is to be prized for its clarity and a certain stubborn honesty. Yet Mill himself does not seem fully conscious of the paradox.

The known conditions of the marriage of John Stuart and Harriet Mill, and his confession of a debt to her that deepens in the 1850s, have prompted many commentators to describe Mill in this phase as intellectually dependent. A sharp formulation of the view was offered by a biographer, Michael St. John Packe, who cannot be accused of hostility to Mill. "Except for the *Logic,*" writes Packe, "the principles underlying the more important works of John Stuart Mill were defined, although not actually composed, by Harriet Taylor. And whatever in them cannot be ascribed to his lucid reasoning must be attributed to the sheer force of her personality."[4] The major works in question are *On Liberty* (1859), *Utilitarianism* (1861), *Considerations on Representative Government* (1863), and *The Subjection of Women* (1869). Some part of Mill's claim of authorship is here being challenged, with Mill's own sanction to some degree. But it is wrong to suppose that at this distance we can correctly assign praise and blame, or settle a precise attribution. What we do know is that John Stuart Mill was the more practiced writer of the two. Harriet Mill was gifted with a more susceptible sympathy and a capacity even greater than his for feeling sure of herself when she was at variance with her earlier views.

Undoubtedly, the great works of Mill's later life — especially *On Liberty,* which she went over sentence by sentence, and *The Subjection of Women,* which had its start in her essay "The Enfranchisement of Women" — owed a great deal to Harriet Mill's thinking. They owed more to a continuous dialogue that prompted Mill's argument even before he sat down to write. She played the part that an intimate friend may often have in friendship, where one says of the other "If she disagrees and thinks *this* way, it is probably some sluggishness or obtuseness of feeling in me that prevented my arriving at a similar thought; and if we go into the matter deeply enough, there is a strong chance that I will come to agree with her after all." Both were adherents of a view in which their teachers Bentham and Shelley oddly agree: in a question of some moment where two thoughtful persons are divided, one with weak predispositions on one side, the other with strong convictions on the other, it is the person who holds the strong convictions (however unsupported by convention) who deserves the more attentive hearing.

In matters concerning imagination, the defense of individuality, and the rights of working men, Mill seems regularly to have accorded priority of perception to his wife, while forming his ultimate opinions for himself. Such a working relationship is far commoner in intellectual life and in the arts than is widely supposed. A certain high-handedness also went with the pride of their mutual sympathy and isolation. The couple, defensive and responding to apparent slights from Mill's sisters after their marriage, took an officious tone which does not consort well with the indifference they professed toward conventional manners; their dealings with Mill's brother George — who admired both of them nearly to veneration — in response to an awkward letter of his were absurdly chastising and unforgiving; while toward Mill's mother (whom his *Autobiography* does not mention) they were cool and unresponsive even in her final days. The sanctity of John Stuart and Harriet Mill in each other's eyes did not improve the alertness of either regarding the society in which they moved. But all things considered, they lived a courageous, if not an unselfish, life together, and by the time of Harriet's death in November 1858 they had run the risk of opprobrium and sustained their group of two with little apparent bitterness. They would have said for their long companionship that it succeeded in holding off "the deep slumber of a decided opinion" — an untraced quotation in the text of *On Liberty* that either John Stuart or Harriet Mill could have written.

Mill's promotion in 1856 to Examiner of India Correspondence gave an added weight to his resignation in 1858 on the ground that the administration of India had become "a thing to be scrambled for by the second and third class of English parliamentary politicians." Echoes of his resistance to the change are still audible in the last chapter of *Representative Government;* in retrospect he seems to have looked on India House as the nearest approach the empire had made to a disinterested civil service. His views on democracy and administration were meant, he says in that book, to achieve "the combination of complete popular control of public affairs, with the greatest attainable perfection of skilled agency"; a description that accords with the summary by A. V. Dicey, in *Law and Public Opinion in England During the Nineteenth Century,* of the objects of Benthamite legislation: "the transference of political power into the hands of the class which it was supposed was large enough and intelligent enough to identify its own interest with the interest of the greatest number — the promotion of humanitarianism — the extension of individual liberty — the creation of adequate legal machinery for the protection of the equal rights of all citizens."[5] Of course, the extension of individual liberty would require growing numbers of people to be taught, by their *experience* of voting and other new rights, to consider themselves as individuals. With the hope of guiding that development, Mill in 1865 arranged for the publication of cheaply available "People's Editions" of his *Political Economy, On Liberty,* and *Representative Government.*

In the same year he was asked by some electors to stand as parliamentary candidate for Westminster. The request had been made once before and politely refused, when Mill felt bound by other commitments, but now he welcomed the opportunity. In a letter of response, he declared his opinions on several subjects, including his belief in women's suffrage. When asked, at a meeting whose audience was mainly working class, whether he had written that the working classes in England "though differing from those of some other countries in being ashamed of lying, are yet generally liars" (he had indeed said as much in 1859 in his "Thoughts on Parliamentary Reform"), Mill answered "I did" and was roundly applauded. The crowd's appreciation of his honesty outweighed any sense of injury. But what sort of candidate were the electors being asked to judge? Mill at this time stood in the vanguard of radical opinion on women's rights, on Irish land reform, and on the rights of workers to organize. He believed that the British empire served on the whole to assist the progress of the nations it subordinated; that it did so with a generosity superior to that of other European nations; and that one of its worst errors was to pretend, with the swagger of *Realpolitik,* to act from more selfish motives than it mostly did act upon.

These last views had been published in 1859, in "A Few Words on Non-Intervention," where Mill asserts it to be the duty of a powerful and prosperous nation to assist freedom and progress where it can, even where it risks self-sacrifice in doing so. What is wrong is for such a nation, by military or commercial intervention, to pretend to create the conditions for liberty among a people who have not yet the spirit or the resources to achieve liberty for themselves. His ideas of foreign policy were benevolent, respectful of autonomy in the already autonomous, and as antipaternalist as is consistent with the perpetuation of empire. In short, the candidate of 1865 was notable for his radicalism, conservatism, heterodoxy. He had stood out most fiercely in recent years for his defense of the Union against the slave power in the American civil war — a radical position to take in England, where middle-class sentiment was preponderantly for the South. "The

South," wrote Mill in 1862, "are in rebellion not for simple slavery; they are in rebellion for the right of burning human creatures alive."[6]

He was one of the Liberals in the House of Commons who kept up the drumbeat for passage of a second reform bill. Two other issues he confronted during his term from 1866 to 1868 bring out the depth of his commitments. Mill was opposed to slavery *in principle* — opposed, that is, to any human bond that threatened coercion, or that narrowed the scope of personal responsibility. In October 1865, in Jamaica, a protest by Negroes against the callous policies of Governor Edward John Eyre had turned into a violent outbreak by an armed band of rebels who killed twenty-two people. In retaliation, Governor Eyre hanged the supposed ringleader, without counsel or witnesses, and enforced martial law for a full month. The governor's soldiers enjoyed unlimited freedom to identify rebels and put them to death, and floggings of men, women, and children became commonplace. By the end of the month, the rule of martial law accounted for the deaths of 586 persons; yet on his return to England, Governor Eyre received a hero's welcome. Memories of the Indian Mutiny of 1857 were still alive, and it was felt that he had dealt wisely and severely, by anticipation, with the menace of an uprising by a subject people. Carlyle among others entertained the idea of the reimposition of slavery. Mill for his part became a leader of the Jamaica Committee, which investigated the conduct of the governor and worked to have him indicted in the months that followed. By seeking the prosecution of Eyre for murder, and, when that proved impossible, for high crimes and misdemeanors, Mill backed his own principle that in a matter of violence by the state against individuals the burden of proof always lies with the state.

Another engagement is as revealing of his politics and his tactical sense. He favored a widening of democracy specifically by the educational means of welcoming the participation of the people in free discussions. On July 23, 1866, a crowd of workingmen, denied permission to assemble at a mass meeting in Hyde Park, wrangled with the police and then became more unruly — picking up railings, trampling flower gardens, and breaking windows in Belgravia. When, in May 1867, the government brought up a bill to prohibit meetings in Hyde Park, Mill was among the small group in Parliament who filibustered to prevent its passage.

Yet he took his greatest intellectual risk on a different front by the publication of *The Subjection of Women*. Mill's argument there interprets the relation of men to women as an instance of the relation of master to slave or, at best, of a member of a superior to that of an inferior class. It shows how the discriminations supposed to arise from nature are in fact the product of artifice, of experience and association, and of the desire of a satisfied group to preserve advantages against a group it has disqualified from representation. This was his father's method, the class analysis of divergent interests, applied to a subject his father had refused to believe would suit the method. Mill's essay of the 1850s on "Nature" (published posthumously in *Three Essays on Religion*) stands as a footnote to *The Subjection of Women,* for it invites the reader to reject the use of "nature" as a mystification, a eulogistic covering on social arrangements which certain people want to assure that others will not inquire into. From the essay on Bentham onward, Mill's sense of the close relation between nature and second nature gives him a perception in common with Hume, Burke, and other thinkers less trustful than he of social reform and democracy. Where these writers on the whole are for granting artificial arrangements a safe passage to acceptance as if they were natural, Mill always demands to know the exact cost: to whose advantage does the arrangement work, among living men and women? If the unhappiness of the result outweighs the happiness, he commonly elects to write a natural history of the practice in question. By showing the arbitrariness of its origin, he is able to suggest the eminent possibility of its eradication. The confidence and the lack of quali- fication with which he narrated *The Subjection of Women* according to this plan, made several reviewers conclude that he had finally lost his bearings. Mill wrote many works that exposed him to ridicule and angry reproach, but none like this had wagered his reputation for probity and sanity.

"Dry argument," says Mill of his early competence as an expositor of doctrine, "was the only thing I could manage, or willingly attempted." That it does not attempt more than it can manage is an impression left by all his writing; and though he may have supposed this a limitation, the clarity and self-sufficiency of his manner earn a reader's trust. His prose can force one back on powerful feelings that one hardly guessed were there, and it often happens that his statement of an unpleasant truth makes a discovery more vivid for its want of heightening — a bleaker contrast is drawn between an atrocious fact and the complacency by which perception was muffled so that one failed to note the fact. The imperturbable style yields the most irresist- ible of calls to attention. This is a broader phenomenon of nineteenth- century prose: one may recognize something like it in Darwin and in Lin- coln (whom Mill greatly admired). To a certain extent, it also has a precedent in the writing of James Mill, especially in the *History of British India* — flattened there to an extreme that can make the effect subtly scandalizing. Yet for James Mill a truth had to have the clarity of a logical proposition. If there is a tendency in his own thought that John Stuart Mill seems anxious to resist, it is this reductive transparency of high rationalism, with its fondness for the inversion of common sentiments.

Mill said of Bentham that "he is the great *subversive* . . . the great *critical* thinker of his age and country." Like Bentham, he himself wished to show a tireless energy in hunting half-truths to their consequences — but without therefore becoming a prey of the subversive half-truths that had assisted him as weapons. Even so, Bentham's individualist formula, "everybody to count for one, nobody for more than one," was a guide that Mill never deserted. He enjoyed his greatest ascendancy in intellectual life between 1860 and 1865, and it was at this period that he chose to publish *Utilitarianism,* the manifesto of a loyal revisionist. Chapter 2 lays down the general rule: "actions are right in proportion as they tend to promote happiness, wrong as they tend to produce the reverse of happiness" (10: 210). There is an important shade of distinction between *promoting* happiness and *producing* the reverse of happiness. Happiness, Mill implies, is to be judged by co-operation with a tendency; the utilitarian confidence in exact calculation has been silently withdrawn. By contrast, unhappiness more sharply and pragmatically is supposed to be knowable by its effects. The distinction aims to discourage intervention against an innocuous practice on the bare chance that it *might* produce unhappiness; and the same skeptical challenge to reformers saturates all of his mature thinking about morals. There remains, for Mill, a larger problem about the connection between utility and happiness, which turns on the definition of happiness itself. "What constitutes happiness?" asked the positivist Frederic Harrison in an appreciative essay written many years later. "How is it created, maintained, and lost? what pleasures are high, what low?" Mill's initial answer is that the ideas of happiness and pleasure are interchangeable; but why in that case allude, as he does expressly, to the distinction between high and low? Harrison thought that Mill's weakness on this point was related to another omission, his failure properly to reconcile "the tone of militant individualism in the *Liberty*" and "the tone of enthusiastic altruism of the *Utilitarianism.*"[7] Granted Mill tells us in many places (though never with much elaboration) that the pleasure of the sage is different and greater than the pleasure of the sensualist. Yet the crisis of his early life had shown that his own higher pleasure, even added to the knowledge that such pleasure would be achieved for the human race generally, could not assure his happiness even for one moment. His return of self-trust depended on the spontaneous work of the affections — a blessing as likely to be enjoyed by the rude as by the refined.

In his essay on Bentham, Mill had tried to meet the problem of definition by classifying all actions into three separate aspects: the moral, the aesthetic, and the sympathetic. The aim was to enrich the utilitarian account of the motives that enter into our judgments of happiness, but the result looks like an attempt to raise utility above itself by subdividing. The main advantages of the greatest-happiness principle had seemed to be simplicity and demystification. But it turns out that people, if left to themselves, are apt to pursue a course that does not add up to a coherent overall benefit to themselves, let alone a benefit for the common good. The definition of happiness must therefore be imposed from above in order to yield any measure of action that can be agreed on; yet it was precisely to avoid such an imposition that Bentham had appealed originally from the language of duties and virtues (which are irrational and prescriptive for all of society) to the language of utility (which can be measured and known by each individual). It is clear in any case, from all Mill's writings, that he does think some goods higher than others, and that his sense of the "capacity for the nobler feelings" includes a capacity for self-sacrifice.

Of the understanding of happiness as the end of life, among philosophers long before the eighteenth century, he has this to say in *Utilitarianism:*

> The happiness which they meant was not a life of rapture; but moments of such, in an existence made up of few and transitory pains, many and various pleasures, with a decided predominance of the active over the passive, and having as the foundation of the whole, not to expect more from life than it is capable of bestowing. A life thus composed, to those who have been fortunate enough to obtain it, has always appeared worthy of the name of happiness. And such an existence is even now the lot of many, during some considerable portion of their lives. The present wretched education, and wretched social arrangements, are the only real hindrance to its being attainable by almost all (10: 215).

It is an idea of moderate attainable happiness, which finds its directives and evidences in the world that surrounds men and women daily; an idea affording a consolation similar to Wordsworth's in the final book of *The Excursion:*

> The primal duties shine aloft — like stars;
> The charities that soothe, and heal, and bless,
> Are scattered at the feet of Man — like flowers.

Mill, as much as Wordsworth, is a believer in the performance of duties that extend beyond self-interest or habitual interest. What he opposes is asceticism or self-renunciation that brings no good to others.

How, then, in utilitarian terms are people to be moved to good acts? A new morality, it would seem, must draw with it a new kind of conscience, an *inward* detestation of "any mental disposition . . . of which the predominant tendency is to produce bad conduct." There seems a tendency woven into human nature itself to admire or to be excited by examples of conduct which we would not in a sober moment elect to follow. An undeclared rhetorical aim of Mill's philosophy, which runs true from *On Liberty* to *Utilitarianism,* is somehow to impart a distaste for such phenomena and to make us share a taste or affection for what is useful. He does not underestimate the difficulty of the task. We come to know conscience, says Mill, as "a mass of feeling which must be broken through in order to do what violates our standard of right, and which, if we do nevertheless violate that standard, will probably have to be encountered afterwards in the form of remorse."

Bentham had defined a law as a rule backed by a sanction, and Mill is here asking what will be the inward sanction against acts that produce more unhappiness than happiness. Can the almost sensational "mass of feeling" that prompts remorse be so directed as make us recoil from acts that violate nothing but the principle of utility? Mill says only that "no reason has ever been shown" why conscience may not work like that; but the candor of his presentation suggests how considerable the obstacle really is. He concludes that there is a "natural basis of sentiment" for the utilitarian morality, a "firm foundation" for its principle of analysis, and that it is to be found simply in "the social feelings of mankind." If that is true, a sentiment of utility ought to suffice to socialize the primitive sense of justice as revenge. We would then resent any harm to society at large, even where it does not touch ourselves; equally, we would applaud a benefit to society even where it includes among its accidental effects some harm to ourselves.

But can such acquired feelings ever supplant the authority of reflex feelings like fear, desire, or sympathy with familiar objects? A penetrating critic of the early utilitarians, William Hazlitt, suggested in "The New School of Reform" that the great weakness of the philosophic radicals lay in their account of motives. "Am I to feel no more," wrote Hazlitt in 1826,

> for a friend or a relative (say) than for an inhabitant of China or of the Moon, because, as a matter of argument, or setting aside their connection with me, and considered absolutely in themselves, the objects are, perhaps, of equal value? Or am I to screw myself up to feel as much for the Antipodes (or God knows who) as for my next-door neighbours, by

such a forced intellectual scale? The last is impossible; and the result of the attempt will be to make the balance even by a diminution of our natural sensibility, instead of an universal and unlimited enlargement of our philosophic benevolence. The feelings cannot be made to keep pace with our bare knowledge of existence or of truth; nor can the affections be disjoined from impressions of time, place, and circumstance, without destroying their vital principle.[8]

It is an acute insight. The whole point of the standard of utility had been to individuate the ascription of pleasure and pain and therefore of right and wrong. Yet for the ultimate good of society, or of mankind at large, the same philosophy now demands that we moderate our feelings concerning the pleasure or suffering of individuals close to ourselves, on the ground that such intimate sensations might prejudice an impartial judgment. The consequence of adopting the system of universal benevolence is to destroy the spring of our sympathy for individuals.

A writer closer to Mill's generation, Walter Bagehot, observed in a remarkable essay, "The Emotion of Conviction," that conviction itself does not so much produce a feeling as require a feeling in order to occur. By this means alone, it is able to override doubt — a state defined by Bagehot as "a hesitation produced by a collision." Mill's philosophy of morals and politics was a system for multiplying doubts, yet without, if possible, sapping the executive will that leads to rational and energetic action. He may have been unusually constituted in being able to thrive in the almost constant state of collision that accompanies the habit of analysis; perhaps he overrated the numbers capable of sharing a condition where the heaviest doubts may be considered without inducing a paralysis of will. The limits of Mill's sympathy with the emotion of conviction are suggested by his remark, in an essay of 1839 on "Reorganization of the Reform Party," that he saw no reason why church reformers within the Christian denominations should not combine politically with atheists to free the church from arbitrary hierarchies and superstitious practices. It seemed to Mill unreasonable that reformers of such admittedly divergent sorts — dissatisfied idealists within the fold and iconoclasts outside it — should not understand the real convergence of their interests. The extreme objects of both parties were clearly unattainable. The result of collaboration was sure to be a compromise assimilable on both sides as an improvement. Mill was blind to the fact that church reformers would naturally distrust atheists as much as they despised the apologists of orthodoxy, while atheists would scorn as feeble the moral capacity of believers who embraced religious faith of any kind. The misjudgment is not an intellectual failure but the result of a failure of contact with a feeling.

Similar charges have sometimes been made against his reasoning about liberty. "Mill and others held," wrote Dicey, "and with truth, that vigorous persecution, either legal or social, may destroy the capacity for free thought. They thence concluded that absolute freedom would stimulate originality and individuality. This inference is of most dubious validity."[9] Mill's view of life was conditioned by his having been made to perceive quite early that a high standard of altruism was normal. "Has a man talents?" Bentham asked. "He owes them to his country in every way in which they can be serviceable."[10] Alongside the assumption that benevolence is a widely distributed virtue, there runs through the writings of Mill an observation in considerable tension with it, namely that the great advances of human kind are mainly owed to the genius of individuals, and that the work of accommodation between such persons and society at large has the unfortunate effect of diluting their achievements. Even though democracy is irresistibly coming, and though its coming is desirable because it reduces slavishness of mind and body and teaches a self-respect that resists the impositions of force, nevertheless democracy is also to be feared. Like aristocracy, but more tyrannically for its strength of numbers, it may add a terrible weight to the sense of voicelessness that inhibits each individual. This was a finding of Tocqueville; but Mill for himself could always venture far on similar lines. He argued in 1831, in "The Spirit of the Age," that qualification for power was not the same as fitness for power; that those who had long possessed the qualification were now steadily losing the fitness; while those who were gaining the fitness had not yet the qualification. He extended the thought in 1836, in "Civilization," to assert that power in modern times was passing from individuals to masses; that the importance of masses was becoming greater, and that of individuals smaller; and that the "weight of the individual" counted for less with the decline of aristocratic society. Mass suffrage rightly expands the qualification for power, but individuality still is needed to assure the fitness.

Yet Mill is pragmatic rather than elegiac when he writes in "Civilization": "All combination is compromise; it is the sacrifice of some portion of individual will, for a common purpose" (18: 122). The word *compromise* offers a quiet way of speaking of self-sacrifice — a moral topic deeply interesting to other mid-Victorian writers. T. H. Green's *Prolegomena to Ethics,* for example, a work that in method and idiom bears little resemblance to *Utilitarianism,* describes individual acts of philanthropy and social assistance as the offspring of a new wakefulness of conscience:

It is indeed in one sense a new type of virtue that has come into being with the recognition of the divine image, of spiritual functions and possibilities, in all forms of weak and suffering humanity. . . . It implies a view of life in which the maintenance of any form of political society scarcely holds a place; in which lives that would be contemptible and valueless, if estimated with reference to the purposes of the state, are invested with a value of their own in virtue of capabilities for some society not seen as yet. . . . The qualities of self-adjustment, of sympathy with inferiors, of tolerance for the weak and foolish, which are exercised in it, are very different from the pride of self-sufficing strength which with Aristotle was inseparable from heroic endurance.[11]

In the manner of Mill's "all combination is compromise," Green asserts that "With every advance towards its universal application comes a complication of the necessity, under which the conscientious man feels himself placed, of sacrificing personal pleasure in satisfaction of the claims of human brotherhood."[12] The conversion to democracy for Mill, like the conversion to "human brotherhood" for Green, carries with it a fresh requirement of self-sacrifice.

Majority rule is reckoned by Mill as a necessary element of democratic society rather than its essence. "There must, we know," he observes in "Bentham," "be some paramount power in society; and that the majority should be that power, is on the whole right, not as being just in itself, but as being less unjust than any other footing on which the matter can be placed" (10: 107–8). The French Revolution was for Mill an example of the delusive gains that follow from attempting sudden changes in a moral environment where neither the paramount minds nor the thoughts and manners of the people have been adequately prepared. But Mill is relentless in denying the presumption that experience, or inheritance, or the need for stability confers on any class in society the right to rule. His powerful essay of 1839 on "Reorganization of the Reform Party" divides society into the privileged or, as Mill also calls them, the satisfied classes, and the disqualified classes; saying of the former, "They have the strongest reason possible for being satisfied with the government; they *are* the government" (6: 470). Again in the review of Tocqueville's second volume, he stresses the importance for the educated middle class of preventing the strongest power, that of the satisfied classes, from becoming the only operative power in society. Even so, Mill came to share with Burke a fear that "the people" may be disposed to identify their will as the standard of right and wrong. He likewise came to share with Tocqueville the judgment that mass opinion shapes the mores of the people in a democracy, so that the right to vote gives the majority, as it were, an extra weight in the scale, which every imaginable constitutional device must be employed to check. "There is no such thing in morals," he writes in 1859, in "Thoughts on Parliamentary Reform," "as a *right* to power over others; and the electoral suffrage is that power" (19: 324). The same essay proposes the adoption of a scheme of plural voting, with more than one vote per person given to those whose work is apt to have rendered them socially responsible, people of advanced education being counted most favorably of all. To heighten further the salutary protection against "false democracy," Mill later borrowed from Thomas Hare the idea of proportional representation. This called for the entire country to share at elections a single register and a single slate of candidates. Each voter was to vote for as many candidates and in whatever order he wished: if his first-ranked candidate had already received a sufficient number of votes, his ballot would be counted for the highest-ranked of his choices who had not yet received a sufficient number, and so on until all seats were filled. The plan is utterly consistent with Bentham's emphasis on intensity of pleasure as a relevant factor in translating the will into action. If one person wants very much to do something, and five persons object, the intensity of the objection in each being very slight, it need not follow axiomatically that the five overrule the one.

Anyway, according to Mill democracy itself, understood as a form of government that vests ultimate power in the people, is appropriate only in a nation that demands a high average of citizenship. By contrast, a nation in which, if a man stabs another in a public street, bystanders ignore the incident "because it is the business of the police to look to the matter and it is safer not to interfere in what does not concern them," is said by Mill to be not yet ready for liberty. Like Tocqueville once more, he suspects that the apathy of mass democracy could lead back to such a state. He does not have in mind only the catastrophe of riot and the menace it brings of anarchy, when, as Herman Melville said, "man rebounds whole aeons back in nature." The fear is rather of an ordinary slackness of moral negligence becoming by degrees a distemper, until the people seek to evade most of their responsibilities and entrust the common good to an oligarchy. All of Mill's optimism, and all of his skeptical reserve about the prospects of democracy, are founded on a plain understanding that government is a contrivance, though one worked out by human beings deliberately to meet the needs of our social nature. That is why he distrusted the idealism associated in the nineteenth century with the disciples of Coleridge: we must always be careful not to confuse our human choice of ameliorative measures with the unalterable course of nature. "We cannot," says Mill in *Representative Government,* "make the river run backwards, but we do not therefore say that watermills 'are not made, but grow.' " Government is an artifice whose good is "to be judged by its action upon men, and by its action upon things; by what it makes of the citizens, and what it does with them" (19: 380, 392).

And so, for all the dangers, a uniquely modern discovery emerges from the system of representative government whose basis lies in democratic suffrage. Public activity and discussion is for Mill, as *Representative Government* makes even clearer than *On Liberty,* a form of life, a culture, put into regular performance by political arrangements, but owing its existence to and deriving continuous energy from a state of manners more deep-seated than politics. "One of the benefits of freedom is that under it the ruler cannot pass by the people's minds, and amend their affairs for them without amending them" (19: 403). The political disaster of lawgivers rendered impotent to transfer an enlightened structure of laws to the people, because the people's minds have not been prepared or because they are distracted by simpler or more violent remedies — this, Mill almost shows to his own satisfaction, has become impossible under a liberal system of representative government. The people and their acts are a legal and necessary medium through which the system reforms itself. Their minds inevitably come to be prepared as, sometimes together, sometimes apart, they live out the reforms which they themselves have approved. In this way too, liberal democracy is able to ward off a mental inertia that threatens any large-scale commercial society. It does so by working against the drift of thoughtless execution and compliance in the individual first. Ultimately, Mill's hope seems to be that, through the operation of the franchise, the appetite for free discussion will pass beyond any need to afford it the protection of the law.

After 1868, still suffering from the tuberculosis he had contracted years before, Mill spent as many seasons as he could at Avignon with Helen Taylor, the daughter of Harriet, who was now his assistant and editor and, in handling a wide correspondence, his collaborator. Throughout his later years, he was a devoted amateur botanist, and gave his spare hours to walks for collecting specimens. He grew more convinced than he once had been of the essential soundness of the democratic aspirations of socialism: the social question of the future was "how to unite the greatest individual liberty of action with a common ownership of the raw materials of the globe, and an equal participation of all in the benefits of combined labour." He was known in his sixties as a venerable and active leader of the campaign for women's rights, playing a significant part in the passage of the Married Women's Property Act, pressing for relaxation of the laws on the irrevocability of marriage, and helping to raise money for women's education. He died on May 7, 1873, saying to Helen Taylor at the end, in an utterance that might have come from him at any time: "You know that I have done my work." The eulogies all speak of his strength of purpose and his generosity — the traits that prompted Frederic Harrison to describe him as "a most strenuous and magnanimous spirit." Mill was less a theorist of experience than a witness in its cause. A defender of the desire for improvement, he taught himself to think with his nerves, to grapple with the unforeseen effects of every improvement, and made the work of reform a secular calling that remains now as an irritant and a summons.

NOTES

1. *Autobiography of John Stuart Mill,* in *The Collected Works of John Stuart Mill,* 31 vols. (Toronto, 1963–91), vol. 1, p. 45. All subsequent references to writings by Mill are to this edition. Where quotations run two sentences or longer, volume and page numbers are inserted parenthetically in the text.

2. Quoted in Elie Halévy, *The Growth of Philosophic Radicalism* (Boston, 1955), pp. 289–90.

3. Quoted in Michael St. John Packe, *The Life of John Stuart Mill* (London, 1954), p. 134.

4. Ibid., p. 317.

5. A. V. Dicey, *Law and Public Opinion in England During the Nineteenth Century* (London, 1952), p. 185.

6. Quoted in Stefan Collini, *Public Moralists* (Oxford, 1991), p. 131.

7. Frederic Harrison, *Tennyson, Ruskin, Mill, and other Literary Estimates* (London, 1899), pp. 304–6.

8. William Hazlitt, "The New School of Reform," in P. P. Howe, ed., *Complete Works of William Hazlitt,* 21 vols. (London, 1930–34), 12: 189.

9. Dicey, *Law and Public Opinion,* p. 438.

10. Quoted ibid., p. 133.

11. T. H. Green, *Prolegomena to Ethics* (New York, 1969), III.v.259, p. 279.

12. Ibid., III.v.271, p. 292.

A Reading of *On Liberty*

GEORGE KATEB

Mill's *On Liberty* is a great work. It has engendered an immense response that began in the year of its publication, 1859. There is no reason to think that any account of the book will ever satisfy all who take the book seriously. Indeed, any single reader is likely to grow dissatisfied after a while with his or her own interpretation. The book is restless, and induces restlessness. The most important source of the book's power to compel commentary is its indefatigable intensity. Mill never lets up. Practically every sentence is freighted, invested by Mill with concentrated meaning. And the sentences often surprise by their inventiveness. Mill suddenly notices a problem or creates one for himself, and proceeds to subdue it. Perhaps irritated by feeling so much gratitude for these displays, one wants to find Mill inconsistent. About his projected book about liberty, Mill said to his wife Harriet, in a letter written in 1855, "We must cram into it as much as possible of what we wish not to leave unsaid" (14: 332). A patient reader will not find it a crammed essay: it is not miscellaneous. But it is almost unmanageably instructive.

I do not suggest that Mill's defense of liberty is definitive. None could be, given the fresh questions about liberty that ever-changing experience continuously raises. Then, too, some of his arguments on the worth of liberty are open to question; his utilitarianism sometimes plays an awkward or an intrusive role; his highest principle, which turns out to be an idea of human dignity, sometimes seems shyly present and has to struggle for primacy. He is too hard on people, singly, or as class members, or as packed in a mass. Some of his fears may appear exaggerated or misplaced for his time, or now out of date. He may have been insensitive to the actual if disguised existence of energies and aspirations that he cherishes. When he makes democracy the new and, one day, possibly the worst enemy of individuality, he may be right, but he is inexperienced, still too much in the old regime. Yet for all the criticisms we can make, his riches are astonishing.

There is no book written in English like *On Liberty*. There was none like it before; there has been none like it since. Mill disclaims originality. Looking back on the book in his *Autobiography* (1873), he says that in it he propounds "the doctrine of the rights of individuality" and adds that "mankind have probably at no time since the beginning of civilisation been entirely without" this doctrine (1: 260). Perhaps he is right to suggest that some effort to defend individuality shows itself through time. But Mill is setting forth a substantially novel idea of the rights of individuality. "Abundant differences in detail" he claims for his conception; but the differences are not merely in detail (1: 261). In its elaboration, the conception becomes radically new, and stays new. Even in comparison to the roughly contemporary attempt led by Emerson in the United States to form an ideal of democratic individuality, Mill's conception is distinctive: differently grounded in part, somewhat different in motive, and different in many of its fears, ambitions, and expectations.

I have no wish to deny, however, that Wilhelm von Humboldt's valuable and engrossing book *The Sphere and Duties of Government* (written in 1791–92, but not available in English until 1854) is a work fit for the company of *On Liberty*. Mill makes use of some of its formulations and leading ideas; the epigraph of *On Liberty* is from Humboldt. There is a closeness of spirit between the two works. Perhaps if Humboldt's book were as well known as Mill's, it would be discussed much more. It certainly deserves greater attention, not all of it historical, and not just for the light it throws on Mill. But reading some of Mill's writings in the period of 1835–40, we see that Mill felt anxiety over the diminishment of humanity well before he read Humboldt. Dealing with this anxiety is the great project of *On Liberty*. The striking difference between Humboldt and Mill is that Mill assigns the people a large part of the blame for their diminishment, while Humboldt locates in the overbearing state the principal source of his anxiety. A constant theme of Mill in such pieces as his two reviews of Tocqueville's *Democracy in America* (1835, 1840), "State of Society in America" (1836), and "Civilization" (1836) is human diminishment and self-diminishment, the way in which, as he says in "Civilization," "by the natural growth of civilization, power passes from individuals to masses" (18: 126). This process, for Mill, is the same as diminishment; and it is, sad to say, abetted by the people who, in their dislike of individuality for themselves and others, show that they welcome being the masses.

We must be prepared, then, to see something unfamiliar, even strange, in *On Liberty*. If it is not politically radical by our standards, it is certainly morally radical by almost any standards. When we think we have learned all its lessons, we may be mistaken. If in no other way, the several grounds of Mill's defense of the rights of individuality separate his doctrine, in significant respects, from any other. But the spirit that animates *On Liberty* is also sometimes surprising. Mill's book is a plea to the world: let there be individuals. There are not enough of them. They are needed. But needed or not, they are in themselves society's highest reason for being. Society exists for them, not the other way around. Yet individuals are as they should be only if they do not trample on others; and only if they feel their refusal to trample as part of their individuality. A true individual will not impair the individuality of any of his fellows or harm their vital interests. Mill's zeal for individuality is (to use one of his favorite words) balanced by a strong concern for fairness or justice. Fairness or justice will conscientiously limit individuality, but ideally the limitation will not be experienced as constraint. The totality of *On Liberty* is thus devoted to the passionate, desperate, immensely resourceful effort to enlarge the possibility that a certain conception of individuality will be acted out in modern life. Unless we see the depth of that passion, we fail to engage properly with Mill's arguments. His rigor is meant to protect his radicalism. The sobriety of his style is at the service of a theory that is anything but sober.

Mill's highest commitment is to individuality. Yet the title's key word is *liberty*. We must try to see how liberty is tied to individuality. But in order to try to make sense of that tie, we have to comprehend the meaning of liberty. The usual negative understanding of liberty as the absence of coercion, of restraint or compulsion, the absence of what Mill often calls "interference," is operative in *On Liberty*. Aside from Mill's concern to require (and if necessary, subsidize) education for the young, material incapacity as an impediment to being free, to doing as one likes, does not play a large role in the book. (Mill addresses this issue in other writings, perhaps not satisfactorily.) When people speak of coercion or interference, they routinely have government in mind as the source. But Mill finds in society itself another powerful source of restriction on liberty. On this point, he therefore departs from the then-prevailing idea.

He is careful to say that the subject of his book is what he calls "Civil or Social Liberty," which is liberty in society, not "Liberty of the Will" (p. 73 of the present edition). In a couple of letters, Mill also distinguishes social liberty from political liberty (15: 534, 581). Writing in French to a correspondent, Mill speaks of his efforts in behalf of "l'autonomie de l'individu" (17: 1831, 1832). Thus his radicalism concentrates itself in his defense of personal liberty as essential to individuality. Only when the vital claims of others are hurt by one's own (and hence inconsistently) expressed individuality can the state or society rightly interfere with one's liberty. If one's liberty harms others, it is no longer only personal; to speak appropriately, it is not even liberty.

On Liberty is a book that defends liberty as essential to individuality. Mill must defend liberty because the majority of people, though they live in a constitutionalist society like Great Britain, dislike the individuality that liberty is associated with. Mill writes as a philosopher whose cause is menaced by those around him. If they cannot have an initial respect for individuality, then perhaps they can at least be reminded of their respect for liberty. After all, they give lip service to liberty. Mill writes, he says in a letter, "to make the many more accessible to all truth by making them more open minded" (15: 631). People who are hostile to individuality and tend to give mainly lip service to liberty are not the only audience that Mill has in mind. Sometimes Mill speaks to his fellow utilitarian philosophers, not because they are necessarily hostile to either liberty or individuality, but to enlarge, if possible, their conceptual reach. And, furthermore, Mill can be taken as fulfilling the vocation of a genius, as he defines it when praising Tocqueville in the second review essay Mill wrote about *Democracy in America:* a genius is one who speaks " to all time" (18: 198). In addition to arguments in behalf of liberty addressed to skeptics or enemies, and to fellow utilitarians, Mill introduces considerations that are more purely philosophical and hence meant to capture the sympathetic attention not only of some of his contemporaries but of thinkers in the future. These considerations, it is hoped, will receive acknowledgment or even confirmation over long periods of time from a few free spirits, here and there — adherents to no school and advocates of no particular cause. These considerations refer to human dignity, and I shall discuss them in due course.

In referring to the different kinds of appeal that Mill makes, I do not mean to suggest that he is ever promoting arguments in which he does not believe. But when he is tactical — as when he defends liberty by means of arguments meant for skeptics and enemies, or for fellow utilitarians — he relies on arguments that matter less to him than other arguments do; and occasionally he indicates that he wishes he did not have to use a particular argument, not because it is false, but because it does not reach to the highest level, which turns out to be the defense of human dignity. And when Mill is being tactical, he expressly says so, as if he has nothing to lose by any extremity of candor. In that respect, he diverges from other thinkers who, he says in *On Liberty,* hide the "general principles and grounds of their convictions" and adjust their conclusions to society's premises, not their own (p.

101). Intimidation distorts their reasoning, but not his, despite the menace that he feels surrounds liberty and individuality. He goes so far as to correct Alexander Bain, one of his friends, who thought that the book contained some esoteric elements. Mill asserts that his aim is emphatically not to say one thing to the many and another to "an intellectual aristocracy of *lumieres.*" To be sure, Mill appears to backtrack a bit when he tells Bain, "Perhaps you were only thinking of the question of religion. On that, certainly I am not anxious to bring over any but really superior intellects & characters to the whole of my own opinions — in the case of all others I would much rather, as things now are, try to improve their religion than to destroy it" (15: 631). However, as his critics pointed out, whether they were religious themselves or just concerned about the subversive effects of freethinking, *On Liberty* is threatening to religious confidence. Mill is incapable of hiding the truth as he sees it. The world did not have to wait until the posthumous publication of "The Utility of Religion" in 1874 (written in the 1850s) to see how tough on religious beliefs he could publicly be. (There is, alas, some concessive retraction in "Theism," written a good deal later, sometime in 1868–70; perhaps toward the end, he was even more willing to "improve" rather than to "destroy" religion.)

What I hope to show is that *On Liberty* contains a tense variety of arguments and considerations intended to defend liberty. It turns out that only considerations that pertain to human dignity defend liberty as essential to individuality. The variety can thus be sorted. After the Introduction, each of the four succeeding chapters makes use of more than one kind of defense of personal liberty, but it may be possible to infer how Mill ranks them. Of course, we may disagree with Mill's own ranking, if we can determine it. That is all to the good: such disagreement is, for Mill, the stuff of moral reasoning. In any case, a preliminary way of sorting the variety of considerations and arguments in defense of liberty is to say that when Mill is confronting skepticism and hostility, he is eloquent and truthful, but not speaking in all respects as he would have most liked. Even when he is addressing his fellow utilitarians, although he is certainly speaking as a utilitarian, he has still not arrived at the level which I believe means the most to him, the defense of liberty as essential to individuality, which means as essential to human dignity. I therefore propose three main audiences for the book and hence three main defenses of liberty. In the same book, Mill is speaking to adversaries, allies, and also to a few others, present and future, who can perhaps respond appreciatively to considerations that must strike most others as vague or insubstantial. The work, however, is not neat in its categories, not distinct in its separate appeals. It takes some work to figure out the scope of Mill's ambition. *On Liberty* is a complex book, so let us try to find our way in it.

In the Introduction, Mill says that his object is "to assert one very simple principle, as entitled to govern absolutely the dealings of society with the individual in the way of compulsion and control. . . . That principle is, that the sole end for which mankind are warranted, individually or collectively, in interfering with the liberty of action of any of their number, is self-protection." Interference is justified only to "prevent harm to others." But whether in the form of legal penalties or coercive public opinion, interference is inadmissible when the concern is the person's own good; such a concern is not "a sufficient warrant." "He cannot rightfully be compelled to do or forbear because it will be better for him to do so, because it will make him happier, because, in the opinions of others, to do so would be wise, or even right" (p. 80). Indeed, in the last chapter, Mill denies unequivocally that society has the right to "decide anything to be wrong which concerns only the individual" (p. 161). Society's warrant does not run that far. "Over himself, over his own body and mind, the individual is sovereign" (p. 81). Personal liberty should be as extensive as individual sovereignty (or individual autonomy or complete self-ownership). The moral radicalism of the book is, precisely, the assertion of such an extent of liberty. Yet to use one's liberty to become an individual does not mean that one is free to inflict injury. The basis of one's moral claim to have absolute personal liberty entails that one must respect the equal claim of others. So far is Mill from believing in the unequal status of human beings that his acceptance of moral equality is axiomatic, even though he is perfectly prepared to judge and even rank people by the degree to which they aspire to become individuals (to insist on their human dignity) and are capable of doing so. In Mill the supreme end of life, the emergence of individuals, cannot be a morally transgressive aspiration, even if the performance of one's moral duties of actions and abstentions does not necessarily, in every incident of life, express or advance one's individuality.

Individual sovereignty (absolute or nearly absolute personal liberty) is integral to Mill's defense of individuality; the defense of individuality is Mill's form of tribute to human dignity. Such sovereignty exists when liberty of speech and publication (freedom of expression, as we now often call it) and liberty of conduct are fully recognized. It is important to emphasize that the concept of "self-regarding" activity is crucially implicated in Mill's claim for both sorts of liberty. Individual sovereignty means the liberty of "self-regarding" activity. On the matter of speech and publication, Mill concedes that publication is not merely a self-regarding activity, that it "concerns other people" (p. 82). That concession is probably ill-advised because the very concept of self-regarding activity, as Mill fully defines it, includes effects on others, provided those effects occur with the "free, voluntary, and undeceived consent and participation" of others (p. 82); alternatively, provided the activity does not "affect them unless they like (all the persons concerned being of full age, and the ordinary amount of understanding)" (p. 139). By Mill's definition of self-regarding activity, written publication and public speech could actually be other-regarding activities only if adults are so susceptible that they tend to be taken in irresistibly by whatever they hear or read, and helplessly agree with it, even when a transmitted expression contradicts the preceding one. Reception of the words of others would typically be involuntary. Mill raises a particular case in which a speaker incites a riot, and agrees that "instigation to some mischievous act" deserves punishment (p. 121). Not the idea but the tone of voice in certain situations is to be punished. The oddity is that a radical speaker exciting an audience is assimilated to a military officer giving orders to obedient subordinates. Is Mill consistent? It seems to me that if the destructive rioters are adults, they are the ones who should be punished, not the speaker who inflamed them. Unless we posit self-control, the notion of self-regarding activity is even more precarious. Of course, if much public expression is dominated by the propaganda of either government or a media oligopoly, and therefore marked by a single and ubiquitous pattern of distortion, it becomes almost irresistibly manipulative. The public would be able to give only deceived consent or assent. Then publication would truly turn into harmful other-regarding activity. But I do not think that Mill, for all his pessimism, works with the background assumption of preponderant manipulative deception, as distinct from vigorously competitive partisanship.

The fact remains that Mill includes publication within the scope of the absolute (or nearly absolute) liberty that he is defending in his book. One's opinions are not "a personal possession of no value except to the owner" (p. 87). Most readers of *On Liberty* are right not to fuss too much as to whether Mill provides the most self-consistent reason for defending liberty of publication when he says in summary that publication "being almost of as much importance as the liberty of thought itself, and resting in great part on the same reasons, is practically inseparable from it" (p. 82).

On liberty of conduct, Mill says, "No one pretends that actions should be as free as opinions" (p. 121). But this remark is also a bit odd, just because Mill wants his readers to subscribe to the view that *self-regarding* actions should be as free as opinions. Part of *On Liberty*'s radicalism consists in that claim. Of course, *other-regarding* actions, which affect other people's interests (especially harmfully and without their consent), cannot be as free as opinions. Mill has been insistent on that point from the start.

The distinction between self-regarding activity and activity that is other-regarding (a term that he does not use in *On Liberty*) is not free of trouble, as numerous critics have pointed out from the beginning of the book's reception. But without it, the book cannot get started. And we cannot get started unless we grant it an initial plausibility, which it surely deserves, despite the oddities that I have just singled out, and other difficulties as well.

Recognition by state and society of individual sovereignty is essential to individuality. The word *individuality* appears in the title of Chapter III. But every chapter is a defense of individuality and of the full exercise of individual sovereignty that is essential to it. What that comes to is that an individual is one who speaks or publishes opinions freely, without inhibition, just as one acts as one pleases, or thinks one has to, or yearns to, short of harming others. The question arises as to whether Mill is interested in only those opinions that people act on. The tie between one's opinions and one's activities is made explicit at the beginning of Chapter III, where Mill says that the same reasons that ground the liberty of expressing one's opinions also "require that men should be free to act upon" them (p. 121). It is clear, however, that Mill's defense of the "liberty of thought and discussion" in Chapter II reaches to all kinds of opinion, many of them having little if anything to do — at least, directly — with how one acts or lives. A person reads and writes poetry and metaphysics, not only religious, moral, and political tracts. In any case, to be an individual, as Mill conceptualizes the ideal, is to think, and also to act and live, independently. To think independently, one must be allowed without interference to speak and listen, read and write freely; while to act and live independently, one's self-regarding choices and activities must not be interfered with by state or society.

Mill is not blind to the many ways in which through the centuries men and women have heroically asserted their independence in thought and conduct in the face of oppression. Indeed, he is memorably sensitive to such heroism, and occasionally even laments the loss of need for that defiant vigor that can flourish only amid oppression. But his effort to promote individuality is suited to unheroic — middle-class, commercial, increasingly democratic — times. To be sure, he can say in regard to expressing one's opinions that to bear "to be ill-thought of and ill-spoken of" should not require "a very heroic mould." But then he says that social penalties for "heretical" opinions — to leave aside government restrictions on them — intimidate (or, as jurists now say, "chill") expression of them. Heretical opinions do not "blaze out far and wide." Hence the general affairs of mankind are not lit with "either a true or a deceptive light" (p. 101). (As if heresy as a sign of courage or energy were a positive good, apart from its truth.) The net result is, he says, "the sacrifice of the entire moral courage of the human mind" (p. 101). In other words, oppression requires too much courage by requiring more than a little. Mill wants independence to flourish, and it can flourish only if heroism is not needed for it; it can flourish only if individual sovereignty (nearly absolute personal liberty) is guaranteed by popular sentiments that are newly made more friendly to it. At least until commercial democracy corrects itself, it tends to be an enemy of individuality.

The first component of individuality is freely forming one's opinions and expressing them to others. Mill assumes that people in England abstractly endorse free speech and free press. But the disposition to suffocate some kinds of expression is never far below the surface, and manifests itself recurrently. What energizes this disposition? In *On Liberty* the important contemporary sources of repression do not include the state's fear of attack on itself or even the state's worry that too much uninhibited discussion may work to undermine the beliefs that supposedly hold society together. Mill does discuss the state's fear and worry at length in a piece (unsigned and never republished) he wrote as a young man in 1825, called "Law of Libel and Liberty of the Press." It is a strong attack on censorship, rebuking officials for their failure to trust the people and learn from them about the condition of society. Mill makes a *political* case for a free press, not embedding it in a defense of personal liberty as essential to individuality, or in a defense of as much liberty (in general) as possible. He says of a free press that "It is equal in value to good government, because without it good government cannot exist" (21: 34).

In *On Liberty* the issue of state persecution of expression is of great, but mostly historical, interest. Despite the imprisonment of a man in 1857 for scrawling blasphemous words on a gate (p. 98), and despite a prosecution in 1858 for the "immoral" doctrine of tyrannicide (p. 86), Mill insists that "the era of pains and penalties for political discussion has, in our own country, passed away" (p. 86). But Mill takes advantage of the attempted prosecution to declare that there must be an unqualified liberty "of professing and discussing, as a matter of ethical conviction, any doctrine, however immoral it may be considered" (p. 86). Mill rejects absolutely the moral right of society to call any opinion "immoral or impious" (p. 93).

If censorship that derives from statist and supervisory motives does not figure in Mill's account as an immediate incentive to defend liberty of thought and discussion, what does worry him? He refers to "the engines of moral repression" through which public opinion exercises its disapproval to punitive lengths (p. 83). It is "natural to mankind" to show "intolerance in whatever they really care about" (p. 79). The overall motive to stifle expression is the wish that certain things never be said, and if said, then made so costly to the speaker or writer that he will henceforth keep his thoughts to himself. The penalties will also deter others. But why such hostility? Mill refers to such particular motives as religious certitude that will not put up with religious difference, and concern for matters of morality, taste, or propriety that may be influenced by religion, even if not always prescribed by it. Religious belief is a main source of hostility to liberty of thought and discussion. And then distaste, disgust, hurt feelings, shock, outrage, and abhorrence are all aroused by the mere fact that someone has *dared* to say or write certain words and express certain attitudes and sentiments, even if no practical consequences ensue. Does Mill detect in the reigning public opinion, as distinct from the state's fear and worry, some solicitude for social order and stability, a sense that uninhibited expression may provoke rebellion or moral decay? That thought is not prominent in the book, though he does refer to a particular view that opinions matter not for their truth but for their usefulness to order and cohesion (p. 92), and that free expression may therefore have "pernicious consequences" (p. 93). It is also obvious that he attributes to religious people a fear that heresy and perhaps unbelief are contagious.

Mill's clearest account of how public opinion works to intimidate and punish expression is found, fittingly enough, in his essay *The Utility of Religion*. There he says, "But the deterring force of the unfavourable sentiments of mankind does not consist solely in the painfulness of knowing oneself to be the object of those sentiments; it includes all the penalties which they can inflict: exclusion from social intercourse and from the innumerable good offices which human beings require from one another; the forfeiture of all that is called success in life; often the great diminution or total loss of means of subsistence; positive ill offices of various kinds, sufficient to render life miserable, and reaching in some states of society as far as actual persecution to death" (10: 411).

Setting up the problem of intolerance in the way that he does, Mill provides his defense of (nearly) absolute liberty of thought and discussion. He must endeavor to increase the tolerance of those strongly disposed to intolerance. He will not take the public's routine remarks about the worth of free expression at face value: tolerance disappears too easily under provocation. Mill says in *Considerations on Representative Government* that religious beliefs remain the most important influence on people's sense of themselves and hence on their attitudes and sentiments in morality, politics, law, and the conduct of life (19: 394). Religion is the principal active adversary to self-regarding liberty of every kind and in every sphere of life. But religion is not a convenient adversary; its hold on people starts at an early age, and reason thereafter often fails to undo the effects of inculcation. Mill must be tactical, but cannot possibly expect a massive immediate change of mind. He must delineate the advantages of free expression to those who cannot abide hearing or reading the expression of certain attitudes and sentiments.

Yet Mill seems to give his audience the credit of wanting to know the truth in religion, morality, politics, law, and the conduct of life. I say *seems* because I think that Mill works with the following ambivalent assumption: most people want what they believe to be the truth. But they acquire their beliefs as it were by chance. Mill says that a person typically "devolves upon his own world the responsibility of being in the right against the dissentient worlds of other people; and it never troubles him that mere accident has decided which of these numerous worlds is the object of his reliance, and that the same causes which make him a Churchman in London, would have made him a Buddhist or Confucian in Pekin" (p. 88). Most people do not arrive at their beliefs from the motive of truth, from honest and self-conscious inquiry, but rather from indoctrination and habituation, sustained by the disposition to conform. Most persons never return to the sources of their beliefs and acquire a self-examined relation to them. One's primary need is not for truth but for the prestige of truth. Once one covers one's beliefs with such prestige, one will cling fiercely to them. That is why there is such resistance to free discussion.

Mill is tactical here, but he cannot assume that even his tactical arguments will work with most people in matters that mean so much to them, especially because of the notion they have of their proper place and role in society. A person, say, can be deeply committed to religious orthodoxy and still not be deeply religious. Such a person cannot be appealed to with any more ease than one who is deeply religious. Is there a rhetoric sufficiently skillful to overpower him or her? Mill tries, certainly. But religious reviewers, whether religious themselves or merely protective of orthodoxy for social reasons, have been among the most severe critics of *On Liberty* from the time of its publication. Only those who are minimally religious are likely to be impressed by Mill's kind of tactical argument. Their minds may be opened. But there is a problem with them, too. They must be persuaded to go from intellectual indifference to thoughtfulness, and such a progression may be as unlikely as going from deep religiousness to intellectual open-mindedness. The target of Mill's tactical arguments is thus not clearly in sight. Yet these arguments can have unpredictable effects. Mill readily agreed to the publication of a cheap People's Edition in order to spread his word about liberty. Who knows how liberty may gain from an opened mind here and there? And if some of those who influence public opinion, like teachers, publicists, officials, and prominent persons, can be won over or fortified by tactical arguments, then eventually greater tolerance may permeate society.

In any case, Mill is intent on showing the advantages of liberty for truth in those areas of doctrine where challenges to one's views are most resented and felt to be most insulting and shocking. One feels oneself assaulted when confronted with serious disagreement; religion, morality, politics, law, and the conduct of life — religion under all and above all — are too personally meaningful to permit an instantly detached response. Restraint, a self-imposed opposition to one's impulses to repress, must be cultivated. Tactical arguments are implements for the cultivation of restraint. To say it again, Mill believes in the correctness of his tactical arguments, even if they are not the arguments he cherishes the most and would most prefer to use. Indeed, he perhaps wishes that he did not have to *argue* for liberty at all. Arguing is best when the liberty to argue can be taken for granted. But Mill will argue for liberty on grounds of truth. His tactical arguments for liberty of thought and discussion as instrumental to truth actually turn out to be the scene of his greatest eloquence, even though the reasons for liberty that are closest to Mill's heart are not instrumental but rather reasons of human dignity, the individuality of speakers and auditors, writers and readers.

Nothing is ever simple, however, in Mill's elaboration of reasons. Specifically, his conception of truth appears to undergo a shift in Chapter II of *On Liberty*. Much of the chapter works with the premise that truth is what everyone thinks it is: on a given issue, full and permanent understanding, proven and incontrovertible. But toward the end of the chapter, truth — doctrinal, not scientific truth — is reconceived as always incomplete and provisional, and sometimes not cumulative. When truth is thus reconceived, the instrumental value of liberty is all the more important, as we shall see. For the time being, let us stay with the ordinary notion of truth.

That Mill's arguments for liberty as instrumental to truth are familiar in outline need not dispel our sense of their continuous power and richness. The history of persecution provides a dramatic backdrop for Mill's lesson that new doctrines are always unpopular, provided they pertain to whatever people "really care about," whether as sincere believers or as sincere or insincere conformists. A new doctrine in religion, morality, politics, law, or the conduct of life is put forth as a new truth (in the ordinary sense of full and permanent truth). If people — a good majority of them — think that they already have the full and permanent truth, they will, if sufficiently appalled, recoil and then strike back. Whenever new doctrines have made their way, it was only by a long and costly struggle. Historically, they have almost always been persecuted. Now in Britain and America, at least, people will use mainly informal but often severe penalties against those who propound them. The important point is that even in the absence of state censorship, there is no "*atmosphere* of freedom" (p. 129). In its absence, fewer new doctrines emerge, and those that emerge do so with greater inhibition or circumspection. There are many books; many small disagreements; but Mill does not find a love — at once passionate and dispassionate — of dispute that he associates with only those few periods of history when for one reason or another orthodoxy was forced to loosen its grip and "the dread of heterodox speculation was for a time suspended" (p. 102).

Mill undergirds his defense of liberty of thought and discussion by the recurrent insistence that people now accept as truth what was once thought false, and that at all times people are prone to find false what is new. Mill is saying that people today are only less drastic in their techniques of persecution. And the future may well look on people's resistance to today's new doctrines as today they look back at the supposed falsehood of old doctrines. Perhaps there has been a growth of understanding, so that present-day doctrines will last. But we cannot be sure; perhaps no society can ever be sure, even a future society now unglimpsed and much better than the present one. Thus even working with the ordinary notion of truth, Mill sometimes weaves in with it a kind of historical relativism that may be found threatening, though covered over by what philosophers call *fallibilism*.

Doctrines have a history. They emerge in time and die out; they are neither eternal nor immortal. Yet the Christian religion, though admittedly emergent, is held by adherents to be the last word. Mill does not say in *On Liberty* that society should anticipate the rise of a successor religion, though he certainly sketches a new religion of humanity in *The Utility of Religion*. (The most striking expression of Mill's own religious sensibility comes, however, not in the advocacy of a religion of humanity but in a letter of

1841 in which he entrusts poetry with the task of inverting Plato by revealing the seen, and making what is real to the senses perceived and felt as real and as sufficient to the purposes of attention and admiration, 13: 469.) What matters is to dwell on the way in which liberty of thought and discussion facilitates the emergence of new general truths; but also of false ideas, which by their challenge, compel a renewed awareness of and commitment to established truths.

Mill first asks his audience to contemplate the possibility that the opinions that now govern the perception and interpretation of life are false. These opinions constitute an outlook that contains residual but important elements of Christianity joined to commercial, middle-class, and incipiently democratic and obsolescently aristocratic elements. By false he means liable to be found false in the future. Mill appeals to the terrible facts that Socrates and Jesus were capitally punished, and to the persecution to death of early Christians by the great and wise Roman emperor Marcus Aurelius. The prevailing judgment now is that Socrates and Jesus suffered for the truth, and that persons who are as wise now as Marcus Aurelius was in his time are sure that he erred profoundly. Mill wants to encourage his audience to look at themselves as the future may look at them. After all, they themselves look back at the expense of the past. Yet he does not attribute this imaginative capacity to any previous society. Mill does not explicitly call for imagination or praise his society for sustaining his presumption that imagination may lie within its capacity. But his tactical argument for free expression, on the ground that liberty facilitates the emergence of new truth that may dispossess prevailing falsehood, does require that society has advanced at least in historical imagination since earlier times.

If people say that they want truth, they should not mobilize the "engines of repression" at society's everyday disposal to punish those who may be the bearers of truth. But didn't the truth of Socrates and Jesus ultimately prevail, in spite of all attempts to punish and silence it? Mill insists that the "dictum that truth always triumphs over persecution" is "one of those pleasant falsehoods . . . which all experience refutes." He says, shockingly, that Christianity need not have survived, but rather could have been "extirpated" by Roman persecution: the Christian God (even if true) has no necessary existence. "It is a piece of idle sentimentality that truth, merely as truth, has any inherent power denied to error" (p. 97). The advantage that truth has is that it can be lost "many times," but "in the course of ages there will generally be found persons to rediscover it" in a time when it can withstand persecution for good (pp. 97–98). But that should be small consolation to the living generation. They should facilitate the emergence of needful truth, or at least not discourage it by intimidation and repression.

Mill goes on to argue for liberty of thought and discussion by working with the assumption that the prevailing composite outlook is true. Here the trace of historical relativism is not relevant. Rather, what is relevant is that Mill wants his audience to believe that truth (in the ordinary sense) benefits from error. If society goes after the proponents of error, it is wounding the truth. Mill collects many considerations to show that the best friend of truth is intelligent error, because any established truth, any established outlook, has an inevitable long-term tendency to be buried alive, to have its original creativity forgotten, its precepts turned into commonplaces. Only when the defenders of truth are forced to reconstruct their views, only when they feel threatened can the truth experience a rebirth. Mill is ingenious in championing error, and we are supposed to think that any champion of truth must also champion error. He would have us believe that truth will probably overcome error in a free and fair contest, even though he does not think that it will, on any given occasion, overcome persecution.

Mill's tactic is to defend liberty of thought and discussion as instrumental to truth. The tactic is precisely to make liberty instrumental, when he would rather not instrumentalize it at all. But Mill must instrumentalize it, if his audience, already ill-disposed to uninhibited expression, will pay attention only to instrumental considerations. Then, too, because his audience characteristically thinks of truth as fully and permanently contained in one comprehensive doctrine or in a set of interconnected doctrines, he will labor to show that doctrines that make such total claims may be judged false by later generations or may have their truth refreshed by a threatening encounter with a system of falsehood that also makes such total claims. Mill will meet the public on its own terms. Naturally, he himself is clear that liberty is indispensably instrumental to truth, if truth is the property of one comprehensive doctrine or a set of interconnected ones. After all, Mill is propounding some basic elements of open-mindedness and historical imagination. He is explaining aspects of his own intellectual method: first, try to imagine what the future will think of your substantive views and see whether it might think the same harsh thoughts as you have about the past; and second, be grateful whenever views you cherish are attacked by an intelligent adversary. Liberty of thought and discussion is instrumentally necessary to practicing this method publicly, and thus to the most widely disseminated advantages of truth, as ordinarily conceived. But does Mill finally believe that the ordinary notion of substantive truth is correct? Does he finally believe that one doctrine or set of interconnected doctrines will have the truth, and all other conflicting doctrines will be false? I have already indicated that I do not think so, and I now turn to his reconception of truth, and how it makes free expression all the more important.

The last part of chapter II works with the premise that no substantive doctrine in religion, morality, politics, law, and the conduct of life is entirely true. Near the start of Chapter III, this premise is restated in a strikingly pejorative tone: mankind's truths "for the most part, are only half-truths" (p. 121). Is a half-truth half of a truth? Even more interesting, Mill says that almost no doctrine is entirely false. But doctrinal truth and falsehood no longer mean what they ordinarily mean. No doctrine (or outlook or theory) can claim to hold the full and permanent truth, proven and incontrovertible, on any main issue that matters greatly to people. Not only is truth of doctrine never full, it is never permanent, and what truth it has can be superseded. That a doctrine's truth is incomplete may be found almost bearable; but that it is provisional is almost impossible to accept. And because a doctrine is put forth as containing the full and permanent truth on some main issue, its truth is always accompanied by the sort of falsehood that is induced by exaggeration, seeing with one eye, oversight, blindness, one-sidedness, imperfect sympathies, rabid partisanship, a failure of imagination, a failure of a sense of historical contingency — and, above all, by a failure to appreciate how time works to unsettle any substantive doctrine. Nevertheless, Mill is confident as well that it is "always probable" that at any given time no substantive doctrine is wholly false (p. 114). Every doctrine, almost no matter how seemingly far-fetched, is in touch with some experience asking for articulation and reception. We might say today that many doctrines have at least symptomatic significance, if no other. Every doctrine is worthy of attention, despite the presumptuous claims it will make for its truth. Only where there is (nearly) absolute liberty of thought and discussion can the fuller range of human experience, at a given time, be voiced.

One qualification concerning the temporariness of doctrines should be noticed. Mill's discussion of justice in the last chapter of *Utilitarianism* seems to indicate that, in rough, some core elements of justice are fairly constant through time. Justice is the absence of injustice: justice is not taking away from people their legal and, ideally, moral rights; not dispossessing them arbitrarily, not dismissing the claims of desert, not breaking faith by violating engagements, and aiming for impartiality in judgment (10: 241–44). These are precepts of ancient lineage and given continuous (if often only nominal) adherence. Yet if Mill sometimes speaks universally, he also insists that "different nations and individuals [have] different notions of justice." Furthermore, there are quite a few contending precepts of justice, all of them "confessedly true" (10: 251–52). Each precept plausibly appeals to the idea of justice, but they all disagree on the way to resolve a particular issue. Each precept captures a fragment of justice. Mill holds that only utility, which supposedly grounds justice, can finally resolve these disputes. Be that as it may, we are led by his immensely sophisticated discussion to see how internally complex, even divided, the concept of justice is. Then, too, justice is only a part of a comprehensive moral code, which rests on a wide-ranging interpretation of life and is usually permeated by religious sentiments. Codes differ in their emphases, omissions, and additions to such an extent that one is led to speak of different moralities. Codes differentiate and rank sectors of the population. Then too, justice, like the rest of morality, is in constant reciprocal relations with mores and manners as the code, at any given time, sponsors them. Yet Mill accords a comparative constancy to what would count as the boundaries of justice and injustice. He retrospectively condemns past practices as "universally stigmatised injustice and tyranny" (10: 259). In regard to justice, he teaches a bounded indeterminacy, whereas for other doctrines, he teaches a much more open-ended changeability.

The clear implication of Mill's reconception of the truth of doctrines is that, hard as it is, a thoughtful person will purge himself or herself of the desire for full and permanent truth in any doctrine, whether specific or comprehensive. To be sure, Mill says only that cases in which truth is dispersed along with error in numerous competing doctrines are "commoner" than cases where there is a simple battle between truth and error (p. 112). But by the time Mill finishes his discussion, nothing seems to be left of the possibility that doctrinal truth can ever be full or permanent. Insofar as a comprehensive doctrine or a world outlook is possible, it must be syncretic or synthetic, and it will be provisional. It will be pieced together by "the calmer and more disinterested bystander," in a philosophical or nonpartisan spirit, from the partisan clamor (p. 117). Only a few persons are able to effect a synthetic outlook that knows its own temporariness, and that always allows for the possibility that it has omitted some significant point or other. If liberty is needed for most people to be partisan, liberty is also needed for the disciplined attempt to wrest from each expression of partisanship its fragment of truth and combine it with the fragments put forth by the opposing partisanship of others.

Mill concedes that the sectarian spirit is "often heightened and exacerbated" by liberty, but the "formidable evil" is not "the violent conflict between parts of the truth, but the quiet suppression of half of it" (p. 117).

"Truth, in the great practical concerns of life, is so much a question of the combining and reconciling of opposites, that very few have minds sufficiently capacious and impartial to make the adjustment with an approach to correctness, and it has to be made by the rough process of a struggle between combatants" (p. 114). The obvious implication is that Mill does not expect disinterested persons to occupy the positions of power. But he does expect that in "an atmosphere of freedom," when opinions enter political life in order to guide public decisions, there will be so much aired disagreement that (putatively beneficent) change will characterize society. There will be — there already are, to an appreciable degree — partisan alternation in power, political and social compromise between excessive claims, and cultural hybridity formed by selective incorporation of borrowed ideas. And even if a particular doctrine is not influential, it will be there as a reminder of an experiential possibility. The great advantage for everybody is that when people's tolerance and perhaps mental expectation create an "atmosphere of freedom," when individuals feel no shame at being outspoken even if they are deviant or heretical, no doctrine, specific or broad, will command the conviction of a long-term homogeneous majority. Diversity will be inescapable. The aesthetic horror of mass like-mindedness will be avoided. Society will not petrify.

It is well to stress that whatever quantity of truth is dispersed throughout the doctrines in contention in even the freest and most diverse society, such truth could only be provisional. Mill means more than that doctrines change. His more insistent view is that every doctrinal truth eventually turns false. He casually speaks of persons who not only discover new truths but also "point out when what were once truths are true no longer" (pp. 128–29). No formulation about the temporariness of doctrinal truth can be blunter than that. Improvement or "progress" in doctrine, "which ought to superadd, for the most part only substitutes" (p. 112). In contrast, correct intellectual *method,* some of whose rules of thumb we have already discussed, may remain correct forever. But every content is perishable. That every doctrine is partly true and partly false — such an assumption may also be correct forever — actually means that its fragment of truth is not true as, say, modern science is true but rather is valuable for advancing a benign social purpose. That is all that doctrinal truth amounts to, when the whole of Mill's discussion is taken in.

I suppose that Mill would be understood as exempting his own (revised) utilitarianism from the fate of supersession, as well as from the charge of incompleteness. One day, it, and perhaps other doctrines, may receive "universal recognition" (p. 110). But that intimation strikes me as consistent with the spirit of Mill's discussion only if we assume, with him, that utilitarianism is based on permanent scientific truth in the form of a correct (hedonistic) psychology. But that psychological theory is worse than dubious. And Mill himself rises above utilitarianism as a philosophical doctrine, and can do so only when he ignores his supposed psychological science.

Mill equates doctrinal truth with a judgment or interpretation that is "more wanted, more adapted to the needs of the time" (p. 112). It is not clear what Mill believes the fraction of society's success in adaptation has so far been. In the movement from barbarism to civilization in Europe and North America, how much needless loss, squandered opportunity, and cruel delay have there been? In any case, liberty of thought and discussion contributes to increasing that fraction. The measure of truth is the power that a doctrine lends adaptation: meeting crises or exploiting or forcing opportunities or igniting innovation. Mill also indicates in *Considerations on Representative Government,* with a noteworthy pessimism, that real progress is not only "moving onward" but "quite as much the prevention of falling back," the prevention of "retrograding," "an unceasing struggle against causes of deterioration" (19: 388). In fact, as he says in *The Subjection of Women,* "Any society which is not improving is deteriorating" (21: 335).

Yet there is a problem. Although Mill unambiguously distinguishes between barbarism and civilization, he remains ambiguous as to whether average people in his society, who make up the large majority, when taken one at a time, may ever be said to be better, more civilized, than their counterparts in barbarism. If conformity exists now and has always existed everywhere, does the quality of the average person's inwardness improve, even from barbarism to civilization? Perhaps only reasonableness improves. Or does conformity to the practices of civilization simply have more fortunate consequences? Yet Mill does speak of social progress, forward movement, and when he does, he is addressing a public that believes in it; he is also addressing his allies in the utilitarian camp; yet he, too, believes in it, but not with an entire heart, perhaps.

Liberty of thought and discussion, then, is instrumental to social adaptation, whether in the form of not regressing or of improving. Most people define progress as increase of wealth and power. Mill believes that liberty does indeed contribute indispensably to progress in this sense. Liberty therefore conduces to the increase of happiness: the decrease of suffering and the increase of pleasure. By doing that, liberty is instrumental to popular desires but also to utility as Benthamite philosophers define it. Made possible by liberty, the proliferation of diverse doctrinal ideas from numerous sources may help to augment wealth and power. But devotion to wealth and power must prove ruthless to doctrines. Mill's implication is that unless doctrines encourage worldly pursuits, or are contorted enough (as Christianity has been) to yield the wished-for conclusions, or at least are not felt as impediments, they will be discarded as false — false because obsolete. Society can be quite revisionist epistemologically, provided, of course, it is not aware of what it is doing. In any case, truth is found only in fragments; the truth of these fragments is only provisional. The compound lesson taught by Mill in the last part of Chapter II of *On Liberty* is a major component of the text's radicalism. Yet that radicalism is put at the service of progress, a value commonly held.

It is fair to say, however, that if liberty of thought and discussion becomes an *atmosphere,* as Mill hopes, it is so mixed in with all expression that to continue thinking of it as an instrument becomes misleading. Liberty is no longer merely permission, reluctantly granted, to speak or write within limits, but is instead an invitation to speak and listen, write and read, without a constant awareness of limits. Adventurousness becomes respectable. And if some persons stay more timid than others, they do not begrudge the frankness of others. Intellectual diversity is the proof that liberty exists. To work for the inception of such an atmosphere is Mill's aim. A few philosophers may step back and take aesthetic pleasure in diversity as such. I think that Mill did. Aestheticism is not concerned with the instrumental value of liberty of thought and discussion to truth, whether in the ordinary or the reconceived sense. Beyond truth, and beyond progress and utility, there lies the beauty of intellectual diversity, the spectacle mounted by the play of free minds. And beyond even beauty lies a consideration that I think matters more to Mill than any other: a commitment to human dignity. Liberty of thought and discussion is essential to individuality; human dignity is inseparable from individuality.

In an atmosphere of liberty, its instrumental value is subordinated in the rank of arguments in its defense. When Mill conceives of liberty as essential to individuality, he means liberty as an atmosphere. An atmosphere is not a mere instrument. Liberty is most properly conceived as the medium of life, the pervasive coloration given every expression. Only when liberty is so conceived can individuality emerge. To be committed to human dignity is to believe that human beings can and should become individuals. That is the highest end, and it is unthinkable without a wholehearted political and social commitment to individual sovereignty, to self-regarding liberty. To ask whether defense of individuality is itself just one more doctrine that time may annul is not a question *On Liberty* can answer. Even where individuality cannot yet be realized — Mill calls these circumstances barbarous—it remains the goal. If in the future, liberty becomes unsuitable, maladaptive, in those parts where it already exists, the world would be enduring a catastrophe beyond Mill's intellectual horizon.

At this point I would like to take up, in a preliminary manner, the inseparability of individuality and human dignity. Mill's highest reason for valuing liberty is that it is essential to individuality. I believe that, in turn, the highest reason for valuing individuality is that only where it exists can we see that human dignity is recognized and cherished. Fully involved in the defense of liberty of thought and discussion in Chapter II, concern for human dignity is fundamental to the defense of liberty of self-regarding conduct, which occupies the rest of the book.

Mill speaks only occasionally of dignity throughout *On Liberty,* but on this matter his use of a keyword is not an adequate register of his meaning. It would be odd indeed for a thinker to insist on the absoluteness of a principle like individual sovereignty (self-regarding liberty) and then content himself with subjecting it exclusively to a defense along instrumentalist lines, as if to say that individual sovereignty is only a means to the end of, say, pleasure or happiness. The philosophical motivation is found in what is held as an absolute. Mill insists on the (near) absoluteness of self-regarding liberty of thought and discussion, as well as conduct.

Nowadays we ordinarily regard human dignity as the basis for the guarantee of fundamental individual human rights. The heart of the idea of human dignity is that adults are to be treated in a way that recognizes that they are not prey, or beasts of burden, or pawns, or mere means or implements for ends beyond themselves. Therefore, the idea obviously precludes gross oppression and injustice. But also precluded is paternalism: the tendency to treat adults as if they are children who can never grow up and hence cannot be trusted with freedom or power or candor. When personal and political rights are respected by government and, furthermore, paternalism is avoided, human dignity is on the way to being recognized. No gain in welfare or pleasure or happiness can count if public policy secures them at the expense of human dignity. The heart of human dignity is thus concern for the equal *status* of every human being. But there is more to human dignity, as Mill (and others) conceive it. There is also concern for the human *stature,* a wish to encourage the extraordinary benign achievements that lie within the capacity of probably no more than a few. But these achievements should give us all reason to affirm and honor humanity. Like personal status, human stature is also favored by respect for fundamental rights.

The language of rights often figures in Mill's book, even though he says that he will "forgo any advantage which could be derived to my argument from the idea of abstract right" (p. 81). Actually, there are several phrases in *Principles of Political Economy* that capture some of the thinking behind the fundamental right of personal liberty. Mill wants a "circle" drawn around every person, which no government should overstep; there should be for every person "some space" that is "entrenched around" and kept "sacred from authoritative intrusion"; there should be a "reserved territory" free of interference. Mill says all this in the name of "human freedom and dignity," not in the name of utility (3: 938). He may as well be a theorist of abstract right.

Mill assumes that western societies tend to respect some rights. Nevertheless, complete respect for human dignity has not yet been reached. Part of the reason for such incompleteness is that, for Mill, people themselves must show, but do not consistently show, some degree of individuality if they are to give evidence that they are aware of the importance of their rights. When instead of arguing at length, Mill simply allows himself to enter a judgment, or when he summons his eloquence to convey some of his deepest fears, the basis strongly resembles the same basis as that for fundamental rights: concern for human dignity. One deep fear is that the human status of every person will fail to be recognized, especially through paternalist measures. The critique of paternalism is a prominent component of the idea of human dignity that figures in *On Liberty* as a whole. Mill complicates our thinking by extending the discussion to include the failure of persons to claim or show respect for their own human status. His disgust at such self-ignorance is in part an aesthetic response, but only in part. Furthermore, the locus of Mill's highest hopes is illustrated by developed individuality, the genius or exceptional attainments of a few. They are the guarantors of the human stature. Individuality is thus not in itself a moral idea, even though it is not a morally transgressive idea. The final purpose of defending self-regarding liberty as essential to individuality is not moral: it is aesthetic and even existential. I mean that although it is morally imperative that state and society recognize "the rights of individuality," the motivation of people when they take advantage of these rights need not be essentially moral, even though they will respect moral limits. Only if self-regarding activity can be segregated from other-regarding activity can nonmoral considerations have a chance. In any case, *status* and *stature* are my terms, but they follow Mill's own intermittent usage. Both terms are traceable to the same Latin word for standing. Together they name the constituents of human dignity, as I find that idea at work in *On Liberty*.

I contend that human dignity usurps the primacy of happiness in *On*

Liberty, despite the fact that Mill says that he writes as a utilitarian, though in a revised sense. "I regard utility as the ultimate appeal on all ethical questions; but it must be utility in the largest sense, grounded on the permanent interests of man as a progressive being" (p. 81). But "the largest sense" of utility gets so stretched that it would be more accurate to say that Mill subordinates utility. It must not only be made compatible with human dignity, a consideration superior to itself; it must also be employed only tactically.

I grant that for a utilitarian thinker happiness should have the primacy, the irreducibility to only instrumental worth, that human dignity has for other thinkers. But Mill's notion of human dignity is not a utilitarian principle of any sort and may exact costs from utility. Mill later says in *Utilitarianism* that it is "better to be Socrates dissatisfied than a fool satisfied" (10: 212). His effort to square that sentiment with utility by revising utility is not persuasive. He makes a strained attempt to concede that when either "unconsciousness" or some habit triumphs over will (which is "the child of pleasure," 10: 239), desire for pleasure and avoidance of pain may be rendered inoperative (10: 238). He feels bound, however, to stay with the dogmatic assumption that human beings, like animals, can be consciously self-moved only by the aim of gaining pleasurable sensations and avoiding painful ones, albeit more complex sensations of pleasure and pain than animals can experience. But Mill knows more than his dogma. In explaining why it is better to be Socrates dissatisfied, he nicely says that the "most appropriate appellation" for the unwillingness to trade complex dissatisfaction for rudimentary satisfaction is "a sense of dignity" (10: 212). This sense, it must be said, does not derive from the pursuit of happiness but rather constrains that pursuit.

Unfortunately, in *The Subjection of Women,* Mill insists that the sentiment of personal dignity derives from the happiness one feels from being in control of one's life and finding outlets for one's talents and energies (21: 336, 338). Utilitarian dogma reasserts itself. The pathos of *On Liberty* is lost: the fear that many people get insufficient pleasure from independence and thus yield to the self-diminishment of conformity. They fail to claim their dignity. They succumb to ease. Mill must therefore and actually does introduce considerations unconnected to pleasure or happiness.

Happiness is incidental to human dignity, even though the soul of human dignity is the absence or attenuation of certain kinds of pain. The kinds of pain that are especially relevant to *On Liberty* are not state injustice and oppression but those that are often not felt, but should be by any self-respecting person. They sometimes have to be pointed out, and even then they may not register on those who should feel them. But if felt, the pain is still not what is decisive — rather, the fact that a person has been treated in a certain way that degrades that person. This is the pain of moral, even existential, insult, not tangible loss. One of Mill's key formulations, found in *Considerations on Representative Government,* is that someone can be "degraded, whether aware of it or not." Mill refers here to regulation by authorities of a person's destiny without "consulting him," but the formulation captures a good part of Mill's overall understanding of human dignity (19: 470).

In *Utilitarianism,* he says that a pursuit like power or fame or money or even virtue can be desired "for its own sake"; if so, "it is, however, desired as part of happiness" (10: 236). That is, each pursuit is desired only because the pleasure it yields is owing to an inextricable psychological association with a pleasure beyond itself, not merely because it is a means to a pleasure beyond itself. But this move does not go in the right direction. How can a philosopher of human growth and development liken virtue to love of power and money and thereby make it a "thing, originally a means, and which if it were not a means to anything else, would be and remain indifferent"? (10: 235) Although individuality is not essentially the practice of other-regarding virtue, personal growth must be in part a growth in virtue. A keen awareness of the possibility of harming others depends on virtue. This is so not only because a disinterested love of virtue is "conducive to the general happiness" (10: 235), and a keen awareness of the possibility of harming others depends on virtue, but also because fullness of individual being requires possession of the traits of character that make up or issue in virtue. A person's life contains much more activity than the self-regarding kind.

Only a zealous utilitarian could want a world in which the virtues were not needed, and would believe that virtues were only instrumentally valuable, whatever the practitioners of virtue themselves believed. In some main respects the worst theoretical enemy of *On Liberty* is *Utilitarianism.* Even though not more than a few people are clearly motivated by human dignity, people must become reachable by considerations that appeal to purposes that, from the beginning, and quite apart from the vagaries of psychological association, disregard pleasure and many kinds of pain. To adapt a formulation from *Utilitarianism,* the desirable must be desired (10: 234). Otherwise, the philosopher could not in good conscience connect the idea of human dignity to realizable human potentialities. It is only dogma to say that happiness inevitably results from actually realized potentialities and can be the only motive of such realization. That some pursuit or activity gives us pleasure or happiness does not mean that our motive must be pleasure or happiness, or that the worth to us of what we do lies in the pleasure or happiness we may happen to feel.

The concern for human dignity as the supreme consideration is in Mill himself. He needs no assistance from Kantian philosophy to understand human dignity, even if he thinks he has to make room for what I call tactical arguments. Throughout much of Mill's work, human dignity subordinates all values that threaten to challenge it for primacy. What? Truth, too? Yes, as long as we see that the truth in question is doctrinal truth, as Mill has reconceived truth. Within broad limits, it matters less what people think than that they are completely free to think. That is to say, self-regarding liberty matters above all because it is essential to individuality: but liberty seen not as an instrument but as an atmosphere, as a medium for and a distinctive coloration of all self-regarding activity, as transformative of human beings.

In regard to liberty of thought and discussion, the freedom of mental activity, society's respect for human dignity will show itself in the practice of (nearly) absolute liberty. Only then does society demonstrate that it respects human beings as persons who are not be treated paternalistically, who can be trusted to hear and read just about anything; and correlatively, to speak and write what they please. In a more free society, persons would then take advantage of impunity to be outspoken. They would individualize themselves by mental exertion. To be treated as an adult, as a person expected to think independently, rather than as a vulnerable or untrustworthy child who is never able to become an adult, is the profoundest meaning of liberty of thought and discussion. Mill also says that it is not "solely, or chiefly, to form great thinkers, that freedom of thinking is required. On the contrary, it is as much and even more indispensable, to enable average human beings to attain the mental stature which they are capable of" (p. 102). This is a more positive way of making the antipaternalist point: one is not to be so constrained as to be kept, through intimidation and active social discouragement, from filling out one's mental potentiality as an independent adult. A person must be allowed to grow up, and must be chided when he or she refuses to. In the defense of liberty of thought and discussion, then, Mill introduces a few aspects of the idea of human dignity that permeates *On Liberty,* even though the bulk of Chapter II is devoted to instrumental arguments. In fact, this idea permeates the chapter as much as it does the rest of the book. Absolute (or nearly absolute) freedom of mind is essential to individuality, and society's encouragement of individuality testifies to its recognition of human dignity.

We turn now to Mill's defense of self-regarding liberty of conduct. The word *individuality* is part of the title of Chapter III, as if to suggest, mis-leadingly, that individuality pertains only to conduct and not to thought. And placing the word at the head of Chapter III could be misleading in another way: it may make us think that the expression of individuality in conduct is shown only when conduct is admirable. In Chapters IV and V, Mill finds far from admirable many of the self-regarding activities that he wants to keep free of interference. Yet these, too, are expressions of individ-uality. Human dignity is the greatest stake in all three chapters on conduct. All other considerations are subordinate. But admirable individuality is just as unpopular as the unadmirable kinds. Once again, Mill feels compelled to employ tactical though truthful arguments in defense of liberty.

Let us notice that Mill begins Chapter III with a defense of admirable individuality that is not tactical at all. His initial arguments are those he prefers; only after that work is done does he turn tactical by introducing considerations that he accepts as correct but says that he wishes he did not have to use. What are the ways he prefers? The highest consideration is human dignity; especially, but not only, the component of human stature. (When Mill defends the liberty of unadmirable conduct in Chapters IV and V, the component of individual status is chiefly in play.) Human stature depends on, is measured by, the exceptional individuality of a few. Mill's passion for what he calls "well-being" or "development" — that is, utility in "the largest sense" — is magnificently elaborated. Originality is cele-brated. Again, however, the revised principle of utility is stretched so far that it ceases being itself and is replaced by the idea of human dignity. Stature has indeed to do with well-being or development of the self; but the highest value of such individuality resides in nothing psychological, whether the pleasure or the happiness of the individual, but in the sheer fact that he or she has attained fullness of realization or creative originality, or has shown resoluteness in a plan of life deliberately carried out; in sum, a person has reached full humanity, which is the highest end. In *Principles of Political Economy,* Mill himself in passing distinguishes between utility and individual development when he places under suspicion any regulation, as such, of *other-regarding* activity. He says that "unless the conscience of the individual goes freely with the legal restraint, it partakes, either in a great or a small degree, of the degradation of slavery" (3: 938). The upshot should be that it matters less that a condition is "irksome" than that it is "degrading" (3: 939). Mill hates slavery, even when it is slavery only in an attenuated sense, because it is a profound injury to human dignity, not only because of its physical pains, which may in some cases be slight.

Ask persons of exceptional development what drives them. I grant that they are not likely to say that they are defending or enhancing human dignity. Typically, only a philosopher is preoccupied with human dignity, even if the notion appears these days in political documents and arguments and circulates as a banal sentiment. Exceptional individuals, however, are not likely to answer, either, with Mill's psychological dogma, that they pursue pleasure or even happiness. They do what they do; they do what they must do; they could not imagine being themselves or living with themselves if they did not do what they do; they are held by an idea of vocation or role or by a sense of indefinite possibility. (Ordinary people, in fact, would often answer in the same way.) In any case, talk of pleasure or happiness is incidental to stature and even tends to cheapen it along with the whole idea of human dignity, and Mill manages importantly to fight free of his psychological dogma.

Mill wars on custom as the great impediment to admirable individuality. He wars on the spirit of conformity that perpetuates custom. And if people give lip service to liberty of speech and press, they do not give even that much to developed individuality. Worse, they give the impression that they are more averse to unusual self-regarding conduct than to some sorts of harmful other-regarding conduct (pp. 83, 169). They may not believe in copying one another exactly. But the hold of custom is despotic. Only a few have the courage and determination to loosen its hold and start living as themselves. A few succeed; more could try, if the situation were not so punitive or self-punitive. And if most people cannot be geniuses — geniuses are "*more* individual than any other people" — or demonstrate a commendable originality; and if the experiments in living of most people would not likely be "any improvement on established practice" if others copied them, the spectacle of massive and unimaginative conformity to custom is disheartening to anyone who cherishes human dignity (p. 129). Mill's aim is to coax people into growing more tolerant of the self-development of those few who attain it, and make people less ready to disown and torment them for their unappreciated departures from the norm.

Mill eventually turns tactical by arguing that just as new challenges to old truth are needed along with new truths, so in the realm of conduct, challenges to custom revivify the reasons for it and may initiate the process of changing it. But first he will defend individuality from the philosophical individualist perspective, for the sake of the individual. (This is not to say

that any individual would act from any of Mill's philosophical considerations.) The social perspective is, oddly enough for a self-described utilitarian, tactical: its truth is for Mill himself less important.

To be an individual means that one will not follow some of the salient
established ways of behaving. (There cannot be total nonconformity, of
course. Mill speaks warmly, for example, of the habits of other-regarding
virtue, which must be instilled and repeatedly exercised to be efficacious,
10: 238–39). If one behaved exactly like all others in one's class (or occupation or region or religion), one would show that one lacked the will to be an
individual. One would be betraying one's potentiality. Custom does not
tailor its specifications for each person; to follow it in all particulars must
result in one's *self-inflicted* injury to one's status as a human being. In
contrast, an individual enhances human stature, the dignity of the human
race, by significant breaks with custom. The spectacle of independent individuals strengthens "the tie which binds every individual to the [human]
race, by making the race infinitely better worth belonging to" (p. 127). It is
as if insisting on and achieving respect for one's human dignity, and enhancing the whole human stature by one's own self-development (if one is
able) were finally the redemption of the honor of humanity in the eyes of the
philosopher. As he says in *Principles of Political Economy,* originality and
individuality are "the only source of any real progress, and of most of the
qualities which make the human race much superior to any herd of animals" (3: 940). What is "real progress" if not the increase of individuality?

The philosopher is an aesthete, surely. In his marvelous essay "Bentham," published twenty years before *On Liberty,* Mill had defined the
aesthetic perspective on conduct by reference to what is admirable (10:
112). To be sure, in *Utilitarianism* he relegates the aesthetic perspective to
judgment of persons and removes it from actions, and seems to tame his
aestheticism for the sake of his fellow utilitarians. Aestheticism is strong,
however, in *On Liberty.* Yet Mill is more than an aesthete. He is a theorist of
human dignity, and not because he is first an aesthete, and not only because
he is dedicated to the cause of the moral treatment of human beings.

What is wrong with custom as such? In a word, it precludes individual
choice and therefore the development of the "mental, moral, and aesthetic
stature" of which a person is capable (p. 132). Mill sometimes also speaks
of mental, moral, and practical faculties, and how the exercise of choice
requires and promotes them in the conduct of life. To follow custom nar-
rows the scope of choice and leaves a person less developed than he or she
could be. Mill says that "to conform to custom, merely *as* custom" does not
contribute to the cultivation of "the distinctive endowment of a human

being" (p. 123). To be sure, he says that an "intelligent" following of custom is better than "a blind and simply mechanical adhesion to it" (p. 124). But that is a scant concession. Mill transforms the conformist into something not human, a creature who has no need for "any other faculty than the ape-like one of imitation" (p. 124). Concern for what is peculiarly individual or human is surely not utilitarian, and it is a main element of Mill's most important argument against custom.

There are other considerations. Just as prevailing opinions may be false, so prevailing customs may reflect narrow or misinterpreted past experience that has congealed, and now block better ways of doing things. Alternatively, just as prevailing opinions may be true but not deemed true by a particular individual, so the interpretation of experience congealed in custom may be correct, or correct for most people, but not for a given person. This latter consideration, when joined to the denunciation of conformity for the sake of conformity, conformity to custom as custom, is the key to Mill's case. A given person, in his or her self-regarding activity, may find a custom oppressive and an impediment to development or self-realization; at the same time, one may feel insulted by the mere fact of doing what others do, and doing it just because they do it and expect one to do it also. To the philosophical observer, both individual status and human stature are involved in an admirable individual's rebellion against conformity. The motives of the nonconformist, the practitioner of what Mill calls "eccentricity," are not necessarily those of the philosophical observer; they would be closer to those we mentioned earlier. In short, utility, as Mill revises it, is not Mill's highest reason, nor is it a reason that nonconformists would recognize as a plausible account of their motivation.

Having dwelt on the notion that "only the cultivation of individuality" can produce "well-developed human beings," Mill says that he "might here close the argument." But such considerations will not "suffice to convince those who most need convincing." Indeed, he assumes that people "do not desire liberty, and would not avail themselves of it." He must offer the prospect of some reward for allowing a few to develop themselves by exercising their individual sovereignty (their self-regarding liberty) to the full (p. 128). The tactical arguments then commence.

We should notice again that Mill regards the condition of developed individuals, taken one at a time, as the supreme end. It is worth remarking, however, that in *Utilitarianism* he says that the utilitarian standard is "not the agent's own greatest happiness, but the greatest amount of happiness altogether." He makes that point precisely to instrumentalize a person of "noble character" who arguably may not always be the happier for his nobleness, but whose nobleness "makes other people happier," makes the world "immensely a gainer by it" (10: 213). Mill may think that as long as one remains committed to utility as the highest standard, the meaning of utility must be not the individual's greatest happiness but rather the greatest total happiness in society. But if Mill transcends his utilitarianism, as I believe he does, then his statement in *Utilitarianism* must be read in the light of that book's project, which is to clarify and deepen utilitarianism and persuade skeptics that this doctrine is not egotistical. The trouble is that we are there presented with a case in which utility — the overall happiness of society — conflicts with and is given precedence to the individualist perspective, which is grounded in human dignity and is nothing egotistical, and which prevails in Chapter III of *On Liberty*. The defense of liberty of thought and discussion in Chapter II does not show such a conflict; it shows only a subordination of utility (in the revised sense) to the idea of human dignity, when the demands of the two principles happen to coincide, as they always or mostly do when free expression is the issue. Perhaps we can say that when Mill turns tactical in Chapter III, he finds a way of showing that here, too, human dignity and utility (in the revised sense in which self-development is part of happiness) may happen to coincide. Perhaps they do. But it is remarkable that even if they do, Mill's heart is not in the utilitarian argument. The moment of reluctantly turning tactical is one of the clearest evidences that Mill's commitment to human dignity is distinct from any utilitarianism and surpasses it in importance. The individualist perspective ranks higher than any social perspective.

In his tactical instrumental defense of admirable individuality — admirable because well-developed — Mill not only believes in the truth of his arguments, in their validity for the present stage of civilization, he is unsparing in his estimation of the majority whom he is supposedly trying to win over to greater tolerance for the liberty they do not themselves exercise. He says that the almost unmediated and unchecked power of the most numerous classes in society "render mediocrity the ascendant power among mankind," and that the "only power deserving of the name is that of masses" (p. 130).

Notwithstanding his pervasive harshness — somewhere or other in his writings, he is harsh to each class in society, from the aristocratic top, down through all gradations, to the very bottom — Mill means to be instructive. Yet the instruction is not very flattering. The advantage of liberty to those now unfriendly to it and not given to its noticeable exercise is that if they grow more tolerant, and an atmosphere of freedom ensues, customs are much more likely to change for the better. Progress can be made. "The initiation of all wise or noble things, comes and must come from individuals; generally at first from some one individual" (p. 131). Stagnation or decay can be avoided, and a society can keep up with the opportunities that present themselves or that can be elicited from a seemingly recalcitrant situation. Innovation can lead "the movement of the world" (p. 136). Mill seems to be referring to progress, as in Chapter II, as increase of wealth and power. He knows that people welcome "new inventions in mechanical things"; even that society is "eager for improvement in politics, in education, even in morals." But people seem ignorant of the preconditions of what they desire. "It is not progress that we object to. . . . It is individuality that we war against . . . forgetting that the unlikeness of one person to another is generally the first thing which draws the attention of either to the imperfection of his own type, and the superiority of another" (p. 135).

Notice that Mill traces progress not to the mutually instructive diversity of groups in society — what we today call cultural pluralism or multiculturalism — but to diverse individuality. Mill does believe in the desirability of classes and in the pluralism of "distinct forces" or "sources of power" in society's structure (20: 269), but this is not the same as affirmative multiculturalism. In any case, he is keenly aware of the dangers of ethnic rivalries, despite his eye for the benefits "to the human race" of the "admixture of nationalities" (19: 549).

When change in custom occurs now, it is like — or it is only — a change of fashion, which "may change once or twice a year." This is merely "change . . . for change's sake," a process of change in which "all change together" (p. 135). (Not that Mill is impervious to the charm of change as such.) Real progress is human improvement, not technical advance or uniform surface alteration. Mill is thus trying to win sympathy for a revised conception of progress, even as he conveys the idea that there are very narrow limits to the degree to which most people can be improved. Indeed, Mill leaves the reader with the impression that even the tactical defense of self-regarding liberty of conduct as essential to individuality will fall on deaf ears. In matters of conduct people are inveterately unreceptive to the idea that the present always derides the past for its ways, and yet the process by which the present got to be what it is depended on a few who dared to be individual, whether or not there was an atmosphere of freedom.

Society exists for human beings to become individuals. By themselves, admirable individuals justify their society and even the whole human race. Individuals may serve society directly or by the influence of their example, but they do not exist for society; society exists for them, for anyone who, without harming others, is able to emerge as a well-developed individual, prepared to be himself or herself fully. For the philosopher of human dignity, no further consideration dealing with self-regarding liberty of conduct is superior to that one. (Only the recognition of everyone's human status matters as much.) For whatever reasons, most people do not, and probably will never, take or force the opportunity to unsettle their relation to prevailing customs. Conformity is their comfort, their stay against confusion, the assurance of their innocence. A few take or force their opportunity and fight free, to some extent, and do so admirably. Yet others (always assumed to constitute, in aggregation, no more than a minority) fight free, but not admirably. They deviate from prevailing custom, but not in a manner that Mill, for one, admires, or would choose for himself. Yet they, too, should not be interfered with, but rather allowed to do what they do, and live as they live, whenever they do not harm others. They must be free even to harm themselves, whether or not they recognize what they do to themselves as harm; or they must be permitted to individuate themselves in an ill-developed or lopsided way. Mill is also the advocate of their liberty. He implicitly extends to unadmirable deviance what he says about (admirably) eccentric individuals: "In this age, the mere example of nonconformity, the mere refusal to bend the knee to custom, is itself a service" (p. 131). Mill's revulsion is directed to the mechanical uniformity that all conformism engenders, and is partly aesthetic, but the major part comes from the thought that uniformity indicates a dreadful mixture of misplaced self-confidence and personal timidity.

Chapters IV and V take up a number of specific cases of unadmirable individuality. The cases are heterogeneous. They include such unlovely habits as gambling, drug taking, casual fornication, and idleness; and such unconventional practices as polygamy, sabbatarian amusements and labor, and un-Christian modes of worship. None of these activities is other-regarding; all are putatively voluntary. All are disliked or abhorred by the majority. Efforts are made to criminalize or otherwise abolish or penalize them. Mill is not averse to minimal regulation in some cases. But his libertarianism is most pronounced in these two chapters, just because he wants liberty granted to what a sizable majority sees no worth in, and often finds unclean, self-destructive, or simply immoral. Just as Mill disallows calling any opinion immoral or impious; so with self-regarding conduct. Morality covers only other-regarding conduct, and Mill does not teach a subjective relativism in moral questions. In religion, on the other hand, one person's impiety is another person's piety. That view is not relativism, either, but absolute respect for religious (or unreligious) conscience.

But shouldn't society or the state take a hand in saving people from themselves? Isn't it true that interference can often rescue an adult from habits and practices that waste one's chance to become happier — habits and practices that once a person is rid of, he or she will feel only gratitude for deliverance from them? Even more, isn't it true that precisely by Mill's own standard of full individual development, interference with a person may be necessary if he or she is to start on the path of development?

Mill is certain that compelling an adult for his or her own good, even when Mill agrees in the judgment of what is good, is unacceptable. What is good for Mill as one particular person, with his tastes and ambitions, may not be good for another. The other may not find it good. His conduct, even when aberrant and perhaps addictive, shows that he finds his good where others see only something wasteful or disgusting. Mill often says, especially in *Principles of Political Economy,* that persons must be presumed to take "a juster and more intelligent view of their own interest" (3: 951). He is here trying to limit state interference in economic affairs, which are other-regarding and which are therefore in principle amenable to such interference. But he probably intends the formulation to be generally applicable to all self-regarding activity as well. Yet I doubt that he is simply saying that a person knows himself better than others can know him, and that therefore the sole wrong of interference in self-regarding matters is that it is likely to be ignorant because presumptuous. That is often true. Each one is "the person most interested in his own well-being" (p. 140). But Mill means more. He certainly does not give primacy to the primitive principle of utility — "all restraint, qua restraint, is an evil" (p. 157). Whatever Bentham may think, Mill does not hold, for example, that the pain of being blocked in the wish to harm another can have moral weight, even if the pain of punishment for harming another may truly have moral weight. There is, he says, "no parity between the desire of a thief to take a purse, and the desire of the right owner to keep it" (p. 147). More to the point, the pain of frustration has no moral weight in Mill's condemnation of interference with self-regarding liberty. This utilitarian precept plays only a small role in *On Liberty,* and it is attributed only to "some" [utilitarians] in *Utilitarianism* (10: 242). His point is rather that the wrong of well-intended and high-minded (what we now call "perfectionist") interference with self-regarding activity is that it treats an adult like a child. It is better for a person to go his own way, even to perdition, than to be improved or saved by paternalist compulsion. "Vigorous and independent characters" will "infallibly rebel" against coercion in self-regarding matters (p. 146). The errors a person makes are "far outweighed by the evil of allowing others to constrain him to what they deem his good" (p. 141). Human dignity is the stake; especially in the aspect of individual status. The human dignity of the undignified requires that they be let alone.

For Mill, proposed interference becomes even worse when it is justified on the grounds that when a person fails to live up to his potentiality, he becomes a drag on the rest, he fails to make the contribution he owes society. Mill summons great angry eloquence when he discusses the rationale offered for the prohibition of alcohol. His anger becomes all the more remarkable when we notice that this rationale converts what Mill sees as self-regarding activity into other-regarding. A representative prohibitionist says that strong drink "destroys my primary right of security, by constantly creating and stimulating social disorder. It invades my right of equality, by deriving a profit from the creation of a misery I am taxed to support. It impedes my right to free moral and intellectual development, by surrounding my path with dangers, and by weakening and demoralizing society, from which I have a right to claim mutual aid and intercourse" (p. 152). One would think that perhaps Mill would concede something to this reasoning, even if he finally rejects the position. But he refuses.

Not merely is it the case that most people who drink do not drink to excess, and that therefore prohibition penalizes the innocent to get at the rest (p. 151). More is at issue. Mill responds that the prohibitionist principle is "monstrous" because "there is no violation of liberty which it would not justify; it acknowledges no right to any freedom whatever, except perhaps to that of holding opinions in secret, without ever disclosing them. . . . The doctrine ascribes to all mankind a vested interest in each other's moral, intellectual, and even physical perfection, to be defined by each claimant according to his own standard" (p. 152). Perfectionism for the many is unthinkable without systematic paternalism, and paternalism is still despotism, even when the paternalistically handled person might eventually concede, after his handling, that the authorities were right. The person is injured in status, even though he may have already injured himself as a functioning human being. Status is altogether beyond functioning in philosophical importance. Of course, if a really sizable minority, or worse, a majority, were to be drunkards or otherwise waste their lives in drug addiction or gambling or idleness, then Mill would have to be prepared to invoke the principle he puts forward in Chapter I; namely, that when a population is not yet sufficiently advanced, an enlightened and paternalist despot is the best fate that can befall them. Individual sovereignty (nearly absolute self-regarding liberty) is a principle fit only for those who have "attained the capacity of being guided to their own improvement by conviction or persuasion." Mill holds that England, Western Europe, and North America have "long since" reached this stage, unlike, say, India (p. 81).

Yet his antipaternalist position may have some inconsistency. There may be more Western personal incapacity (backwardness) than he chooses to observe. Numbers of people are unable to improve themselves: their ingrained and inescapable habits and practices place them beyond the improving reach of "free and equal discussion" (p. 81). Wouldn't it be sensible to contemplate policies that were aimed at the personal enhancement and moral rescue of (only) certain sectors of the population? Mill firmly believes in requiring and, if need be, subsidizing universal primary education. He balks, however, at any proposal that interferes with the self-regarding liberty of adults.

Mill says, in response to the scandalized hatred shown the polygamous Mormons, "I am not aware that any community has a right to force another to be civilized" (p. 154). Suppose, however, that there are pockets of barbarism in the midst of civilization, rather than in geographically remote enclaves. Isn't that a threat to civilization? All Mill can say is that if barbarism could return victoriously, civilization would already be "degenerate" and deserve to go under. "If society lets any considerable number of its members grow up children, incapable of being acted on by rational consideration of distant motives, society has itself to blame for the consequences" (p. 146). Barbarism is not so much a threat as a deservedly mortal disgrace to the society in whose midst it has returned.

I think that Mill's background assumption is that only a minority (in aggregation) waste their lives, as judged by some external, perhaps aesthetic standard. To waste one's life is to be addicted to drink or drugs or some other ruinous habit. I also think that Mill would wish to see them saved against their will, if need be, but does not say so. Does the matter come down to the following calculation? It is better *for others* that a minority be let alone rather than saved against their will. Why is it better for others? Perhaps once any sector of the population is treated paternalistically, a precedent is set for treating the whole society in this manner, for one purpose or another, and more and more. But this "slippery-slope" argument signifies that a social perspective has replaced the individualist perspective; or at least that the (paternalist) rescue of a minority from fundamental incapacity is rejected for the sake of demonstrating respect for the individual status, the human dignity, of persons in the majority. If, on the other hand, a majority of a population lead dissolute lives, I cannot imagine that Mill would intend his theory of individual sovereignty to apply. Worry over the paternalist insult to human status would then seem altogether misguided.

Throughout my discussion, I have repeatedly referred to the idea of human dignity, and to its two aspects, individual status and human stature. I shall conclude by reassembling the considerations that Mill uses to build up a defense of human dignity. To repeat: human dignity is acknowledged and respected when (nearly) absolute self-regarding liberty is seen as essential to individuality, with the result that an atmosphere of freedom is created. In that atmosphere, people feel free to think and speak out, and numbers of people feel free to become themselves more fully, whether admirably or not. An act done in a free society is not the same act when done in an unfree society. Liberty changes every meaning. A free society is the setting for human dignity. The problem of poverty must be faced if the preconditions of human dignity are to be met and its setting is truly to be established; but Mill earnestly addresses this problem in other writings, however unsatisfactorily. Then, too, a background assumption of *On Liberty* is that the state does not administer oppression or systematic injustice. To that extent, and it is considerable, the status of each individual as an equal human being is recognized by the political system. Fundamental individual human rights are respected. But there is more to individual status than the absence of oppression and systematic injustice, ungrateful as it may sound to say so. And there is also more to human dignity than individual status: there is also human stature. I shall now concern myself with human dignity only as it is implicated in the enjoyment of the moral right of self-regarding liberty in regard to conduct.

Let us take the aspect of status first. As we have seen, paternalism is the one policy (enacted by the state, but often owing to social pressure) that works most harshly against self-regarding liberty and hence against individuality, to which liberty is essential. But the damage done by paternalism is not the only consideration. Although many people seem not to want to become individuals and discourage others from the pursuit, Mill nonetheless hopes for some incremental advance. For the sake of that increment, he celebrates institutions and arrangements that favor the appetite for individuality — specifically, the individuality of average human beings. Put negatively, the net effect of new and better political and social practices would be resistance to an ever greater threat, a society of "cramped and dwarfed" people (p. 127). The avoidance of human dwarfing, of diminishment and self-diminishment, is a prominent theme in *On Liberty* (and other writings by Mill) because dwarfing appears to be inherent in many social tendencies that relentlessly remove diversity from the world (pp. 136–37). To be sure, Mill must side with some of these tendencies, like greater mass education, increased prosperity, and easier movement and communication. But all these tendencies "tend to raise the low and to lower the high" (p. 137). Their underside is therefore the potentiality for a society of interchangeable people. To retard this kind of painless and unresented dwarfing, Mill urges practices that awaken and reward energy. (The influence on Mill of Tocqueville's concept of democratic despotism is profound.) These practices involve voluntary cooperation with others and hence are often not self-regarding activities. But without them, the emergence into even a minimal individuality, so to speak, is not likely. Undertaken for one common purpose or another, these practices — to use Mill's phrase of approval about private business enterprise — are "further recommended by all the advantages which have been set forth in this Essay as belonging to individuality of development, and diversity of modes of action" (p. 170). Mill ends *On Liberty* with a discussion of reasons for discouraging governmental activity when private activity can take its place, even though the government, by acting, would not infringe either self-regarding or other-regarding liberty (pp. 169 ff.). Mill wants more energy, more vitality in people. Passivity contributes to dwarfing. Energetic cooperation with others may awaken an appetite for one's own use of self-regarding liberty, and a respect for everyone else's. People give proof that their rights matter to them by exercising them. Thereby they show awareness of their human status.

Respect for individual status necessitates political and social arrangements that work to inspire a distaste for passivity, especially that which ensues from a system in which all the main benefits of life are distributed by an apparently beneficent central agency. The point is to promote a society whose arrangements and institutions are inclusive and participatory. (Mill defended universal adult suffrage, for example, when women and many men could not vote.) From the perspective of individuality, especially the minimal individuality of the average person, the great advantage is that inclusion and participation confer recognition and acceptance on all adults; and thence, relief from enclosure within one's narrow and obscure circle. Greater individual energy must result. This view reflects not only Tocqueville's influence but Mill's intense admiration of democratic Athens. A person's mental, moral, and practical faculties are strengthened by participating with others and helping them to decide common affairs. More developed, one can think better of oneself and hence of one's liberty. One can attain one's life as one's own. If individuality is to be a common aspiration, provision must be made for significant voluntary association, for the web of freely chosen relationships. Exceptional individuals often need solitude and may express their individuality in conduct that is exclusive. But the average and the exceptional are, for Mill, two distinct categories.

Exceptional individuals show what humanity is capable of, especially for the good. This is what human stature is about. Their experiments in thinking and living enlarge our sense of human capacity. Both their spontaneity and their deliberate effort to design and live a life show how keenly aware they are that liberty is essential to their individuality. They take humanity outside itself. If energy is a desirable characteristic of the raised average, creativity marks the exceptional. Their strong nature, their genius, drives them beyond boundaries, and makes the solid and stable look fluid and surpassable. A society that means to respect human dignity must take care not to stifle or penalize creativity. Ideally, society would do so for the sake of the exceptional few, and not for its own advantage. Only if society does not instrumentalize, Mill seems to say, is liberty authentically established; and when it is, advantages to every individual, exceptional as well as average, will flow inevitably.

I would add my own tactical point. Mill's tactical arguments, whether utilitarian or not, are instrumental. But instrumental arguments, howsoever truthfully urged, are always open to rebuttal on plausible empirical grounds, and are not just a target of hostile sophistry or bluster. These arguments seem to be the most hard-headed and therefore to have the strongest appeal. Yet they are the most vulnerable. The idea of human dignity, apparently vaporous or insubstantial and addressed to only a few, may turn out to be the least vulnerable and hence the most eligible as a "fall-back" position, after all attempted empirical rebuttals. The highest principle is the safest, even if it is itself vulnerable to snobbish aesthetic distaste or philosophical skepticism. Or it would be the safest if a version of it that especially emphasized individual status could be popularly absorbed. Mill did not think it could be in his time — were the democratic revolutions of the eighteenth century and after in vain? — but maybe it is what helps to keep the wish for liberty going in ours.

Once the idea of human dignity is seen as Mill's most important reason for self-regarding liberty, a certain irony in Mill's work discloses itself. Mill is determined to defend the dignity of people who, whatever they may say, are insensitive to its claims. Indeed, Mill writes as if most people want to be dwarfed. To be sure, they run the danger of being dwarfed by tendencies in modern life that they have no control over — except for their avidity for goods and pleasures that grow increasingly available. They appear, however, to accept enlistment as mere members, conforming to external expectations, and finding sufficient recompense for their conformity. If they could imagine their dignity at stake, they would not be so active in enforcing passivity, enforcing submission to custom and to mutually (if not fully consciously) dictated terms and channels of endeavor. They could not possibly be skeptical or hostile toward self-regarding liberty, as they are now. Mill wants people to have what they apparently do not want. He is on the side of their potential selves in the war that *On Liberty* declares against their actual selves.

That such a fight is necessary at all fills Mill with chagrin. Of course, Mill could not and would not force an awareness of their dignity on people: such an ambition goes against the teaching of the whole book. But step by step, greater open-mindedness may lead to greater tolerance of the uses that others make of their self-regarding liberty. With greater tolerance may come less conformity, less timidity. With more inclusion and participation, also, may come less timidity. And from these possibilities an awakened sense of their own dignity may take hold. People would cease thinking of liberty as a dangerous instrument and live in it as an exhilarating atmosphere. People would cling to the thought that human nature is not a machine constructed to do a job of work, but "a tree, which requires to grow and develope itself on all sides, according to the tendency of the inward forces which make it a living thing" (p. 124). At the extreme of hope, "human beings become a noble and beautiful object of contemplation" (p. 127). (Aesthetic considerations are rarely absent from Mill's understanding of human dignity.)

Similarly, the exceptional few may not give a thought to the abstract principle of human stature; their motives, their drives, are what they must be. But it does not matter: they do not fight their own potentiality. The philosopher of human dignity need not give them encouragement, only defense. He has nothing to reproach them for. Indeed, they provide the examples that inspire the philosopher to conceptualize human dignity.

In short, human dignity is a philosopher's idea in Mill's work. Its audience is assumed to be small and made up only of those who are given to ruminate on the human condition, and who do so as free spirits — that is, as thinkers who are committed to the belief that without the aspiration to individuality, the very idea of what it means to be human remains impoverished, and in whom a general sense of decline or decadence, in spite of and yet because of technical progress, becomes too tempting.

On Liberty
John Stuart Mill

A Note on the Text

The present text reprints the first edition of *On Liberty* (1859). Notes by the editors appear as numbered footnotes. Mill's own footnotes are signaled by asterisks. In a few cases, the editors have appended, in brackets, comments after Mill's notes.

The grand, leading principle, towards which every argument unfolded in these pages directly converges, is the absolute and essential importance of human development in its richest diversity.

WILHELM VON HUMBOLDT: *Sphere and Duties of Government.*

To the beloved and deplored memory of her who was the inspirer, and in part the author, of all that is best in my writings — the friend and wife whose exalted sense of truth and right was my strongest incitement, and whose approbation was my chief reward — I dedicate this volume. Like all that I have written for many years, it belongs as much to her as to me; but the work as it stands has had, in a very insufficient degree, the inestimable advantage of her revision; some of the most important portions having been reserved for a more careful re-examination, which they are now never destined to receive. Were I but capable of interpreting to the world one half the great thoughts and noble feelings which are buried in her grave, I should be the medium of a greater benefit to it, than is ever likely to arise from anything that I can write, unprompted and unassisted by her all but un-rivalled wisdom.

CHAPTER I

INTRODUCTORY

The subject of this Essay is not the so-called Liberty of the Will, so unfortunately opposed to the misnamed doctrine of Philosophical Necessity; but Civil, or Social Liberty: the nature and limits of the power which can be legitimately exercised by society over the individual. A question seldom stated, and hardly ever discussed, in general terms, but which profoundly influences the practical controversies of the age by its latent presence, and is likely soon to make itself recognised as the vital question of the future. It is so far from being new, that in a certain sense, it has divided mankind, almost from the remotest ages; but in the stage of progress into which the more civilized portions of the species have now entered, it presents itself under new conditions, and requires a different and more fundamental treatment.

The struggle between Liberty and Authority is the most conspicuous feature in the portions of history with which we are earliest familiar, particularly in that of Greece, Rome, and England. But in old times this contest was between subjects, or some classes of subjects, and the government. By liberty, was meant protection against the tyranny of the political rulers. The rulers were conceived (except in some of the popular governments of Greece) as in a necessarily antagonistic position to the people whom they ruled. They consisted of a governing One, or a governing tribe or caste, who derived their authority from inheritance or conquest, who, at all events, did not hold it at the pleasure of the governed, and whose supremacy men did not venture, perhaps did not desire, to contest, whatever precautions might be taken against its oppressive exercise. Their power was regarded as necessary, but also as highly dangerous; as a weapon which they would attempt to use against their subjects, no less than against external enemies. To prevent the weaker members of the community from being preyed upon by innumerable vultures, it was needful that there should be an animal of prey stronger than the rest, commissioned to keep them down. But as the king of the vultures would be no less bent upon preying on the flock, than any of the minor harpies, it was indispensable to be in a perpetual attitude of defence against his beak and claws. The aim, therefore, of patriots, was to set limits to the power which the ruler should be suffered to exercise over the community; and this limitation was what they meant by liberty. It was attempted in two ways. First, by obtaining a recognition of certain immunities, called political liberties or rights, which it was to be regarded as a breach of duty in the ruler to infringe, and which if he did infringe, specific resistance, or general rebellion, was held to be justifiable. A second, and generally a later expedient, was the establishment of constitutional checks; by which the consent of the community, or of a body of some sort, supposed to represent its interests, was made a necessary condition to some of the more important acts of the governing power. To the first of these modes of limitation, the ruling power, in most European countries, was compelled, more or less, to submit. It was not so with the second; and to attain this, or when already in some degree possessed, to attain it more completely, became everywhere the principal object of the lovers of liberty. And so long as mankind were content to combat one enemy by another, and to be ruled by a master, on condition of being guaranteed more or less efficaciously against his tyranny, they did not carry their aspirations beyond this point.

A time, however, came, in the progress of human affairs, when men ceased to think it a necessity of nature that their governors should be an independent power, opposed in interest to themselves. It appeared to them much better that the various magistrates of the State should be their tenants or delegates, revocable at their pleasure. In that way alone, it seemed, could they have complete security that the powers of government would never be abused to their disadvantage. By degrees, this new demand for elective and temporary rules became the prominent object of the exertions of the popular party, wherever any such party existed; and superseded, to a considerable extent, the previous efforts to limit the power of rulers. As the struggle proceeded for making the ruling power emanate from the periodical choice of the ruled, some persons began to think that too much importance had been attached to the limitation of the power itself. *That* (it might seem) was a resource against rulers whose interests were habitually opposed to those of the people. What was now wanted was, that the rulers should be identified with the people; that their interest and will should be the interest and will of the nation. The nation did not need to be protected against its own will. There was no fear of its tyrannizing over itself. Let the rulers be effectually responsible to it, promptly removable by it, and it could afford to trust them with power of which it could itself dictate the use to be made. Their power was but the nation's own power, concentrated, and in a form convenient for exercise. This mode of thought, or rather perhaps of feeling, was common among the last generation of European liberalism, in the

Continental section of which, it still apparently predominates. Those who admit any limit to what a government may do, except in the case of such governments as they think ought not to exist, stand out as brilliant exceptions among the political thinkers of the Continent. A similar tone of sentiment might by this time have been prevalent in our own country, if the circumstances which for a time encouraged it, had continued unaltered.

But, in political and philosophical theories, as well as in persons, success discloses faults and infirmities which failure might have concealed from observation. The notion, that the people have no need to limit their power over themselves, might seem axiomatic, when popular government was a thing only dreamed about, or read of as having existed at some distant period of the past. Neither was that notion necessarily disturbed by such temporary aberrations as those of the French Revolution, the worst of which were the work of an usurping few,[1] and which, in any case, belonged, not to the permanent working of popular institutions, but to a sudden and convulsive outbreak against monarchical and aristocratic despotism. In time, however, a democratic republic came to occupy a large portion of the earth's surface, and made itself felt as one of the most powerful members of the community of nations; and elective and responsible government became subject to the observations and criticisms which wait upon a great existing fact. It was now perceived that such phrases as "self-government," and "the power of the people over themselves," do not express the true state of the case. The "people" who exercise the power, are not always the same people with those over whom it is exercised; and the "self-government" spoken of, is not the government of each by himself, but of each by all the rest. The will of the people, moreover, practically means, the will of the most numerous or the most active *part* of the people; the majority, or those who succeed in making themselves accepted as the majority: the people, consequently, *may* desire to oppress a part of their number; and precautions

1. Mill grants the essential justice of the French Revolution and its consistency with the progress of liberty. He reserves his objection for the "aberrations" of the revolution: that is, those of its episodes that tended toward the consolidation of state power at the sacrifice of personal liberty. A conspicuous instance of such a reversal was the assumption of unrestricted control over public life by the Committee of Public Safety from June 1793 through July 1794, a period sometimes referred to by historians as the Reign of Terror. Mill would have been aware that the way was opened to such abuses by antilibertarian legislation — for example, the Law of Suspects, passed in September 1793, which meted out severe punishments not only for treason against the revolution but for insufficient zeal in its service.

are as much needed against this, as against any other abuse of power. The limitation, therefore, of the power of government over individuals, loses none of its importance when the holders of power are regularly accountable to the community, that is, to the strongest party therein. This view of things, recommending itself equally to the intelligence of thinkers and to the inclination of those important classes in European society to whose real or supposed interests democracy is adverse, has had no difficulty in establishing itself; and in political speculations "the tyranny of the majority" is now generally included among the evils against which society requires to be on its guard.

Like other tyrannies, the tyranny of the majority was at first, and is still vulgarly, held in dread, chiefly as operating through the acts of the public authorities. But reflecting persons perceived that when society is itself the tyrant — society collectively, over the separate individuals who compose it — its means of tyrannizing are not restricted to the acts which it may do by the hands of its political functionaries. Society can and does execute its own mandates: and if it issues wrong mandates instead of right, or any mandates at all in things with which it ought not to meddle, it practises a social tyranny more formidable than many kinds of political oppression, since, though not usually upheld by such extreme penalties, it leaves fewer means of escape, penetrating much more deeply into the details of life, and enslaving the soul itself. Protection, therefore, against the tyranny of the magistrate is not enough: there needs protection also against the tyranny of the prevailing opinion and feeling; against the tendency of society to impose, by other means than civil penalties, its own ideas and practices as rules of conduct on those who dissent from them; to fetter the development, and, if possible, prevent the formation, of any individuality not in harmony with its ways, and compel all characters to fashion themselves upon the model of its own. There is a limit to the legitimate interference of collective opinion with individual independence: and to find that limit, and maintain it against encroachment, is as indispensable to a good condition of human affairs, as protection against political despotism.

But though this proposition is not likely to be contested in general terms, the practical question, where to place the limit — how to make the fitting adjustment between individual independence and social control — is a subject on which nearly everything remains to be done. All that makes existence valuable to any one, depends on the enforcement of restraints upon the actions of other people. Some rules of conduct, therefore, must be imposed, by law in the first place, and by opinion on many things which are not fit subjects for the operation of law. What these rules should be, is the principal question in human affairs; but if we except a few of the most obvious cases, it is one of those which least progress has been made in resolving. No two ages, and scarcely any two countries, have decided it alike; and the decision of one age or country is a wonder to another. Yet the people of any given age and country no more suspect any difficulty in it, than if it were a subject on which mankind had always been agreed. The rules which obtain among themselves appear to them self-evident and self-justifying. This all but universal illusion is one of the examples of the magical influence of custom, which is not only, as the proverb says, a second nature, but is continually mistaken for the first. The effect of custom, in preventing any misgiving respecting the rules of conduct which mankind impose on one another, is all the more complete because the subject is one on which it is not generally considered necessary that reasons should be given, either by one person to others, or by each to himself. People are accustomed to believe, and have been encouraged in the belief by some who aspire to the character of philosophers, that their feelings, on subjects of this nature, are better than reasons, and render reasons unnecessary. The practical principle which guides them to their opinions on the regulation of human conduct, is the feeling in each person's mind that everybody should be required to act as he, and those with whom he sympathizes, would like them to act. No one, indeed, acknowledges to himself that his standard of judgment is his own liking; but an opinion on a point of conduct, not supported by reasons, can only count as one person's preference; and if the reasons, when given, are a mere appeal to a similar preference felt by other people, it is still only many people's liking instead of one. To an ordinary man, however, his own preference, thus supported, is not only a perfectly satisfactory reason, but the only one he generally has for any of his notions of morality, taste, or propriety, which are not expressly written in his religious creed; and his chief guide in the interpretation even of that. Men's opinions, accordingly, on what is laudable or blameable, are affected by all the multifarious causes which influence their wishes in regard to the conduct of others, and which are as numerous as those which determine their wishes on any other subject. Sometimes their reason — at other times their prejudices or superstitions: often their social affections, not seldom their antisocial ones, their envy or jealousy, their arrogance or contemptuousness: but most commonly, their desires or fears for themselves — their legitimate or illegitimate self-interest. Wherever there is an ascendant class, a large portion of the morality of the country emanates from its class interests, and its feelings of class superiority. The morality between Spartans and Helots, between planters and negroes, between princes and subjects, between nobles and roturiers,[2] between men and women, has been for the most part the creation of these class interests and feelings: and the sentiments thus generated, react in turn upon the moral feelings of the members of the ascendant class, in their relations among themselves. Where, on the other hand, a class, formerly ascendant, has lost its ascendancy, or where its ascendancy is unpopular, the prevailing moral sentiments frequently bear the impress of an impatient dislike of superiority. Another grand determining principle of the rules of conduct, both in act and forbearance, which have been enforced by law or opinion, has been the servility of mankind towards the supposed preferences or aversions of their temporal masters, or of their gods. This servility, though essentially selfish, is not hypocrisy; it gives rise to perfectly genuine sentiments of abhorrence; it made men burn magicians and heretics. Among so many baser influences, the general and obvious interests of society have of course had a share, and a large one, in the direction of the moral sentiments: less, however, as a matter of reason, and on their own account, than as a consequence of the sympathies and antipathies which grew out of them: and sympathies and antipathies which had little or nothing to do with the interests of society, have made themselves felt in the establishment of moralities with quite as great force.

The likings and dislikings of society, or of some powerful portion of it, are thus the main thing which has practically determined the rules laid down for general observance, under the penalties of law or opinion. And in general, those who have been in advance of society in thought and feeling, have left this condition of things unassailed in principle, however they may have come into conflict with it in some of its details. They have occupied themselves rather in inquiring what things society ought to like or dislike, than in questioning whether its likings or dislikings should be a law to individuals. They preferred endeavouring to alter the feelings of mankind on the particular points on which they were themselves heretical, rather than make common cause in defence of freedom, with heretics generally. The only case in which the higher ground has been taken on principle and maintained with consistency, by any but an individual here and there, is that of religious belief: a case instructive in many ways, and not least so as forming a most striking instance of the fallibility of what is called the moral sense: for the *odium theologicum*,[3] in a sincere bigot, is one of the most unequivocal cases of moral feeling. Those who first broke the yoke of what

2. Commoners.
3. Theological hatred.

called itself the Universal Church,[4] were in general as little willing to permit difference of religious opinion as that church itself. But when the heat of the conflict was over, without giving a complete victory to any party, and each church or sect was reduced to limit its hopes to retaining possession of the ground it already occupied; minorities, seeing that they had no chance of becoming majorities, were under the necessity of pleading to those whom they could not convert, for permission to differ. It is accordingly on this battle field, almost solely, that the rights of the individual against society have been asserted on broad grounds of principle, and the claim of society to exercise authority over dissentients, openly controverted. The great writers to whom the world owes what religious liberty it possesses, have mostly asserted freedom of conscience as an indefeasible right, and denied absolutely that a human being is accountable to others for his religious belief. Yet so natural to mankind is intolerance in whatever they really care about, that religious freedom has hardly anywhere been practically realized, except where religious indifference, which dislikes to have its peace disturbed by theological quarrels, has added its weight to the scale. In the minds of almost all religious persons, even in the most tolerant countries, the duty of toleration is admitted with tacit reserves. One person will bear with dissent in matters of church government, but not of dogma; another can tolerate everybody, short of a Papist or an Unitarian; another, every one who believes in revealed religion; a few extend their charity a little further, but stop at the belief in a God and in a future state. Wherever the sentiment of the majority is still genuine and intense, it is found to have abated little of its claim to be obeyed.

In England, from the peculiar circumstances of our political history, though the yoke of opinion is perhaps heavier, that of law is lighter, than in most other countries of Europe; and there is considerable jealousy of direct interference, by the legislative or the executive power, with private conduct; not so much from any just regard for the independence of the individual, as from the still subsisting habit of looking on the government as representing an opposite interest to the public. The majority have not yet learnt to feel the power of the government their power, or its opinions their opinions. When they do so, individual liberty will probably be as much exposed to invasion from the government, as it already is from public opinion. But, as yet, there is a considerable amount of feeling ready to be

4. Followers of Martin Luther (1483–1546), John Calvin (1509–64), and John Knox (1505–72) who demanded a thoroughgoing reformation of the Catholic Church.

called forth against any attempt of the law to control individuals in things in which they have not hitherto been accustomed to be controlled by it; and this with very little discrimination as to whether the matter is, or is not, within the legitimate sphere of legal control; insomuch that the feeling, highly salutary on the whole, is perhaps quite as often misplaced as well grounded in the particular instances of its application. There is, in fact, no recognised principle by which the propriety or impropriety of government interference is customarily tested. People decide according to their personal preferences. Some, whenever they see any good to be done, or evil to be remedied, would willingly instigate the government to undertake the business; while others prefer to bear almost any amount of social evil, rather than add one to the departments of human interests amenable to governmental control. And men range themselves on one or the other side in any particular case, according to this general direction of their sentiments; or according to the degree of interest which they feel in the particular thing which it is proposed that the government should do, or according to the belief they entertain that the government would, or would not, do it in the manner they prefer; but very rarely on account of any opinion to which they consistently adhere, as to what things are fit to be done by a government. And it seems to me that in consequence of this absence of rule or principle, one side is at present as often wrong as the other; the interference of government is, with about equal frequency, improperly invoked and improperly condemned.

The object of this Essay is to assert one very simple principle, as entitled to govern absolutely the dealings of society with the individual in the way of compulsion and control, whether the means used be physical force in the form of legal penalties, or the moral coercion of public opinion. That principle is, that the sole end for which mankind are warranted, individually or collectively, in interfering with the liberty of action of any of their number, is self-protection. That the only purpose for which power can be rightfully exercised over any member of a civilized community, against his will, is to prevent harm to others. His own good, either physical or moral, is not a sufficient warrant. He cannot rightfully be compelled to do or forbear because it will be better for him to do so, because it will make him happier, because, in the opinions of others, to do so would be wise, or even right. These are good reasons for remonstrating with him, or reasoning with him, or persuading him, or entreating him, but not for compelling him, or visiting him with any evil in case he do otherwise. To justify that, the conduct from which it is desired to deter him, must be calculated to produce evil to some one else. The only part of the conduct of any one, for which he is amenable to society, is that which concerns others. In the part which merely concerns himself, his independence is, of right, absolute. Over himself, over his own body and mind, the individual is sovereign.

It is, perhaps, hardly necessary to say that this doctrine is meant to apply only to human beings in the maturity of their faculties. We are not speaking of children, or of young persons below the age which the law may fix as that of manhood or womanhood. Those who are still in a state to require being taken care of by others, must be protected against their own actions as well as against external injury. For the same reason, we may leave out of consideration those backward states of society in which the race itself may be considered as in its nonage. The early difficulties in the way of spontaneous progress are so great, that there is seldom any choice of means for overcoming them; and a ruler full of the spirit of improvement is warranted in the use of any expedients that will attain an end, perhaps otherwise unattainable. Despotism is a legitimate mode of government in dealing with barbarians, provided the end be their improvement, and the means justified by actually effecting that end. Liberty, as a principle, has no application to any state of things anterior to the time when mankind have become capable of being improved by free and equal discussion. Until then, there is nothing for them but implicit obedience to an Akbar or a Charlemagne, if they are so fortunate as to find one. But as soon as mankind have attained the capacity of being guided to their own improvement by conviction or persuasion (a period long since reached in all nations with whom we need here concern ourselves), compulsion, either in the direct form or in that of pains and penalties for non-compliance, is no longer admissible as a means to their own good, and justifiable only for the security of others.

It is proper to state that I forego any advantage which could be derived to my argument from the idea of abstract right, as a thing independent of utility. I regard utility as the ultimate appeal on all ethical questions; but it must be utility in the largest sense, grounded on the permanent interests of man as a progressive being. Those interests, I contend, authorize the subjection of individual spontaneity to external control, only in respect to those actions of each, which concern the interest of other people. If any one does an act hurtful to others, there is a *primâ facie* case for punishing him, by law, or, where legal penalties are not safely applicable, by general disapprobation. There are also many positive acts for the benefit of others, which he may rightfully be compelled to perform; such as, to give evidence in a court of justice; to bear his fair share in the common defence, or in any other joint work necessary to the interest of the society of which he enjoys the protection; and to perform certain acts of individual beneficence, such as saving a fellow-creature's life, or interposing to protect the defenceless against ill-usage, things which whenever it is obviously a man's duty to do, he may rightfully be made responsible to society for not doing. A person may cause evil to others not only by his actions but by his inaction, and in either case he is justly accountable to them for the injury. The latter case, it is true, requires a much more cautious exercise of compulsion than the former. To make any one answerable for doing evil to others, is the rule; to make him answerable for not preventing evil, is, comparatively speaking, the exception. Yet there are many cases clear enough and grave enough to justify that exception. In all things which regard the external relations of the individual, he is *de jure*[5] amenable to those whose interests are concerned, and if need be, to society as their protector. There are often good reasons for not holding him to the responsibility; but these reasons must arise from the special expediencies of the case: either because it is a kind of case in which he is on the whole likely to act better, when left to his own discretion, than when controlled in any way in which society have it in their power to control him; or because the attempt to exercise control would produce other evils, greater than those which it would prevent. When such reasons as these preclude the enforcement of responsibility, the conscience of the agent himself should step into the vacant judgment seat, and protect those interests of others which have no external protection; judging himself all the more rigidly, because the case does not admit of his being made accountable to the judgment of his fellow-creatures.

But there is a sphere of action in which society, as distinguished from the individual, has, if any, only an indirect interest; comprehending all that portion of a person's life and conduct which affects only himself, or if it also affects others, only with their free, voluntary, and undeceived consent and participation. When I say only himself, I mean directly, and in the first instance: for whatever affects himself, may affect others *through* himself; and the objection which may be grounded on this contingency, will receive consideration in the sequel. This, then, is the appropriate region of human liberty. It comprises, first, the inward domain of consciousness; demanding liberty of conscience, in the most comprehensive sense; liberty of thought and feeling; absolute freedom of opinion and sentiment on all subjects, practical or speculative, scientific, moral, or theological. The liberty of expressing and publishing opinions may seem to fall under a different principle, since it belongs to that part of the conduct of an individual which concerns other people; but, being almost of as much importance as the

5. By law.

liberty of thought itself, and resting in great part on the same reasons, is practically inseparable from it. Secondly, the principle requires liberty of tastes and pursuits; of framing the plan of our life to suit our own character; of doing as we like, subject to such consequences as may follow: without impediment from our fellow-creatures, so long as what we do does not harm them, even though they should think our conduct foolish, perverse, or wrong. Thirdly, from this liberty of each individual, follows the liberty, within the same limits, of combination among individuals; freedom to unite, for any purpose not involving harm to others: the persons combining being supposed to be of full age, and not forced or deceived.

No society in which these liberties are not, on the whole, respected, is free, whatever may be its form of government; and none is completely free in which they do not exist absolute and unqualified. The only freedom which deserves the name, is that of pursuing our own good in our own way, so long as we do not attempt to deprive others of theirs, or impede their efforts to obtain it. Each is the proper guardian of his own health, whether bodily, or mental and spiritual. Mankind are greater gainers by suffering each other to live as seems good to themselves, than by compelling each to live as seems good to the rest.

Though this doctrine is anything but new, and, to some persons, may have the air of a truism, there is no doctrine which stands more directly opposed to the general tendency of existing opinion and practice. Society has expended fully as much effort in the attempt (according to its lights) to compel people to conform to its notions of personal, as of social excellence. The ancient commonwealths thought themselves entitled to practise, and the ancient philosophers countenanced, the regulation of every part of private conduct by public authority, on the ground that the State had a deep interest in the whole bodily and mental discipline of every one of its citizens; a mode of thinking which may have been admissible in small republics surrounded by powerful enemies, in constant peril of being subverted by foreign attack or internal commotion, and to which even a short interval of relaxed energy and self-command might so easily be fatal, that they could not afford to wait for the salutary permanent effects of freedom. In the modern world, the greater size of political communities, and above all, the separation between spiritual and temporal authority (which placed the direction of men's consciences in other hands than those which controlled their worldly affairs), prevented so great an interference by law in the details of private life; but the engines of moral repression have been wielded more strenuously against divergence from the reigning opinion in self-regarding, than even in social matters; religion, the most powerful of the elements which have entered into the formation of moral feeling, having almost always been governed either by the ambition of a hierarchy, seeking control over every department of human conduct, or by the spirit of Puritanism. And some of those modern reformers who have placed themselves in strongest opposition to the religions of the past, have been noway behind either churches or sects in their assertion of the right of spiritual domination: M. Comte,[6] in particular, whose social system, as unfolded in his *Traité de Politique Positive,* aims at establishing (though by moral more than by legal appliances) a despotism of society over the individual, surpassing anything contemplated in the political ideal of the most rigid disciplinarian among the ancient philosophers.

Apart from the peculiar tenets of individual thinkers, there is also in the world at large an increasing inclination to stretch unduly the powers of society over the individual, both by the force of opinion and even by that of legislation: and as the tendency of all the changes taking place in the world is to strengthen society, and diminish the power of the individual, this encroachment is not one of the evils which tend spontaneously to disappear, but, on the contrary, to grow more and more formidable. The disposition of mankind, whether as rulers or as fellow-citizens, to impose their own opinions and inclinations as a rule of conduct on others, is so energetically supported by some of the best and by some of the worst feelings incident to human nature, that it is hardly ever kept under restraint by anything but want of power;[7] and as the power is not declining, but growing, unless a strong barrier of moral conviction can be raised against the mischief, we must expect, in the present circumstances of the world, to see it increase.

It will be convenient for the argument, if, instead of at once entering upon the general thesis, we confine ourselves in the first instance to a single branch of it, on which the principle here stated is, if not fully, yet to a certain point, recognised by the current opinions. This one branch is the Liberty of Thought: from which it is impossible to separate the cognate liberty of speaking and of writing. Although these liberties, to some considerable amount, form part of the political morality of all countries which profess religious toleration and free institutions, the grounds, both philosophical and practical, on which they rest, are perhaps not so familiar to the general

6. Auguste Comte (1798–1857), in his *Système de Politique Positive* (the first word of the title is misquoted by Mill) and in other works, laid down the Positivist theory of human progress to be achieved through the scientific understanding of society.

7. Compare Thomas Paine in *The Rights of Man:* "Man is so naturally a creature of society, that it is almost impossible to put him out of it."

mind, nor so thoroughly appreciated by many even of the leaders of opinion, as might have been expected. Those grounds, when rightly understood, are of much wider application than to only one division of the subject, and a thorough consideration of this part of the question will be found the best introduction to the remainder. Those to whom nothing which I am about to say will be new, may therefore, I hope, excuse me, if on a subject which for now three centuries has been so often discussed, I venture on one discussion more.

CHAPTER II

OF THE LIBERTY OF THOUGHT AND DISCUSSION

The time, it is to be hoped, is gone by, when any defence would be necessary of the "liberty of the press" as one of the securities against corrupt or tyrannical government. No argument, we may suppose, can now be needed, against permitting a legislature or an executive, not identified in interest with the people, to prescribe opinions to them, and determine what doctrines or what arguments they shall be allowed to hear. This aspect of the question, besides, has been so often and so triumphantly enforced by preceding writers, that it needs not be specially insisted on in this place. Though the law of England, on the subject of the press, is as servile to this day as it was in the time of the Tudors, there is little danger of its being actually put in force against political discussion, except during some temporary panic, when fear of insurrection drives ministers and judges from their propriety;* and, speaking generally, it is not, in constitutional coun-

---

*These words had scarcely been written, when, as if to give them an emphatic contradiction, occurred the Government Press Prosecutions of 1858. That ill-judged interference with the liberty of public discussion has not, however, induced me to alter a single word in the text, nor has it at all weakened my conviction that, moments of panic excepted, the era of pains and penalties for political discussion has, in our own country, passed away. For, in the first place, the prosecutions were not persisted in; and, in the second, they were never, properly speaking, political prosecutions. The offence charged was not that of criticising institutions, or the acts or persons of rulers, but of circulating what was deemed an immoral doctrine, the lawfulness of Tyrannicide.

If the arguments of the present chapter are of any validity, there ought to exist the fullest liberty of professing and discussing, as a matter of ethical conviction, any doctrine, however immoral it may be considered. It would, therefore, be irrelevant and out of place to examine here, whether the doctrine of Tyrannicide deserves that title. I shall content myself with saying, that the subject has been at all times one of the open questions of morals; that the act of a private citizen in striking down a criminal, who, by raising himself above the law, has placed himself beyond the reach of legal punishment or control, has been accounted by whole nations, and by some of the best and wisest of men,

tries, to be apprehended, that the government, whether completely responsible to the people or not, will often attempt to control the expression of
opinion, except when in doing so it makes itself the organ of the general
intolerance of the public. Let us suppose, therefore, that the government is
entirely at one with the people, and never thinks of exerting any power of
coercion unless in agreement with what it conceives to be their voice. But I
deny the right of the people to exercise such coercion, either by themselves
or by their government. The power itself is illegitimate. The best government has no more title to it than the worst. It is as noxious, or more noxious,
when exerted in accordance with public opinion, than when in opposition to
it. If all mankind minus one, were of one opinion, and only one person were
of the contrary opinion, mankind would be no more justified in silencing
that one person, than he, if he had the power, would be justified in silencing
mankind. Were an opinion a personal possession of no value except to the
owner; if to be obstructed in the enjoyment of it were simply a private
injury, it would make some difference whether the injury was inflicted only
on a few persons or on many. But the peculiar evil of silencing the expression of an opinion is, that it is robbing the human race; posterity as well as
the existing generation; those who dissent from the opinion, still more than
those who hold it. If the opinion is right, they are deprived of the opportunity of exchanging error for truth: if wrong, they lose, what is almost as
great a benefit, the clearer perception and livelier impression of truth, produced by its collision with error.

It is necessary to consider separately these two hypotheses, each of

---

not a crime, but an act of exalted virtue; and that, right or wrong, it is not of the nature of
assassination, but of civil war. As such, I hold that the instigation to it, in a specific case,
may be a proper subject of punishment, but only if an overt act has followed, and at least a
probable connexion can be established between the act and the instigation. Even then, it is
not a foreign government, but the very government assailed, which alone, in the exercise
of self-defence, can legitimately punish attacks directed against its own existence.

[Mill refers to the arrest by government warrant of the London publisher Edward
Truelove for publication of W. E. Adams's pamphlet *Tyrannicide: Is it justifiable?* This
work offered arguments in support of the attempt by the Italian revolutionary Orsini to
assassinate Napoleon III — a brutally conceived and miscarried act of political violence
that killed eight people and injured many others. Truelove's rights as a publisher were
defended by the Secular Movement (which had published Harriet Mill's pamphlet *Are
Women Fit for Politics?*). A committee was formed by Charles Bradlaugh to defray the
costs of the legal defense; eventually, the government withdrew from prosecution in
exchange for Truelove's promise to discontinue Adams's pamphlet. — *Ed.*]

which has a distinct branch of the argument corresponding to it. We can never be sure that the opinion we are endeavouring to stifle is a false opinion; and if we were sure, stifling it would be an evil still.

First: the opinion which it is attempted to suppress by authority may possibly be true. Those who desire to suppress it, of course deny its truth; but they are not infallible. They have no authority to decide the question for all mankind, and exclude every other person from the means of judging. To refuse a hearing to an opinion, because they are sure that it is false, is to assume that *their* certainty is the same thing as *absolute* certainty. All silencing of discussion is an assumption of infallibility. Its condemnation may be allowed to rest on this common argument, not the worse for being common.

Unfortunately for the good sense of mankind, the fact of their fallibility is far from carrying the weight in their practical judgment, which is always allowed to it in theory; for while every one well knows himself to be fallible, few think it necessary to take any precautions against their own fallibility, or admit the supposition that any opinion, of which they feel very certain, may be one of the examples of the error to which they acknowledge themselves to be liable. Absolute princes, or others who are accustomed to unlimited deference, usually feel this complete confidence in their own opinions on nearly all subjects. People more happily situated, who sometimes hear their opinions disputed, and are not wholly unused to be set right when they are wrong, place the same unbounded reliance only on such of their opinions as are shared by all who surround them, or to whom they habitually defer: for in proportion to a man's want of confidence in his own solitary judgment, does he usually repose, with implicit trust, on the infallibility of "the world" in general. And the world, to each individual, means the part of it with which he comes in contact; his party, his sect, his church, his class of society: the man may be called, by comparison, almost liberal and large-minded to whom it means anything so comprehensive as his own country or his own age. Nor is his faith in this collective authority at all shaken by his being aware that other ages, countries, sects, churches, classes, and parties have thought, and even now think, the exact reverse. He devolves upon his own world the responsibility of being in the right against the dissentient worlds of other people; and it never troubles him that mere accident has decided which of these numerous worlds is the object of his reliance, and that the same causes which make him a Churchman in London, would have made him a Buddhist or a Confucian in Pekin. Yet it is as evident in itself, as any amount of argument can make it, that ages are no more infallible than individuals; every age having held many opinions which subsequent ages have deemed not only false but absurd; and it is as certain that many opinions, now general, will be rejected by future ages, as it is that many, once general, are rejected by the present.

The objection likely to be made to this argument, would probably take some such form as the following. There is no greater assumption of infallibility in forbidding the propagation of error, than in any other thing which is done by public authority on its own judgment and responsibility. Judgment is given to men that they may use it. Because it may be used erroneously, are men to be told that they ought not to use it at all? To prohibit what they think pernicious, is not claiming exemption from error, but fulfilling the duty incumbent on them, although fallible, of acting on their conscientious conviction. If we were never to act on our opinions, because those opinions may be wrong, we should leave all our interests uncared for, and all our duties unperformed. An objection which applies to all conduct, can be no valid objection to any conduct in particular. It is the duty of governments, and of individuals, to form the truest opinions they can; to form them carefully, and never impose them upon others unless they are quite sure of being right. But when they are sure (such reasoners may say), it is not conscientiousness but cowardice to shrink from acting on their opinions, and allow doctrines which they honestly think dangerous to the welfare of mankind, either in this life or in another, to be scattered abroad without restraint, because other people, in less enlightened times, have persecuted opinions now believed to be true. Let us take care, it may be said, not to make the same mistake: but governments and nations have made mistakes in other things, which are not denied to be fit subjects for the exercise of authority: they have laid on bad taxes, made unjust wars. Ought we therefore to lay on no taxes, and, under whatever provocation, make no wars? Men, and governments, must act to the best of their ability. There is no such thing as absolute certainty, but there is assurance sufficient for the purposes of human life. We may, and must, assume our opinion to be true for the guidance of our own conduct: and it is assuming no more when we forbid bad men to pervert society by the propagation of opinions which we regard as false and pernicious.

I answer, that it is assuming very much more. There is the greatest difference between presuming an opinion to be true, because, with every opportunity for contesting it, it has not been refuted, and assuming its truth for the purpose of not permitting its refutation. Complete liberty of contradicting and disproving our opinion, is the very condition which justifies us in assuming its truth for purposes of action; and on no other terms can a being with human faculties have any rational assurance of being right.

When we consider either the history of opinion, or the ordinary conduct of human life, to what is it to be ascribed that the one and the other are no worse than they are? Not certainly to the inherent force of the human understanding; for, on any matter not self-evident, there are ninety-nine persons totally incapable of judging of it, for one who is capable; and the capacity of the hundredth person is only comparative; for the majority of the eminent men of every past generation held many opinions now known to be erroneous, and did or approved numerous things which no one will now justify. Why is it, then, that there is on the whole a preponderance among mankind of rational opinions and rational conduct? If there really is this preponderance — which there must be, unless human affairs are, and have always been, in an almost desperate state — it is owing to a quality of the human mind, the source of everything respectable in man either as an intellectual or as a moral being, namely, that his errors are corrigible. He is capable of rectifying his mistakes, by discussion and experience. Not by experience alone. There must be discussion, to show how experience is to be interpreted. Wrong opinions and practices gradually yield to fact and argument: but facts and arguments, to produce any effect on the mind, must be brought before it. Very few facts are able to tell their own story, without comments to bring out their meaning. The whole strength and value, then, of human judgment, depending on the one property, that it can be set right when it is wrong, reliance can be placed on it only when the means of setting it right are kept constantly at hand. In the case of any person whose judgment is really deserving of confidence, how has it become so? Because he has kept his mind open to criticism of his opinions and conduct. Because it has been his practice to listen to all that could be said against him; to profit by as much of it as was just, and expound to himself, and upon occasion to others, the fallacy of what was fallacious. Because he has felt, that the only way in which a human being can make some approach to knowing the whole of a subject, is by hearing what can be said about it by persons of every variety of opinion, and studying all modes in which it can be looked at by every character of mind. No wise man ever acquired his wisdom in any mode but this; nor is it in the nature of human intellect to become wise in any other manner. The steady habit of correcting and completing his own opinion by collating it with those of others, so far from causing doubt and hesitation in carrying it into practice, is the only stable foundation for a just reliance on it: for, being cognisant of all that can, at least obviously, be said against him, and having taken up his position against all gainsayers — knowing that he has sought for objections and difficulties, instead of avoiding them, and has shut out no light which can be thrown upon the subject from any quarter — he has a right to think his judgment better than that of any person, or any multitude, who have not gone through a similar process.

It is not too much to require that what the wisest of mankind, those who are best entitled to trust their own judgment, find necessary to warrant their relying on it, should be submitted to by that miscellaneous collection of a few wise and many foolish individuals, called the public. The most intolerant of churches, the Roman Catholic Church, even at the canonization of a saint, admits, and listens patiently to, a "devil's advocate." The holiest of men, it appears, cannot be admitted to posthumous honours, until all that the devil could say against him is known and weighed. If even the Newtonian philosophy were not permitted to be questioned, mankind could not feel as complete assurance of its truth as they now do. The beliefs which we have most warrant for, have no safeguard to rest on, but a standing invitation to the whole world to prove them unfounded. If the challenge is not accepted, or is accepted and the attempt fails, we are far enough from certainty still; but we have done the best that the existing state of human reason admits of; we have neglected nothing that could give the truth a chance of reaching us: if the lists are kept open, we may hope that if there be a better truth, it will be found when the human mind is capable of receiving it; and in the meantime we may rely on having attained such approach to truth, as is possible in our own day. This is the amount of certainty attainable by a fallible being, and this the sole way of attaining it.

Strange it is, that men should admit the validity of the arguments for free discussion, but object to their being "pushed to an extreme"; not seeing that unless the reasons are good for an extreme case, they are not good for any case. Strange that they should imagine that they are not assuming infallibility, when they acknowledge that there should be free discussion on all subjects which can possibly be *doubtful*, but think that some particular principle or doctrine should be forbidden to be questioned because it is *so certain*, that is, because *they are certain* that it is certain. To call any proposition certain, while there is any one who would deny its certainty if permitted, but who is not permitted, is to assume that we ourselves, and those who agree with us, are the judges of certainty, and judges without hearing the other side.

In the present age — which has been described as "destitute of faith, but terrified at scepticism"[8] — in which people feel sure, not so much that their opinions are true, as that they should not know what to do without them —

8. The quotation is from Thomas Carlyle's review of the *Life of Scott* by J. G. Lockhart.

the claims of an opinion to be protected from public attack are rested not so much on its truth, as on its importance to society. There are, it is alleged, certain beliefs, so useful, not to say indispensable to well-being, that it is as much the duty of governments to uphold those beliefs, as to protect any other of the interests of society. In a case of such necessity, and so directly in the line of their duty, something less than infallibility may, it is maintained, warrant, and even bind, governments, to act on their own opinion, con-firmed by the general opinion of mankind. It is also often argued, and still oftener thought, that none but bad men would desire to weaken these salu-tary beliefs; and there can be nothing wrong, it is thought, in restraining bad men, and prohibiting what only such men would wish to practise. This mode of thinking makes the justification of restraints on discussion not a question of the truth of doctrines, but of their usefulness; and flatters itself by that means to escape the responsibility of claiming to be an infallible judge of opinions. But those who thus satisfy themselves, do not perceive that the assumption of infallibility is merely shifted from one point to another. The usefulness of an opinion is itself matter of opinion: as disputa-ble, as open to discussion, and requiring discussion as much, as the opinion itself. There is the same need of an infallible judge of opinions to decide an opinion to be noxious, as to decide it to be false, unless the opinion con-demned has full opportunity of defending itself. And it will not do to say that the heretic may be allowed to maintain the utility or harmlessness of his opinion, though forbidden to maintain its truth. The truth of an opinion is part of its utility. If we would know whether or not it is desirable that a proposition should be believed, is it possible to exclude the consideration of whether or not it is true? In the opinion, not of bad men, but of the best men, no belief which is contrary to truth can be really useful: and can you prevent such men from urging that plea, when they are charged with culpability for denying some doctrine which they are told is useful, but which they believe to be false? Those who are on the side of received opinions, never fail to take all possible advantage of this plea; you do not find *them* handling the question of utility as if it could be completely abstracted from that of truth: on the contrary, it is, above all, because their doctrine is "the truth," that the knowledge or the belief of it is held to be so indispensable. There can be no fair discussion of the question of usefulness, when an argument so vital may be employed on one side, but not on the other. And in point of fact, when law or public feeling do not permit the truth of an opinion to be disputed, they are just as little tolerant of a denial of its usefulness. The utmost they allow is an extenuation of its absolute necessity, or of the positive guilt of rejecting it.

In order more fully to illustrate the mischief of denying a hearing to opinions because we, in our own judgment, have condemned them, it will be desirable to fix down the discussion to a concrete case; and I choose, by preference, the cases which are least favourable to me — in which the argument against freedom of opinion, both on the score of truth and on that of utility, is considered the strongest. Let the opinions impugned be the belief in a God and in a future state, or any of the commonly received doctrines of morality. To fight the battle on such ground, gives a great advantage to an unfair antagonist; since he will be sure to say (and many who have no desire to be unfair will say it internally), Are these the doctrines which you do not deem sufficiently certain to be taken under the protection of law? Is the belief in a God one of the opinions, to feel sure of which, you hold to be assuming infallibility? But I must be permitted to observe, that it is not the feeling sure of a doctrine (be it what it may) which I call an assumption of infallibility. It is the undertaking to decide that question *for others*, without allowing them to hear what can be said on the contrary side. And I denounce and reprobate this pretension not the less, if put forth on the side of my most solemn convictions. However positive any one's persuasion may be, not only of the falsity, but of the pernicious consequences — not only of the pernicious consequences, but (to adopt expressions which I altogether condemn) the immorality and impiety of an opinion; yet if, in pursuance of that private judgment, though backed by the public judgment of his country or his cotemporaries, he prevents the opinion from being heard in its defence, he assumes infallibility. And so far from the assumption being less objectionable or less dangerous because the opinion is called immoral or impious, this is the case of all others in which it is most fatal. These are exactly the occasions on which the men of one generation commit those dreadful mistakes, which excite the astonishment and horror of posterity. It is among such that we find the instances memorable in history, when the arm of the law has been employed to root out the best men and the noblest doctrines; with deplorable success as to the men, though some of the doctrines have survived to be (as if in mockery) invoked, in defence of similar conduct towards those who dissent from *them*, or from their received interpretation.

Mankind can hardly be too often reminded, that there was once a man named Socrates, between whom and the legal authorities and public opinion of his time, there took place a memorable collision. Born in an age and country abounding in individual greatness, this man has been handed down to us by those who best knew both him and the age, as the most virtuous man in it; while *we* know him as the head and prototype of all subsequent teachers of virtue, the source equally of the lofty inspiration of Plato and the judicious utilitarianism of Aristotle, "*i maëstri di color che sanno,*" the two headsprings of ethical as of all other philosophy.[9] This acknowledged master of all the eminent thinkers who have since lived — whose fame, still growing after more than two thousand years, all but outweighs the whole remainder of the names which make his native city illustrious — was put to death by his countrymen, after a judicial conviction, for impiety and immorality. Impiety, in denying the gods recognised by the State; indeed his accuser asserted (see the "Apologia") that he believed in no gods at all. Immorality, in being, by his doctrines and instructions, a "corruptor of youth." Of these charges the tribunal, there is every ground for believing, honestly found him guilty, and condemned the man who probably of all then born had deserved best of mankind, to be put to death as a criminal.

To pass from this to the only other instance of judicial iniquity, the mention of which, after the condemnation of Socrates, would not be an anticlimax: the event which took place on Calvary rather more than eighteen hundred years ago. The man who left on the memory of those who witnessed his life and conversation, such an impression of his moral grandeur, that eighteen subsequent centuries have done homage to him as the Almighty in person, was ignominiously put to death, as what? As a blasphemer. Men did not merely mistake their benefactor; they mistook him for the exact contrary of what he was, and treated him as that prodigy of impiety, which they themselves are now held to be, for their treatment of him. The feelings with which mankind now regard these lamentable transactions, especially the later of the two, render them extremely unjust in their judgment of the unhappy actors. These were, to all appearance, not bad men — not worse than men commonly are, but rather the contrary; men who possessed in a full, or somewhat more than a full measure, the religious, moral, and patriotic feelings of their time and people: the very kind of men who, in all times, our own included, have every chance of passing through life blameless and respected. The high-priest who rent his garments when the words were pronounced, which, according to all the ideas of his country, constituted the blackest guilt, was in all probability quite as sincere in his horror and indignation, as the generality of respectable and pious men now

9. The self-defense of Socrates at his trial is recollected in Plato's *Apology*. The phrase *il maestro di color che sanno,* "the master of those who know," is from Dante's description of Aristotle at *Inferno* 4.131; rendered plural by Mill, "the masters," so as to include Plato, who is presented by Dante soon after along with Democritus, Diogenes, Anaxagoras, Thales, Empedocles, Heraclitus, and Zeno.

are in the religious and moral sentiments they profess; and most of those who now shudder at his conduct, if they had lived in his time, and been born Jews, would have acted precisely as he did. Orthodox Christians who are tempted to think that those who stoned to death the first martyrs must have been worse men than they themselves are, ought to remember that one of those persecutors was Saint Paul.

Let us add one more example, the most striking of all, if the impressiveness of an error is measured by the wisdom and virtue of him who falls into it. If ever any one, possessed of power, had grounds for thinking himself the best and most enlightened among his cotemporaries, it was the Emperor Marcus Aurelius. Absolute monarch of the whole civilized world, he preserved through life not only the most unblemished justice, but what was less to be expected from his Stoical breeding, the tenderest heart. The few failings which are attributed to him, were all on the side of indulgence: while his writings, the highest ethical product of the ancient mind, differ scarcely perceptibly, if they differ at all, from the most characteristic teachings of Christ.[10] This man, a better Christian in all but the dogmatic sense of the word, than almost any of the ostensibly Christian sovereigns who have since reigned, persecuted Christianity. Placed at the summit of all the previous attainments of humanity, with an open, unfettered intellect, and a character which led him of himself to embody in his moral writings the Christian ideal, he yet failed to see that Christianity was to be a good and not an evil to the world, with his duties to which he was so deeply penetrated. Existing society he knew to be in a deplorable state. But such as it was, he saw, or thought he saw, that it was held together, and prevented from being worse, by belief and reverence of the received divinities. As a ruler of mankind, he deemed it his duty not to suffer society to fall in pieces; and saw not how, if its existing ties were removed, any others could be formed which could again knit it together. The new religion openly aimed at dissolving these ties: unless, therefore, it was his duty to adopt that religion, it seemed to be his duty to put it down. Inasmuch then as the theology of Christianity did not appear to him true or of divine origin; inasmuch as this strange history of a crucified God was not credible to him, and a system which purported to rest entirely upon a foundation to him so wholly unbelievable, could not be foreseen by him to be that renovating agency which, after all abatements, it has in fact proved to be; the gentlest and most amiable of philosophers and rulers, under a solemn sense of duty, autho-

10. Marcus Aurelius (121–80), whose *Meditations* are among the masterpieces of the Stoical philosophy, was emperor from 161 to 180.

rized the persecution of Christianity. To my mind this is one of the most tragical facts in all history. It is a bitter thought, how different a thing the Christianity of the world might have been, if the Christian faith had been adopted as the religion of the empire under the auspices of Marcus Aurelius instead of those of Constantine. But it would be equally unjust to him and false to truth, to deny, that no one plea which can be urged for punishing anti-Christian teaching, was wanting to Marcus Aurelius for punishing, as he did, the propagation of Christianity. No Christian more firmly believes that Atheism is false, and tends to the dissolution of society, than Marcus Aurelius believed the same things of Christianity; he who, of all men then living, might have been thought the most capable of appreciating it. Unless any one who approves of punishment for the promulgation of opinions, flatters himself that he is a wiser and better man than Marcus Aurelius — more deeply versed in the wisdom of his time, more elevated in his intellect above it — more earnest in his search for truth, or more single-minded in his devotion to it when found; — let him abstain from that assumption of the joint infallibility of himself and the multitude, which the great Antoninus made with so unfortunate a result.

Aware of the impossibility of defending the use of punishment for restraining irreligious opinions, by any argument which will not justify Marcus Antoninus, the enemies of religious freedom, when hard pressed, occasionally accept this consequence, and say, with Dr. Johnson, that the persecutors of Christianity were in the right; that persecution is an ordeal through which truth ought to pass, and always passes successfully, legal penalties being, in the end, powerless against truth, though sometimes beneficially effective against mischievous errors. This is a form of the argument for religious intolerance, sufficiently remarkable not to be passed without notice.

A theory which maintains that truth may justifiably be persecuted because persecution cannot possibly do it any harm, cannot be charged with being intentionally hostile to the reception of new truths; but we cannot commend the generosity of its dealing with the persons to whom mankind are indebted for them. To discover to the world something which deeply concerns it, and of which it was previously ignorant; to prove to it that it had been mistaken on some vital point of temporal or spiritual interest, is as important a service as a human being can render to his fellow-creatures, and in certain cases, as in those of the early Christians and of the Reformers, those who think with Dr. Johnson believe it to have been the most precious gift which could be bestowed on mankind. That the authors of such splendid benefits should be requited by martyrdom; that their reward should be to be dealt with as the vilest of criminals, is not, upon this theory, a deplorable error and misfortune, for which humanity should mourn in sackcloth and ashes, but the normal and justifiable state of things. The propounder of a new truth, according to this doctrine, should stand, as stood, in the legislation of the Locrians, the proposer of a new law, with a halter round his neck, to be instantly tightened if the public assembly did not, on hearing his reasons, then and there adopt his proposition.[11] People who defend this mode of treating benefactors, cannot be supposed to set much value on the benefit; and I believe this view of the subject is mostly confined to the sort of persons who think that new truths may have been desirable once, but that we have had enough of them now.

But, indeed, the dictum that truth always triumphs over persecution, is one of those pleasant falsehoods which men repeat after one another till they pass into commonplaces, but which all experience refutes. History teems with instances of truth put down by persecution. If not suppressed for ever, it may be thrown back for centuries. To speak only of religious opinions: the Reformation broke out at least twenty times before Luther, and was put down. Arnold of Brescia was put down. Fra Dolcino was put down. Savonarola was put down. The Albigeois were put down. The Vaudois were put down. The Lollards were put down. The Hussites were put down. Even after the era of Luther, wherever persecution was persisted in, it was successful. In Spain, Italy, Flanders, the Austrian empire, Protestantism was rooted out; and, most likely, would have been so in England, had Queen Mary lived, or Queen Elizabeth died. Persecution has always succeeded, save where the heretics were too strong a party to be effectually persecuted. No reasonable person can doubt that Christianity might have been extirpated in the Roman Empire. It spread, and became predominant, because the persecutions were only occasional, lasting but a short time, and separated by long intervals of almost undisturbed propagandism. It is a piece of idle sentimentality that truth, merely as truth, has any inherent power denied to error, of prevailing against the dungeon and the stake. Men are not more zealous for truth than they often are for error, and a sufficient application of legal or even of social penalties will generally succeed in stopping the propagation of either. The real advantage which truth has, consists in this, that when an opinion is true, it may be extinguished once, twice, or many times, but in the course of ages there will generally be found persons to rediscover it, until some one of its reappearances falls on a time when

11. The citizens of Locri, a colony of Greece in southern Italy, drafted the first legal code of Europe and discouraged its revision.

from favourable circumstances it escapes persecution until it has made such head as to withstand all subsequent attempts to suppress it.

It will be said, that we do not now put to death the introducers of new opinions: we are not like our fathers who slew the prophets, we even build sepulchres to them. It is true we no longer put heretics to death; and the amount of penal infliction which modern feeling would probably tolerate, even against the most obnoxious opinions, is not sufficient to extirpate them. But let us not flatter ourselves that we are yet free from the stain even of legal persecution. Penalties for opinion, or at least for its expression, still exist by law; and their enforcement is not, even in these times, so unexampled as to make it at all incredible that they may some day be revived in full force. In the year 1857, at the summer assizes of the county of Cornwall, an unfortunate man,* said to be of unexceptionable conduct in all relations of life, was sentenced to twenty-one months imprisonment, for uttering, and writing on a gate, some offensive words concerning Christianity. Within a month of the same time, at the Old Bailey, two persons, on two separate occasions,† were rejected as jurymen, and one of them grossly insulted by the judge and by one of the counsel, because they honestly declared that they had no theological belief; and a third, a foreigner,‡ for the same reason, was denied justice against a thief. This refusal of redress took place in virtue of the legal doctrine, that no person can be allowed to give evidence in a court of justice, who does not profess belief in a God (any god is sufficient) and in a future state; which is equivalent to declaring such persons to be outlaws, excluded from the protection of the tribunals; who may not only be robbed or assaulted with impunity, if no one but themselves, or persons of similar opinions, be present, but any one else may be robbed or assaulted with impunity, if the proof of the fact depends on their evidence. The assumption on which this is grounded, is that the oath is worthless, of a person who does not believe in a future state; a proposition which betokens much ignorance of history in those who assent to it (since it is historically true that a large proportion of infidels in all ages have been persons of distinguished integrity and honour); and would be maintained by no one who had the smallest conception how many of the persons in greatest repute with the world, both for virtues and for attainments, are well known, at least to their intimates, to be unbelievers. The rule, besides, is

---

*Thomas Pooley, Bodmin Assizes, July 31, 1857. In December following, he received a free pardon from the Crown.

†George Jacob Holyoake, August 17, 1857; Edward Truelove, July, 1857.

‡Baron de Gleichen, Marlborough-street Police Court, August 4, 1857.

suicidal, and cuts away its own foundation. Under pretence that atheists must be liars, it admits the testimony of all atheists who are willing to lie, and rejects only those who brave the obloquy of publicly confessing a detested creed rather than affirm a falsehood. A rule thus self-convicted of absurdity so far as regards its professed purpose, can be kept in force only as a badge of hatred, a relic of persecution; a persecution, too, having the perculiarity, that the qualification for undergoing it, is the being clearly proved not to deserve it. The rule, and the theory it implies, are hardly less insulting to believers than to infidels. For if he who does not believe in a future state, necessarily lies, it follows that they who do believe are only prevented from lying, if prevented they are, by the fear of hell. We will not do the authors and abettors of the rule the injury of supposing, that the conception which they have formed of Christian virtue is drawn from their own consciousness.

These, indeed, are but rags and remnants of persecution, and may be thought to be not so much an indication of the wish to persecute, as an example of that very frequent infirmity of English minds, which makes them take a preposterous pleasure in the assertion of a bad principle, when they are no longer bad enough to desire to carry it really into practice. But unhappily there is no security in the state of the public mind, that the suspension of worse forms of legal persecution, which has lasted for about the space of a generation, will continue. In this age the quiet surface of routine is as often ruffled by attempts to resuscitate past evils, as to introduce new benefits. What is boasted of at the present time as the revival of religion, is always, in narrow and uncultivated minds, at least as much the revival of bigotry; and where there is the strong permanent leaven of intolerance in the feelings of a people, which at all times abides in the middle classes of this country, it needs but little to provoke them into actively persecuting those whom they have never ceased to think proper objects of persecution.* For it is this — it is the opinions men entertain, and the feel-

---

*Ample warning may be drawn from the large infusion of the passions of a persecutor, which mingled with the general display of the worst parts of our national character on the occasion of the Sepoy insurrection. The ravings of fanatics or charlatans from the pulpit may be unworthy of notice; but the heads of the Evangelical party have announced as their principle, for the government of Hindoos and Mahomedans, that no schools be supported by public money in which the Bible is not taught, and by necessary consequence that no public employment be given to any but real or pretended Christians. An Under-Secretary of State, in a speech delivered to his constituents on the 12th of November, 1857, is reported to have said: "Toleration of their faith" (the faith of a hundred

ings they cherish, respecting those who disown the beliefs they deem important, which makes this country not a place of mental freedom. For a long time past, the chief mischief of the legal penalties is that they strengthen the social stigma. It is that stigma which is really effective, and so effective is it, that the profession of opinions which are under the ban of society is much less common in England, than is, in many other countries, the avowal of those which incur risk of judicial punishment. In respect to all persons but those whose pecuniary circumstances make them independent of the good will of other people, opinion, on this subject, is as efficacious as law; men might as well be imprisoned, as excluded from the means of earning their bread. Those whose bread is already secured, and who desire no favours from men in power, or from bodies of men, or from the public, have nothing to fear from the open avowal of any opinions, but to be ill-thought of and ill-spoken of, and this it ought not to require a very heroic mould to enable them to bear. There is no room for any appeal *ad misericordiam*[12] in behalf of such persons. But though we do not now inflict so much evil on those who think differently from us, as it was formerly our custom to do, it may be that we do ourselves as much evil as ever by our treatment of them. Socrates was put to death, but the Socratic philosophy rose like the sun in heaven, and spread its illumination over the whole intellectual firmament. Christians were cast to the lions, but the Christian church grew up a stately and spreading tree, overtopping the older and less vigorous growths, and stifling them by its shade. Our merely social intolerance kills no one, roots out no

---

millions of British subjects), "the superstition which they called religion, by the British Government, had had the effect of retarding the ascendancy of the British name, and preventing the salutary growth of Christianity. . . . Toleration was the great corner-stone of the religious liberties of this country; but do not let them abuse that precious word toleration. As he understood it, it meant the complete liberty to all, freedom of worship, *among Christians, who worshipped upon the same foundation.* It meant toleration of all sects and denominations of *Christians who believed in the one mediation.*" I desire to call attention to the fact, that a man who has been deemed fit to fill a high office in the government of this country, under a liberal Ministry, maintains the doctrine that all who do not believe in the divinity of Christ are beyond the pale of toleration. Who, after this imbecile display, can indulge the illusion that religious persecution has passed away, never to return?

[The mutiny in 1857 of "sepoy" or native Indian soldiers serving in the British army sent a shock through the empire whose reverberations were still felt two years later. — *Ed.*]

12. To mercy.

opinions, but induces men to disguise them, or to abstain from any active effort for their diffusion. With us, heretical opinions do not perceptibly gain, or even lose, ground in each decade or generation; they never blaze out far and wide, but continue to smoulder in the narrow circles of thinking and studious persons among whom they originate, without ever lighting up the general affairs of mankind with either a true or a deceptive light. And thus is kept up a state of things very satisfactory to some minds, because, without the unpleasant process of fining or imprisoning anybody, it maintains all prevailing opinions outwardly undisturbed, while it does not absolutely interdict the exercise of reason by dissentients afflicted with the malady of thought. A convenient plan for having peace in the intellectual world, and keeping all things going on therein very much as they do already. But the price paid for this sort of intellectual pacification, is the sacrifice of the entire moral courage of the human mind. A state of things in which a large portion of the most active and inquiring intellects find it advisable to keep the genuine principles and grounds of their convictions within their own breasts, and attempt, in what they address to the public, to fit as much as they can of their own conclusions to premises which they have internally renounced, cannot send forth the open, fearless characters, and logical, consistent intellects who once adorned the thinking world. The sort of men who can be looked for under it, are either mere conformers to commonplace, or time-servers for truth, whose arguments on all great subjects are meant for their hearers, and are not those which have convinced themselves. Those who avoid this alternative, do so by narrowing their thoughts and interest to things which can be spoken of without venturing within the region of principles, that is, to small practical matters, which would come right of themselves, if but the minds of mankind were strengthened and enlarged, and which will never be made effectually right until then: while that which would strengthen and enlarge men's minds, free and daring speculation on the highest subjects, is abandoned.

Those in whose eyes this reticence on the part of heretics is no evil, should consider in the first place, that in consequence of it there is never any fair and thorough discussion of heretical opinions; and that such of them as could not stand such a discussion, though they may be prevented from spreading, do not disappear. But it is not the minds of heretics that are deteriorated most, by the ban placed on all inquiry which does not end in the orthodox conclusions. The greatest harm done is to those who are not heretics, and whose whole mental development is cramped, and their reason cowed, by the fear of heresy. Who can compute what the world loses in the multitude of promising intellects combined with timid characters, who dare not follow out any bold, vigorous, independent train of thought, lest it should land them in something which would admit of being considered irreligious or immoral? Among them we may occasionally see some man of deep conscientiousness, and subtle and refined understanding, who spends a life in sophisticating with an intellect which he cannot silence, and exhausts the resources of ingenuity in attempting to reconcile the promptings of his conscience and reason with orthodoxy, which yet he does not, perhaps, to the end succeed in doing. No one can be a great thinker who does not recognise, that as a thinker it is his first duty to follow his intellect to whatever conclusions it may lead. Truth gains more even by the errors of one who, with due study and preparation, thinks for himself, than by the true opinions of those who only hold them because they do not suffer themselves to think. Not that it is solely, or chiefly, to form great thinkers, that freedom of thinking is required. On the contrary, it is as much, and even more indispensable, to enable average human beings to attain the mental stature which they are capable of. There have been, and may again be, great individual thinkers, in a general atmosphere of mental slavery. But there never has been, nor ever will be, in that atmosphere, an intellectually active people. Where any people has made a temporary approach to such a character, it has been because the dread of heterodox speculation was for a time suspended. Where there is a tacit convention that principles are not to be disputed; where the discussion of the greatest questions which can occupy humanity is considered to be closed, we cannot hope to find that generally high scale of mental activity which has made some periods of history so remarkable. Never when controversy avoided the subjects which are large and important enough to kindle enthusiasm, was the mind of a people stirred up from its foundations, and the impulse given which raised even persons of the most ordinary intellect to something of the dignity of thinking beings. Of such we have had an example in the condition of Europe during the times immediately following the Reformation; another, though limited to the Continent and to a more cultivated class, in the speculative movement of the latter half of the eighteenth century; and a third, of still briefer duration, in the intellectual fermentation of Germany during the Goethian and Fichtean period.[13] These periods differed widely in the particular opinions which they developed; but were alike in this, that during all

13. The Romantic movement in German literature and philosophy, associated with the productive maturity of Johann Wolfgang Goethe (1749–1832) and Johann Gottlieb Fichte (1762–1814) — roughly, the last two decades of the eighteenth century and the first of the nineteenth.

three the yoke of authority was broken. In each, an old mental despotism had been thrown off, and no new one had yet taken its place. The impulse given at these three periods has made Europe what it now is. Every single improvement which has taken place either in the human mind or in institutions, may be traced distinctly to one or other of them. Appearances have for some time indicated that all three impulses are well nigh spent; and we can expect no fresh start, until we again assert our mental freedom.

Let us now pass to the second division of the argument, and dismissing the supposition that any of the received opinions may be false, let us assume them to be true, and examine into the worth of the manner in which they are likely to be held, when their truth is not freely and openly canvassed. However unwillingly a person who has a strong opinion may admit the possibility that his opinion may be false, he ought to be moved by the consideration that however true it may be, if it is not fully, frequently, and fearlessly discussed, it will be held as a dead dogma, not a living truth.

There is a class of persons (happily not quite so numerous as formerly) who think it enough if a person assents undoubtingly to what they think true, though he has no knowledge whatever of the grounds of the opinion, and could not make a tenable defence of it against the most superficial objections. Such persons, if they can once get their creed taught from authority, naturally think that no good, and some harm, comes of its being allowed to be questioned. Where their influence prevails, they make it nearly impossible for the received opinion to be rejected wisely and considerately, though it may still be rejected rashly and ignorantly; for to shut out discussion entirely is seldom possible, and when it once gets in, beliefs not grounded on conviction are apt to give way before the slightest semblance of an argument. Waving, however, this possibility — assuming that the true opinion abides in the mind, but abides as a prejudice, a belief independent of, and proof against, argument — this is not the way in which truth ought to be held by a rational being. This is not knowing the truth. Truth, thus held, is but one superstition the more, accidentally clinging to the words which enunciate a truth.

If the intellect and judgment of mankind ought to be cultivated, a thing which Protestants at least do not deny, on what can these faculties be more appropriately exercised by any one, than on the things which concern him so much that it is considered necessary for him to hold opinions on them? If the cultivation of the understanding consists in one thing more than in another, it is surely in learning the ground of one's own opinions. Whatever people believe, on subjects on which it is of the first importance to believe rightly, they ought to be able to defend against at least the common objections. But, some one may say, "Let them be *taught* the grounds of their opinions. It does not follow that opinions must be merely parroted because they are never heard controverted. Persons who learn geometry do not simply commit the theorems to memory, but understand and learn likewise the demonstrations; and it would be absurd to say that they remain ignorant of the grounds of geometrical truths, because they never hear any one deny, and attempt to disprove them." Undoubtedly: and such teaching suffices on a subject like mathematics, where there is nothing at all to be said on the wrong side of the question. The peculiarity of the evidence of mathematical truths is, that all the argument is on one side. There are no objections, and no answers to objections. But on every subject on which difference of opinion is possible, the truth depends on a balance to be struck between two sets of conflicting reasons. Even in natural philosophy, there is always some other explanation possible of the same facts; some geocentric theory instead of heliocentric, some phlogiston instead of oxygen; and it has to be shown why that other theory cannot be the true one: and until this is shown, and until we know how it is shown, we do not understand the grounds of our opinion. But when we turn to subjects infinitely more complicated, to morals, religion, politics, social relations, and the business of life, three-fourths of the arguments for every disputed opinion consist in dispelling the appearances which favour some opinion different from it. The greatest orator, save one, of antiquity, has left it on record that he always studied his adversary's case with as great, if not with still greater, intensity than even his own. What Cicero practised as the means of forensic success, requires to be imitated by all who study any subject in order to arrive at the truth. He who knows only his own side of the case, knows little of that. His reasons may be good, and no one may have been able to refute them. But if he is equally unable to refute the reasons on the opposite side; if he does not so much as know what they are, he has no ground for preferring either opinion. The rational position for him would be suspension of judgment, and unless he contents himself with that, he is either led by authority, or adopts, like the generality of the world, the side to which he feels most inclination. Nor is it enough that he should hear the arguments of adversaries from his own teachers, presented as they state them, and accompanied by what they offer as refutations. That is not the way to do justice to the arguments, or bring them into real contact with his own mind. He must be able to hear them from persons who actually believe them; who defend them in earnest, and do their very utmost for them. He must know them in their most plausible and persuasive form; he must feel the whole force of the difficulty which the true view of the subject has to encounter and dispose of; else he will never really possess himself of the portion of truth which meets and removes that difficulty. Ninety-nine in a hundred of what are called educated men are in this condition; even of those who can argue fluently for their opinions. Their conclusion may be true, but it might be false for anything they know: they have never thrown themselves into the mental position of those who think differently from them, and considered what such persons may have to say; and consequently they do not, in any proper sense of the word, know the doctrine which they themselves profess. They do not know those parts of it which explain and justify the remainder; the considerations which show that a fact which seemingly conflicts with another is reconcilable with it, or that, of two apparently strong reasons, one and not the other ought to be preferred. All that part of the truth which turns the scale, and decides the judgment of a completely informed mind, they are strangers to; nor is it ever really known, but to those who have attended equally and impartially to both sides, and endeavoured to see the reasons of both in the strongest light. So essential is this discipline to a real understanding of moral and human subjects, that if opponents of all important truths do not exist, it is indispensable to imagine them, and supply them with the strongest arguments which the most skilful devil's advocate can conjure up.

To abate the force of these considerations, an enemy of free discussion may be supposed to say, that there is no necessity for mankind in general to know and understand all that can be said against or for their opinions by philosophers and theologians. That it is not needful for common men to be able to expose all the misstatements or fallacies of an ingenious opponent. That it is enough if there is always somebody capable of answering them, so that nothing likely to mislead uninstructed persons remains unrefuted. That simple minds, having been taught the obvious grounds of the truths inculcated on them, may trust to authority for the rest, and being aware that they have neither knowledge nor talent to resolve every difficulty which can be raised, may repose in the assurance that all those which have been raised have been or can be answered, by those who are specially trained to the task.

Conceding to this view of the subject the utmost that can be claimed for it by those most easily satisfied with the amount of understanding of truth which ought to accompany the belief of it; even so, the argument for free discussion is no way weakened. For even this doctrine acknowledges that mankind ought to have a rational assurance that all objections have been satisfactorily answered; and how are they to be answered if that which requires to be answered is not spoken? or how can the answer be known to be satisfactory, if the objectors have no opportunity of showing that it is unsatisfactory? If not the public, at least the philosophers and theologians who are to resolve the difficulties, must make themselves familiar with those difficulties in their most puzzling form; and this cannot be accomplished unless they are freely stated, and placed in the most advantageous light which they admit of. The Catholic Church has its own way of dealing with this embarrassing problem. It makes a broad separation between those who can be permitted to receive its doctrines on conviction, and those who must accept them on trust. Neither, indeed, are allowed any choice as to what they will accept; but the clergy, such at least as can be fully confided in, may admissibly and meritoriously make themselves acquainted with the arguments of opponents, in order to answer them, and may, therefore, read heretical books; the laity, not unless by special permission, hard to be obtained. This discipline recognises a knowledge of the enemy's case as beneficial to the teachers, but finds means, consistent with this, of denying it to the rest of the world: thus giving to the *élite* more mental culture, though not more mental freedom, than it allows to the mass. By this device it succeeds in obtaining the kind of mental superiority which its purposes require; for though culture without freedom never made a large and liberal mind, it can make a clever *nisi prius*[14] advocate of a cause. But in countries professing Protestantism, this resource is denied; since Protestants hold, at least in theory, that the responsibility for the choice of a religion must be borne by each for himself, and cannot be thrown off upon teachers. Besides, in the present state of the world, it is practically impossible that writings which are read by the instructed can be kept from the uninstructed. If the teachers of mankind are to be cognisant of all that they ought to know, everything must be free to be written and published without restraint.

If, however, the mischievous operation of the absence of free discussion, when the received opinions are true, were confined to leaving men ignorant of the grounds of those opinions, it might be thought that this, if an intellectual, is no moral evil, and does not affect the worth of the opinions, regarded in their influence on the character. The fact, however, is, that not only the grounds of the opinion are forgotten in the absence of discussion, but too often the meaning of the opinion itself. The words which convey it, cease to suggest ideas, or suggest only a small portion of those they were originally employed to communicate. Instead of a vivid conception and a living belief, there remain only a few phrases retained by rote; or, if any part, the shell and husk only of the meaning is retained, the finer essence being lost. The

14. Unless earlier; taken in law to mean that a particular law is valid unless shown otherwise.

great chapter in human history which this fact occupies and fills, cannot be too earnestly studied and meditated on.

It is illustrated in the experience of almost all ethical doctrines and religious creeds. They are all full of meaning and vitality to those who originate them, and to the direct disciples of the originators. Their meaning continues to be felt in undiminished strength, and is perhaps brought out into even fuller consciousness, so long as the struggle lasts to give the doctrine or creed an ascendancy over other creeds. At last it either prevails, and becomes the general opinion, or its progress stops; it keeps possession of the ground it has gained, but ceases to spread further. When either of these results has become apparent, controversy on the subject flags, and gradually dies away. The doctrine has taken its place, if not as a received opinion, as one of the admitted sects or divisions of opinion: those who hold it have generally inherited, not adopted it; and conversion from one of these doctrines to another, being now an exceptional fact, occupies little place in the thoughts of their professors. Instead of being, as at first, constantly on the alert either to defend themselves against the world, or to bring the world over to them, they have subsided into acquiescence, and neither listen, when they can help it, to arguments against their creed, nor trouble dissentients (if there be such) with arguments in its favour. From this time may usually be dated the decline in the living power of the doctrine. We often hear the teachers of all creeds lamenting the difficulty of keeping up in the minds of believers a lively apprehension of the truth which they nominally recognise, so that it may penetrate the feelings, and acquire a real mastery over the conduct. No such difficulty is complained of while the creed is still fighting for its existence: even the weaker combatants then know and feel what they are fighting for, and the difference between it and other doctrines; and in that period of every creed's existence, not a few persons may be found, who have realized its fundamental principles in all the forms of thought, have weighed and considered them in all their important bearings, and have experienced the full effect on the character, which belief in that creed ought to produce in a mind thoroughly imbued with it. But when it has come to be an hereditary creed, and to be received passively, not actively — when the mind is no longer compelled, in the same degree as at first, to exercise its vital powers on the questions which its belief presents to it, there is a progressive tendency to forget all of the belief except the formularies, or to give it a dull and torpid assent, as if accepting it on trust dispensed with the necessity of realizing it in consciousness, or testing it by personal experience; until it almost ceases to connect itself at all with the inner life of the human being. Then are seen the cases, so frequent in this age of the world as almost to form the majority, in which the creed remains as it were outside the mind, encrusting and petrifying it against all other influences addressed to the higher parts of our nature; manifesting its power by not suffering any fresh and living conviction to get in, but itself doing nothing for the mind or heart, except standing sentinel over them to keep them vacant.

To what an extent doctrines intrinsically fitted to make the deepest impression upon the mind may remain in it as dead beliefs, without being ever realized in the imagination, the feelings, or the understanding, is exemplified by the manner in which the majority of believers hold the doctrines of Christianity. By Christianity I here mean what is accounted such by all churches and sects — the maxims and precepts contained in the New Testament. These are considered sacred, and accepted as laws, by all professing Christians. Yet it is scarcely too much to say that not one Christian in a thousand guides or tests his individual conduct by reference to those laws. The standard to which he does refer it, is the custom of his nation, his class, or his religious profession. He has thus, on the one hand, a collection of ethical maxims, which he believes to have been vouchsafed to him by infallible wisdom as rules for his government; and on the other, a set of every-day judgments and practices, which go a certain length with some of those maxims, not so great a length with others, stand in direct opposition to some, and are, on the whole, a compromise between the Christian creed and the interests and suggestions of worldly life. To the first of these standards he gives his homage; to the other his real allegiance. All Christians believe that the blessed are the poor and humble, and those who are ill-used by the world; that it is easier for a camel to pass through the eye of a needle than for a rich man to enter the kingdom of heaven; that they should judge not, lest they be judged; that they should swear not at all; that they should love their neighbour as themselves; that if one take their cloak, they should give him their coat also; that they should take no thought for the morrow; that if they would be perfect, they should sell all that they have and give it to the poor. They are not insincere when they say that they believe these things. They do believe them, as people believe what they have always heard lauded and never discussed. But in the sense of that living belief which regulates conduct, they believe these doctrines just up to the point to which it is usual to act upon them. The doctrines in their integrity are serviceable to pelt adversaries with; and it is understood that they are to be put forward (when possible) as the reasons for whatever people do that they think laudable. But any one who reminded them that the maxims require an infinity of things which they never even think of doing, would gain nothing but to be classed among those very unpopular characters who affect to be better than other people. The doctrines have no hold on ordinary believers — are not a power in their minds. They have an habitual respect for the sound of them, but no feeling which spreads from the words to the things signified, and forces the mind to take *them* in, and make them conform to the formula. Whenever conduct is concerned, they look round for Mr. A and B to direct them how far to go in obeying Christ.

Now we may be well assured that the case was not thus, but far otherwise, with the early Christians. Had it been thus, Christianity never would have expanded from an obscure sect of the despised Hebrews into the religion of the Roman empire. When their enemies said, "See how these Christians love one another" (a remark not likely to be made by anybody now), they assuredly had a much livelier feeling of the meaning of their creed than they have ever had since. And to this cause, probably, it is chiefly owing that Christianity now makes so little progress in extending its domain, and after eighteen centuries, is still nearly confined to Europeans and the descendants of Europeans. Even with the strictly religious, who are much in earnest about their doctrines, and attach a greater amount of meaning to many of them than people in general, it commonly happens that the part which is thus comparatively active in their minds is that which was made by Calvin, or Knox, or some such person much nearer in character to themselves. The sayings of Christ coexist passively in their minds, producing hardly any effect beyond what is caused by mere listening to words so amiable and bland. There are many reasons, doubtless, why doctrines which are the badge of a sect retain more of their vitality than those common to all recognised sects, and why more pains are taken by teachers to keep their meaning alive; but one reason certainly is, that the peculiar doctrines are more questioned, and have to be oftener defended against open gainsayers. Both teachers and learners go to sleep at their post, as soon as there is no enemy in the field.

The same thing holds true, generally speaking, of all traditional doctrines — those of prudence and knowledge of life, as well as of morals or religion. All languages and literatures are full of general observations on life, both as to what it is, and how to conduct oneself in it; observations which everybody knows, which everybody repeats, or hears with acquiescence, which are received as truisms, yet of which most people first truly learn the meaning, when experience, generally of a painful kind, has made it a reality to them. How often, when smarting under some unforeseen misfortune or disappointment, does a person call to mind some proverb or common saying, familiar to him all his life, the meaning of which, if he had ever before felt it as he does now, would have saved him from the calamity. There are indeed reasons for this, other than the absence of discussion: there are many truths of which the full meaning *cannot* be realized, until personal experience has brought it home. But much more of the meaning even of these would have been understood, and what was understood would have been far more deeply impressed on the mind, if the man had been accustomed to hear it argued *pro* and *con* by people who did understand it. The fatal tendency of mankind to leave off thinking about a thing when it is no longer doubtful, is the cause of half their errors. A cotemporary author has well spoken of "the deep slumber of a decided opinion."

But what! (it may be asked) Is the absence of unanimity an indispensable condition of true knowledge? Is it necessary that some part of mankind should persist in error, to enable any to realize the truth? Does a belief cease to be real and vital as soon as it is generally received — and is a proposition never thoroughly understood and felt unless some doubt of it remains? As soon as mankind have unanimously accepted a truth, does the truth perish within them? The highest aim and best result of improved intelligence, it has hitherto been thought, is to unite mankind more and more in the acknowledgment of all important truths: and does the intelligence only last as long as it has not achieved its object? Do the fruits of conquest perish by the very completeness of the victory?

I affirm no such thing. As mankind improve, the number of doctrines which are no longer disputed or doubted will be constantly on the increase: and the well-being of mankind may almost be measured by the number and gravity of the truths which have reached the point of being uncontested. The cessation, on one question after another, of serious controversy, is one of the necessary incidents of the consolidation of opinion; a consolidation as salutary in the case of true opinions, as it is dangerous and noxious when the opinions are erroneous. But though this gradual narrowing of the bounds of diversity of opinion is necessary in both senses of the term, being at once inevitable and indispensable, we are not therefore obliged to conclude that all its consequences must be beneficial. The loss of so important an aid to the intelligent and living apprehension of a truth, as is afforded by the necessity of explaining it to, or defending it against, opponents, though not sufficient to outweigh, is no trifling drawback from, the benefit of its universal recognition. Where this advantage can no longer be had, I confess I should like to see the teachers of mankind endeavouring to provide a substitute for it; some contrivance for making the difficulties of the question as present to the learner's consciousness, as if they were pressed upon him by a dissentient champion, eager for his conversion.

But instead of seeking contrivances for this purpose, they have lost those they formerly had. The Socratic dialectics, so magnificently exemplified in the dialogues of Plato, were a contrivance of this description. They were essentially a negative discussion of the great questions of philosophy and life, directed with consummate skill to the purpose of convincing any one who had merely adopted the commonplaces of received opinion, that he did not understand the subject — that he as yet attached no definite meaning to the doctrines he professed; in order that, becoming aware of his ignorance, he might be put in the way to attain a stable belief, resting on a clear apprehension both of the meaning of doctrines and of their evidence. The school disputations of the middle ages had a somewhat similar object. They were intended to make sure that the pupil understood his own opinion, and (by necessary correlation) the opinion opposed to it, and could enforce the grounds of the one and confute those of the other. These last-mentioned contests had indeed the incurable defect, that the premises appealed to were taken from authority, not from reason; and, as a discipline to the mind, they were in every respect inferior to the powerful dialectics which formed the intellects of the "Socratici viri":[15] but the modern mind owes far more to both than it is generally willing to admit, and the present modes of education contain nothing which in the smallest degree supplies the place either of the one or of the other. A person who derives all his instruction from teachers or books, even if he escape the besetting temptation of contenting himself with cram, is under no compulsion to hear both sides; accordingly it is far from a frequent accomplishment, even among thinkers, to know both sides; and the weakest part of what everybody says in defence of his opinion, is what he intends as a reply to antagonists. It is the fashion of the present time to disparage negative logic — that which points out weaknesses in theory or errors in practice, without establishing positive truths. Such negative criticism would indeed be poor enough as an ultimate result; but as a means to attaining any positive knowledge or conviction worthy the name, it cannot be valued too highly; and until people are again systematically trained to it, there will be few great thinkers, and a low general average of intellect, in any but the mathematical and physical departments of speculation. On any other subject no one's opinions deserve the name of knowledge, except so far as he has either had forced upon him by others, or gone through of himself, the same mental process which would have been required of him in carrying on an active controversy with opponents. That, therefore, which when absent, it is so indispensable, but so difficult, to

15. Students of Socrates.

create, how worse than absurd is it to forego, when spontaneously offering itself! If there are any persons who contest a received opinion, or who will do so if law or opinion will let them, let us thank them for it, open our minds to listen to them, and rejoice that there is some one to do for us what we otherwise ought, if we have any regard for either the certainty or the vitality of our convictions, to do with much greater labour for ourselves.

It still remains to speak of one of the principal causes which make diversity of opinion advantageous, and will continue to do so until mankind shall have entered a stage of intellectual advancement which at present seems at an incalculable distance. We have hitherto considered only two possibilities: that the received opinion may be false, and some other opinion, consequently, true; or that, the received opinion being true, a conflict with the opposite error is essential to a clear apprehension and deep feeling of its truth. But there is a commoner case than either of these; when the conflicting doctrines, instead of being one true and the other false, share the truth between them; and the nonconforming opinion is needed to supply the remainder of the truth, of which the received doctrine embodies only a part. Popular opinions, on subjects not palpable to sense, are often true, but seldom or never the whole truth. They are a part of the truth; sometimes a greater, sometimes a smaller part, but exaggerated, distorted, and disjoined from the truths by which they ought to be accompanied and limited. Heretical opinions, on the other hand, are generally some of these suppressed and neglected truths, bursting the bonds which kept them down, and either seeking reconciliation with the truth contained in the common opinion, or fronting it as enemies, and setting themselves up, with similar exclusiveness, as the whole truth. The latter case is hitherto the most frequent, as, in the human mind, one-sidedness has always been the rule, and many-sidedness the exception. Hence, even in revolutions of opinion, one part of the truth usually sets while another rises. Even progress, which ought to superadd, for the most part only substitutes one partial and incomplete truth for another; improvement consisting chiefly in this, that the new fragment of truth is more wanted, more adapted to the needs of the time, than that which it displaces. Such being the partial character of prevailing opinions, even when resting on a true foundation; every opinion which embodies somewhat of the portion of truth which the common opinion omits, ought to be considered precious, with whatever amount of error and confusion that truth may be blended. No sober judge of human affairs will feel bound to be indignant because those who force on our notice truths which we should otherwise have overlooked, overlook some of those which we see. Rather, he will think that so long as popular truth is onesided, it is more desirable than otherwise that unpopular truth should have onesided asserters too; such being usually the most energetic, and the most likely to compel reluctant attention to the fragment of wisdom which they proclaim as if it were the whole.

Thus, in the eighteenth century, when nearly all the instructed, and all those of the uninstructed who were led by them, were lost in admiration of what is called civilization, and of the marvels of modern science, literature, and philosophy, and while greatly overrating the amount of unlikeness between the men of modern and those of ancient times, indulged the belief that the whole of the difference was in their own favour; with what a salutary shock did the paradoxes of Rousseau explode like bombshells in the midst, dislocating the compact mass of onesided opinion, and forcing its elements to recombine in a better form and with additional ingredients. Not that the current opinions were on the whole farther from the truth than Rousseau's were; on the contrary they were nearer to it; they contained more of positive truth, and very much less of error. Nevertheless there lay in Rousseau's doctrine, and has floated down the stream of opinion along with it, a considerable amount of exactly those truths which the popular opinion wanted; and these are the deposit which was left behind when the flood subsided. The superior worth of simplicity of life, the enervating and demoralizing effect of the trammels and hypocrisies of artificial society, are ideas which have never been entirely absent from cultivated minds since Rousseau wrote; and they will in time produce their due effect, though at present needing to be asserted as much as ever, and to be asserted by deeds, for words, on this subject, have nearly exhausted their power.[16]

In politics, again, it is almost a commonplace, that a party of order or stability, and a party of progress or reform, are both necessary elements of a healthy state of political life; until the one or the other shall have so enlarged its mental grasp as to be a party equally of order and of progress, knowing and distinguishing what is fit to be preserved from what ought to be swept away. Each of these modes of thinking derives its utility from the deficiencies of the other; but it is in a great measure the opposition of the other that keeps each within the limits of reason and sanity. Unless opinions

16. Mill seems to have had in mind particularly Rousseau's *Discourse on the Sciences and Arts,* which argues that the technical progress of mankind has been a catastrophe because it reduces all thought of self to a craving for distinction; and his *Discourse on Inequality,* which argues that every social convention, including property, is necessarily at war with feeling and robs human beings of the power to begin to know who they are.

favourable to democracy and to aristocracy, to property and to equality, to co-operation and to competition, to luxury and to abstinence, to sociality and individuality, to liberty and discipline, and all the other standing antagonisms of practical life, are expressed with equal freedom, and enforced and defended with equal talent and energy, there is no chance of both elements obtaining their due; one scale is sure to go up, and the other down. Truth, in the great practical concerns of life, is so much a question of the reconciling and combining of opposites, that very few have minds sufficiently capacious and impartial to make the adjustment with an approach to correctness, and it has to be made by the rough process of a struggle between combatants fighting under hostile banners. On any of the great open questions just enumerated, if either of the two opinions has a better claim than the other, not merely to be tolerated, but to be encouraged and countenanced, it is the one which happens at the particular time and place to be in a minority. That is the opinion which, for the time being, represents the neglected interests, the side of human well-being which is in danger of obtaining less than its share. I am aware that there is not, in this country, any intolerance of differences of opinion on most of these topics. They are adduced to show, by admitted and multiplied examples, the universality of the fact, that only through diversity of opinion is there, in the existing state of human intellect, a chance of fair play to all sides of the truth. When there are persons to be found, who form an exception to the apparent unanimity of the world on any subject, even if the world is in the right, it is always probable that dissentients have something worth hearing to say for themselves, and that truth would lose something by their silence.

It may be objected, "But *some* received principles, especially on the highest and most vital subjects, are more than half-truths. The Christian morality, for instance, is the whole truth on that subject, and if any one teaches a morality which varies from it, he is wholly in error." As this is of all cases the most important in practice, none can be fitter to test the general maxim. But before pronouncing what Christian morality is or is not, it would be desirable to decide what is meant by Christian morality. If it means the morality of the New Testament, I wonder that any one who derives his knowledge of this from the book itself, can suppose that it was announced, or intended, as a complete doctrine of morals. The Gospel always refers to a pre-existing morality, and confines its precepts to the particulars in which that morality was to be corrected, or superseded by a wider and higher; expressing itself, moreover, in terms most general, often impossible to be interpreted literally, and possessing rather the impressiveness of poetry or eloquence than the precision of legislation. To extract from

it a body of ethical doctrine, has never been possible without eking it
out from the Old Testament, that is, from a system elaborate indeed, but
in many respects barbarous, and intended only for a barbarous people.
St. Paul, a declared enemy to this Judaical mode of interpreting the doctrine
and filling up the scheme of his Master, equally assumes a pre-existing
morality, namely that of the Greeks and Romans; and his advice to Christians is in a great measure a system of accommodation to that; even to the
extent of giving an apparent sanction to slavery. What is called Christian,
but should rather be termed theological, morality, was not the work of
Christ or the Apostles, but is of much later origin, having been gradually
built up by the Catholic church of the first five centuries, and though not
implicitly adopted by moderns and Protestants, has been much less modified by them than might have been expected. For the most part, indeed, they
have contented themselves with cutting off the additions which had been
made to it in the middle ages, each sect supplying the place by fresh additions, adapted to its own character and tendencies. That mankind owe a
great debt to this morality, and to its early teachers, I should be the last
person to deny; but I do not scruple to say of it, that it is, in many important
points, incomplete and onesided, and that unless ideas and feelings, not
sanctioned by it, had contributed to the formation of European life and
character, human affairs would have been in a worse condition than they
now are. Christian morality (so called) has all the characters of a reaction; it
is, in great part, a protest against Paganism. Its ideal is negative rather than
positive; passive rather than active; Innocence rather than Nobleness; Abstinence from Evil, rather than energetic Pursuit of Good: in its precepts (as
has been well said) "thou shalt not" predominates unduly over "thou
shalt." In its horror of sensuality, it made an idol of asceticism, which has
been gradually compromised away into one of legality. It holds out the hope
of heaven and the threat of hell, as the appointed and appropriate motives to
a virtuous life: in this falling far below the best of the ancients, and doing
what lies in it to give to human morality an essentially selfish character, by
disconnecting each man's feelings of duty from the interests of his fellow-
creatures, except so far as a self-interested inducement is offered to him for
consulting them. It is essentially a doctrine of passive obedience; it incul-
cates submission to all authorities found established; who indeed are not to
be actively obeyed when they command what religion forbids, but who are
not to be resisted, far less rebelled against, for any amount of wrong to
ourselves. And while, in the morality of the best Pagan nations, duty to the
State holds even a disproportionate place, infringing on the just liberty of
the individual; in purely Christian ethics, that grand department of duty is

scarcely noticed or acknowledged. It is in the Koran, not the New Testament, that we read the maxim — "A ruler who appoints any man to an office, when there is in his dominions another man better qualified for it, sins against God and against the State." What little recognition the idea of obligation to the public obtains in modern morality, is derived from Greek and Roman sources, not from Christian; as, even in the morality of private life, whatever exists of magnanimity, highmindedness, personal dignity, even the sense of honour, is derived from the purely human, not the religious part of our education, and never could have grown out of a standard of ethics in which the only worth, professedly recognised, is that of obedience.

I am as far as any one from pretending that these defects are necessarily inherent in the Christian ethics, in every manner in which it can be conceived, or that the many requisites of a complete moral doctrine which it does not contain, do not admit of being reconciled with it. Far less would I insinuate this of the doctrines and precepts of Christ himself. I believe that the sayings of Christ are all, that I can see any evidence of their having been intended to be; that they are irreconcileable with nothing which a comprehensive morality requires; that everything which is excellent in ethics may be brought within them, with no greater violence to their language than has been done to it by all who have attempted to deduce from them any practical system of conduct whatever. But it is quite consistent with this, to believe that they contain, and were meant to contain, only a part of the truth; that many essential elements of the highest morality are among the things which are not provided for, nor intended to be provided for, in the recorded deliverances of the Founder of Christianity, and which have been entirely thrown aside in the system of ethics erected on the basis of those deliverances by the Christian Church. And this being so, I think it a great error to persist in attempting to find in the Christian doctrine that complete rule for our guidance, which its author intended it to sanction and enforce, but only partially to provide. I believe, too, that this narrow theory is becoming a grave practical evil, detracting greatly from the value of the moral training and instruction, which so many well-meaning persons are now at length exerting themselves to promote. I much fear that by attempting to form the mind and feelings on an exclusively religious type, and discarding those secular standards (as for want of a better name they may be called) which heretofore co-existed with and supplemented the Christian ethics, receiving some of its spirit, and infusing into it some of theirs, there will result, and is even now resulting, a low, abject, servile type of character, which, submit itself as it may to what it deems the Supreme Will, is incapable of rising to or sympathizing in the conception of Supreme Goodness. I believe that other ethics than any which can be evolved from exclusively Christian sources, must exist side by side with Christian ethics to produce the moral regeneration of mankind; and that the Christian system is no exception to the rule, that in an imperfect state of the human mind, the interests of truth require a diversity of opinions. It is not necessary that in ceasing to ignore the moral truths not contained in Christianity, men should ignore any of those which it does contain. Such prejudice, or oversight, when it occurs, is altogether an evil; but it is one from which we cannot hope to be always exempt, and must be regarded as the price paid for an inestimable good. The exclusive pretension made by a part of the truth to be the whole, must and ought to be protested against, and if a reactionary impulse should make the protestors unjust in their turn, this onesidedness, like the other, may be lamented, but must be tolerated. If Christians would teach infidels to be just to Christianity, they should themselves be just to infidelity. It can do truth no service to blink the fact, known to all who have the most ordinary acquaintance with literary history, that a large portion of the noblest and most valuable moral teaching has been the work, not only of men who did not know, but of men who knew and rejected, the Christian faith.

I do not pretend that the most unlimited use of the freedom of enunciating all possible opinions would put an end to the evils of religious or philosophical sectarianism. Every truth which men of narrow capacity are in earnest about, is sure to be asserted, inculcated, and in many ways even acted on, as if no other truth existed in the world, or at all events none that could limit or qualify the first. I acknowledge that the tendency of all opinions to become sectarian is not cured by the freest discussion, but is often heightened and exacerbated thereby; the truth which ought to have been, but was not, seen, being rejected all the more violently because proclaimed by persons regarded as opponents. But it is not on the impassioned partisan, it is on the calmer and more disinterested bystander, that this collision of opinions works its salutary effect. Not the violent conflict between parts of the truth, but the quiet suppression of half of it, is the formidable evil: there is always hope when people are forced to listen to both sides; it is when they attend only to one that errors harden into prejudices, and truth itself ceases to have the effect of truth, by being exaggerated into falsehood. And since there are few mental attributes more rare than that judicial faculty which can sit in intelligent judgment between two sides of a question, of which only one is represented by an advocate before it, truth has no chance but in proportion as every side of it, every opinion which embodies any fraction of the truth, not only finds advocates, but is so advocated as to be listened to.

■

We have now recognised the necessity to the mental well-being of mankind (on which all their other well-being depends) of freedom of opinion, and freedom of the expression of opinion, on four distinct grounds; which we will now briefly recapitulate.

First, if any opinion is compelled to silence, that opinion may, for aught we can certainly know, be true. To deny this is to assume our own infallibility.

Second, though the silenced opinion be an error, it may, and very commonly does, contain a portion of truth; and since the general or prevailing opinion on any subject is rarely or never the whole truth, it is only by the collision of adverse opinions that the remainder of the truth has any chance of being supplied.

Thirdly, even if the received opinion be not only true, but the whole truth; unless it is suffered to be, and actually is, vigorously and earnestly contested, it will, by most of those who receive it, be held in the manner of a prejudice, with little comprehension or feeling of its rational grounds. And not only this, but, fourthly, the meaning of the doctrine itself will be in danger of being lost, or enfeebled, and deprived of its vital effect on the character and conduct: the dogma becoming a mere formal profession, inefficacious for good, but cumbering the ground, and preventing the growth of any real and heartfelt conviction, from reason or personal experience.

Before quitting the subject of freedom of opinion, it is fit to take some notice of those who say, that the free expression of all opinions should be permitted, on condition that the manner be temperate, and do not pass the bounds of fair discussion. Much might be said on the impossibility of fixing where these supposed bounds are to be placed; for if the test be offence to those whose opinion is attacked, I think experience testifies that this offence is given whenever the attack is telling and powerful, and that every opponent who pushes them hard, and whom they find it difficult to answer, appears to them, if he shows any strong feeling on the subject, an intemperate opponent. But this, though an important consideration in a practical point of view, merges in a more fundamental objection. Undoubtedly the manner of asserting an opinion, even though it be a true one, may be very objectionable, and may justly incur severe censure. But the principal offences of the kind are such as it is mostly impossible, unless by accidental self-betrayal, to bring home to conviction. The gravest of them is, to argue sophistically, to suppress facts or arguments, to misstate the elements of the case, or misrepresent the opposite opinion. But all this, even to the most aggravated degree, is so continually done in perfect good faith, by persons who are not considered, and in many other respects may not deserve to be considered, ignorant or incompetent, that it is rarely possible on adequate grounds conscientiously to stamp the misrepresentation as morally culpable; and still less could law presume to interfere with this kind of controversial misconduct. With regard to what is commonly meant by intemperate discussion, namely invective, sarcasm, personality, and the like, the denunciation of these weapons would deserve more sympathy if it were ever proposed to interdict them equally to both sides; but it is only desired to restrain the employment of them against the prevailing opinion: against the unprevailing they may not only be used without general disapproval, but will be likely to obtain for him who uses them the praise of honest zeal and righteous indignation. Yet whatever mischief arises from their use, is greatest when they are employed against the comparatively defenceless; and whatever unfair advantage can be derived by any opinion from this mode of asserting it, accrues almost exclusively to received opinions. The worst offence of this kind which can be committed by a polemic, is to stigmatize those who hold the contrary opinion as bad and immoral men. To calumny of this sort, those who hold any unpopular opinion are peculiarly exposed, because they are in general few and uninfluential, and nobody but themselves feels much interest in seeing justice done them; but this weapon is, from the nature of the case, denied to those who attack a prevailing opinion: they can neither use it with safety to themselves, nor, if they could, would it do anything but recoil on their own cause. In general, opinions contrary to those commonly received can only obtain a hearing by studied moderation of language, and the most cautious avoidance of unnecessary offence, from which they hardly ever deviate even in a slight degree without losing ground: while unmeasured vituperation employed on the side of the prevailing opinion, really does deter people from professing contrary opinions, and from listening to those who profess them. For the interest, therefore, of truth and justice, it is far more important to restrain this employment of vituperative language than the other; and, for example, if it were necessary to choose, there would be much more need to discourage offensive attacks on infidelity, than on religion. It is, however, obvious that law and authority have no business with restraining either, while opinion ought, in every instance, to determine its verdict by the circumstances of the individual case; condemning every one, on whichever side of the argument he places himself, in whose mode of advocacy either want of candour, or malignity, bigotry, or intolerance of feeling manifest themselves; but not inferring these vices from the side which a person takes, though it be the contrary side of the question to our own: and giving merited honour to every one, whatever opinion he may hold, who has calmness to see and honesty to state what his opponents and their opinions really are, exaggerating nothing to their discredit, keeping nothing back which tells, or can be supposed to tell, in their favour. This is the real morality of public discussion; and if often violated, I am happy to think that there are many controversialists who to a great extent observe it, and a still greater number who conscientiously strive towards it.

CHAPTER III

OF INDIVIDUALITY, AS ONE OF THE

ELEMENTS OF WELL-BEING

Such being the reasons which make it imperative that human beings should be free to form opinions, and to express their opinions without reserve; and such the baneful consequences to the intellectual, and through that to the moral nature of man, unless this liberty is either conceded, or asserted in spite of prohibition; let us next examine whether the same reasons do not require that men should be free to act upon their opinions—to carry these out in their lives, without hindrance, either physical or moral, from their fellow-men, so long as it is at their own risk and peril. This last proviso is of course indispensable. No one pretends that actions should be as free as opinions. On the contrary, even opinions lose their immunity, when the circumstances in which they are expressed are such as to constitute their expression a positive instigation to some mischievous act. An opinion that corn-dealers are starvers of the poor, or that private property is robbery, ought to be unmolested when simply circulated through the press, but may justly incur punishment when delivered orally to an excited mob assembled before the house of a corn-dealer, or when handed about among the same mob in the form of a placard. Acts, of whatever kind, which, without justifiable cause, do harm to others, may be, and in the more important cases absolutely require to be, controlled by the unfavourable sentiments, and, when needful, by the active interference of mankind. The liberty of the individual must be thus far limited; he must not make himself a nuisance to other people. But if he refrains from molesting others in what concerns them, and merely acts according to his own inclination and judgment in things which concern himself, the same reasons which show that opinion should be free, prove also that he should be allowed, without molestation, to carry his opinions into practice at his own cost. That mankind are not infallible; that their truths, for the most part, are only half-truths; that unity of opinion, unless resulting from the fullest and freest comparison of opposite opinions, is not desirable, and diversity not an evil, but a good, until mankind are much more capable than at present of recognising all sides of the truth, are principles applicable to men's modes of action, not less than to their opinions. As it is useful that while mankind are imperfect there should be different opinions, so is it that there should be different experiments of living; that free scope should be given to varieties of character, short of injury to others; and that the worth of different modes of life should be proved practically, when any one thinks fit to try them. It is desirable, in short, that in things which do not primarily concern others, individuality should assert itself. Where, not the person's own character, but the traditions or customs of other people are the rule of conduct, there is wanting one of the principal ingredients of human happiness, and quite the chief ingredient of individual and social progress.

In maintaining this principle, the greatest difficulty to be encountered does not lie in the appreciation of means toward an acknowledged end, but in the indifference of persons in general to the end itself. If it were felt that the free development of individuality is one of the leading essentials of well-being; that it is not only a co-ordinate element with all that is designated by the terms civilization, instruction, education, culture, but is itself a necessary part and condition of all those things; there would be no danger that liberty should be undervalued, and the adjustment of the boundaries between it and social control would present no extraordinary difficulty. But the evil is, that individual spontaneity is hardly recognized by the common modes of thinking, as having any intrinsic worth, or deserving any regard on its own account. The majority, being satisfied with the ways of mankind as they now are (for it is they who make them what they are), cannot comprehend why those ways should not be good enough for everybody; and what is more, spontaneity forms no part of the ideal of the majority of moral and social reformers, but is rather looked on with jealousy, as a troublesome and perhaps rebellious obstruction to the general acceptance of what these reformers, in their own judgment, think would be best for mankind. Few persons, out of Germany, even comprehend the meaning of the doctrine which Wilhelm Von Humboldt, so eminent both as a *savant* and as a politician, made the text of a treatise — that "the end of man, or that which is prescribed by the eternal or immutable dictates of reason, and not suggested by vague and transient desires, is the highest and most harmonious developement of his powers to a complete and consistent whole"; that, therefore, the object "towards which every human being must ceaselessly direct his efforts, and on which especially those who design to influence their fellow-men must ever keep their eyes, is the individuality of power and developement"; that for this there are two requisites, "freedom, and a variety of situations"; and that from the union of these arise "individual vigour and manifold diversity," which combine themselves in "originality."*

Little, however, as people are accustomed to a doctrine like that of Von Humboldt, and surprising as it may be to them to find so high a value attached to individuality, the question, one must nevertheless think, can only be one of degree. No one's idea of excellence in conduct is that people should do absolutely nothing but copy one another. No one would assert that people ought not to put into their mode of life, and into the conduct of their concerns, any impress whatever of their own judgment, or of their own individual character. On the other hand, it would be absurd to pretend that people ought to live as if nothing whatever had been known in the world before they came into it; as if experience had as yet done nothing towards showing that one mode of existence, or of conduct, is preferable to another. Nobody denies that people should be so taught and trained in youth, as to know and benefit by the ascertained results of human experience. But it is the privilege and proper condition of a human being, arrived at the maturity of his faculties, to use and interpret experience in his own way. It is for him to find out what part of recorded experience is properly applicable to his own circumstances and character. The traditions and customs of other people are, to a certain extent, evidence of what their experience has taught *them;* presumptive evidence, and as such, have a claim to his deference: but, in the first place, their experience may be too narrow; or they may not have interpreted it rightly. Secondly, their interpretation of experience may be correct, but unsuitable to him. Customs are made for customary circumstances, and customary characters: and his circumstances or his character may be uncustomary. Thirdly, though the customs be both good as customs, and suitable to him, yet to conform to custom, merely *as* custom, does not educate or develope in him any of the qualities which are the distinctive endowment of a human being. The human faculties of perception, judgment, discriminative feeling, mental activity, and even moral preference, are exercised only in making a choice. He who does anything because it is the custom, makes no choice. He gains no practice either in discerning or in

---

* *The Sphere and Duties of Government,* from the German of Baron Wilhelm von Humboldt, pp. 11–13.

[Wilhelm von Humboldt (1767–1835), in the work cited by Mill, has in view the diversity of forces and impulses that go to form an individual, rather than the diversity of individuals that compose a group or the diversity of groups that constitute a society. — *Ed.*]

desiring what is best. The mental and moral, like the muscular powers, are improved only by being used. The faculties are called into no exercise by doing a thing merely because others do it, no more than by believing a thing only because others believe it. If the grounds of an opinion are not conclusive to the person's own reason, his reason cannot be strengthened, but is likely to be weakened by his adopting it: and if the inducements to an act are not such as are consentaneous to his own feelings and character (where affection, or the rights of others, are not concerned) it is so much done towards rendering his feelings and character inert and torpid, instead of active and energetic.

He who lets the world, or his own portion of it, choose his plan of life for him, has no need of any other faculty than the ape-like one of imitation. He who chooses his plan for himself, employs all his faculties. He must use observation to see, reasoning and judgment to foresee, activity to gather materials for decision, discrimination to decide, and when he has decided, firmness and self-control to hold to his deliberate decision. And these qualities he requires and exercises exactly in proportion as the part of his conduct which he determines according to his own judgment and feelings is a large one. It is possible that he might be guided in some good path, and kept out of harm's way, without any of these things. But what will be his comparative worth as a human being? It really is of importance, not only what men do, but also what manner of men they are that do it. Among the works of man, which human life is rightly employed in perfecting and beautifying, the first in importance surely is man himself. Supposing it were possible to get houses built, corn grown, battles fought, causes tried, and even churches erected and prayers said, by machinery—by automatons in human form—it would be a considerable loss to exchange for these automatons even the men and women who at present inhabit the more civilized parts of the world, and who assuredly are but starved specimens of what nature can and will produce. Human nature is not a machine to be built after a model, and set to do exactly the work prescribed for it, but a tree, which requires to grow and develope itself on all sides, according to the tendency of the inward forces which make it a living thing.

It will probably be conceded that it is desirable people should exercise their understandings, and that an intelligent following of custom, or even occasionally an intelligent deviation from custom, is better than a blind and simply mechanical adhesion to it. To a certain extent it is admitted, that our understanding should be our own: but there is not the same willingness to admit that our desires and impulses should be our own likewise; or that to possess impulses of our own, and of any strength, is anything but a peril and a snare. Yet desires and impulses are as much a part of a perfect human being, as beliefs and restraints: and strong impulses are only perilous when not properly balanced; when one set of aims and inclinations is developed into strength, while others, which ought to co-exist with them, remain weak and inactive. It is not because men's desires are strong that they act ill; it is because their consciences are weak. There is no natural connexion between strong impulses and a weak conscience. The natural connexion is the other way. To say that one person's desires and feelings are stronger and more various than those of another, is merely to say that he has more of the raw material of human nature, and is therefore capable, perhaps of more evil, but certainly of more good. Strong impulses are but another name for energy. Energy may be turned to bad uses; but more good may always be made of an energetic nature, than of an indolent and impassive one. Those who have most natural feeling, are always those whose cultivated feelings may be made the strongest. The same strong susceptibilities which make the personal impulses vivid and powerful, are also the source from whence are generated the most passionate love of virtue, and the sternest self-control. It is through the cultivation of these, that society both does its duty and protects its interests: not by rejecting the stuff of which heroes are made, because it knows not how to make them. A person whose desires and impulses are his own — are the expression of his own nature, as it has been developed and modified by his own culture[17] — is said to have a character. One whose desires and impulses are not his own, has no character, no more than a steam-engine has a character. If, in addition to being his own, his impulses are strong, and are under the government of a strong will, he has an energetic character. Whoever thinks that individuality of desires and impulses should not be encouraged to unfold itself, must maintain that society has no need of strong natures — is not the better for containing many persons who have much character — and that a high general average of energy is not desirable.

In some early states of society, these forces might be, and were, too much ahead of the power which society then possessed of disciplining and controlling them. There has been a time when the element of spontaneity and individuality was in excess, and the social principle had a hard struggle with it. The difficulty then was, to induce men of strong bodies or minds to pay obedience to any rules which required them to control their impulses. To overcome this difficulty, law and discipline, like the Popes struggling against the Emperors, asserted a power over the whole man, claiming to

17. Self-cultivation.

control all his life in order to control his character — which society had not found any other sufficient means of binding. But society has now fairly got the better of individuality; and the danger which threatens human nature is not the excess, but the deficiency, of personal impulses and preferences. Things are vastly changed, since the passions of those who were strong by station or by personal endowment were in a state of habitual rebellion against laws and ordinances, and required to be rigorously chained up to enable the persons within their reach to enjoy any particle of security. In our times, from the highest class of society down to the lowest, every one lives as under the eye of a hostile and dreaded censorship. Not only in what concerns others, but in what concerns only themselves, the individual, or the family, do not ask themselves — what do I prefer? or, what would suit my character and disposition? or, what would allow the best and highest in me to have fair play, and enable it to grow and thrive? They ask themselves, what is suitable to my position? what is usually done by persons of my station and pecuniary circumstances? or (worse still) what is usually done by persons of a station and circumstances superior to mine? I do not mean that they choose what is customary, in preference to what suits their own inclination. It does not occur to them to have any inclination, except for what is customary. Thus the mind itself is bowed to the yoke: even in what people do for pleasure, conformity is the first thing thought of; they like in crowds; they exercise choice only among things commonly done: peculiarity of taste, eccentricity of conduct, are shunned equally with crimes: until by dint of not following their own nature, they have no nature to follow: their human capacities are withered and starved: they become incapable of any strong wishes or native pleasures, and are generally without either opinions or feelings of home growth, or properly their own. Now is this, or is it not, the desirable condition of human nature?

It is so, on the Calvinistic theory. According to that, the one great offence of man is Self-will. All the good of which humanity is capable, is comprised in Obedience. You have no choice; thus you must do, and no otherwise: "whatever is not a duty, is a sin." Human nature being radically corrupt, there is no redemption for any one until human nature is killed within him. To one holding this theory of life, crushing out any of the human faculties, capacities, and susceptibilities, is no evil: man needs no capacity, but that of surrendering himself to the will of God: and if he uses any of his faculties for any other purpose but to do that supposed will more effectually, he is better without them. That is the theory of Calvinism; and it is held, in a mitigated form, by many who do not consider themselves Calvinists; the mitigation consisting in giving a less ascetic interpretation to the alleged will of God; asserting it to be his will that mankind should gratify some of their inclinations; of course not in the manner they themselves prefer, but in the way of obedience, that is, in a way prescribed to them by authority; and, therefore, by the necessary conditions of the case, the same for all. In some such insidious form there is at present a strong tendency to this narrow theory of life, and to the pinched and hidebound type of human character which it patronizes. Many persons, no doubt, sincerely think that human beings thus cramped and dwarfed, are as their Maker designed them to be; just as many have thought that trees are a much finer thing when clipped into pollards, or cut out into figures of animals, than as nature made them. But if it be any part of religion to believe that man was made by a good being, it is more consistent with that faith to believe, that this Being gave all human faculties that they might be cultivated and unfolded, not rooted out and consumed, and that he takes delight in every nearer approach made by his creatures to the ideal conception embodied in them, every increase in any of their capabilities of comprehension, of action, or of enjoyment. There is a different type of human excellence from the Calvinistic; a conception of humanity as having its nature bestowed on it for other purposes than merely to be abnegated. "Pagan self-assertion" is one of the elements of human worth, as well as "Christian self-denial."* There is a Greek ideal of self-development, which the Platonic and Christian ideal of self-government blends with, but does not supersede. It may be better to be a John Knox than an Alcibiades, but it is better to be a Pericles than either; nor would a Pericles, if we had one in these days, be without anything good which belonged to John Knox.[18]

It is not by wearing down into uniformity all that is individual in themselves, but by cultivating it and calling it forth, within the limits imposed by the rights and interests of others, that human beings become a noble and beautiful object of contemplation; and as the works partake the character of those who do them, by the same process human life also becomes rich, diversified, and animating, furnishing more abundant aliment to high thoughts and elevating feelings, and strengthening the tie which binds every individual to the race, by making the race infinitely better worth belonging to. In

* Sterling's *Essays.*

[John Sterling (1806–44) was a man of letters known for his poetry, fiction, and essays. A close friend of Mill's, he contributed much to the posthumous revival of interest in Coleridge. — *Ed.*]

18. Alcibiades is named as a demagogue and traitor to Athens in the Peloponnesian War, Pericles as a self-sacrificing leader and statesman.

proportion to the development of his individuality, each person becomes more valuable to himself, and is therefore capable of being more valuable to others. There is a greater fulness of life about his own existence, and when there is more life in the units there is more in the mass which is composed of them. As much compression as is necessary to prevent the stronger specimens of human nature from encroaching on the rights of others, cannot be dispensed with; but for this there is ample compensation even in the point of view of human development. The means of development which the individual loses by being prevented from gratifying his inclinations to the injury of others, are chiefly obtained at the expense of the development of other people. And even to himself there is a full equivalent in the better development of the social part of his nature, rendered possible by the restraint put upon the selfish part. To be held to rigid rules of justice for the sake of others, developes the feelings and capacities which have the good of others for their object. But to be restrained in things not affecting their good, by their mere displeasure, developes nothing valuable, except such force of character as may unfold itself in resisting the restraint. If acquiesced in, it dulls and blunts the whole nature. To give any fair play to the nature of each, it is essential that different persons should be allowed to lead different lives. In proportion as this latitude has been exercised in any age, has that age been noteworthy to posterity. Even despotism does not produce its worst effects, so long as Individuality exists under it; and whatever crushes individuality is despotism, by whatever name it may be called, and whether it professes to be enforcing the will of God or the injunctions of men.

Having said that Individuality is the same thing with development, and that it is only the cultivation of individuality which produces, or can produce, well-developed human beings, I might here close the argument: for what more or better can be said of any condition of human affairs, than that it brings human beings themselves nearer to the best thing they can be? or what worse can be said of any obstruction to good, than that it prevents this? Doubtless, however, these considerations will not suffice to convince those who most need convincing; and it is necessary further to show, that these developed human beings are of some use to the undeveloped — to point out to those who do not desire liberty, and would not avail themselves of it, that they may be in some intelligible matter rewarded for allowing other people to make use of it without hindrance.

In the first place, then, I would suggest that they might possibly learn something from them. It will not be denied by anybody, that originality is a valuable element in human affairs. There is always need of persons not only to discover new truths, and point out when what were once truths are true no longer, but also to commence new practices, and set the example of more enlightened conduct, and better taste and sense in human life. This cannot well be gainsaid by anybody who does not believe that the world has already attained perfection in all its ways and practices. It is true that this benefit is not capable of being rendered by everybody alike: there are but few persons, in comparison with the whole of mankind, whose experiments, if adopted by others, would be likely to be any improvement on established practice. But these few are the salt of the earth; without them, human life would become a stagnant pool. Not only is it they who introduce good things which did not before exist; it is they who keep the life in those which already existed. If there were nothing new to be done, would human intellect cease to be necessary? Would it be a reason why those who do the old things should forget why they are done, and do them like cattle, not like human beings? There is only too great a tendency in the best beliefs and practices to degenerate into the mechanical; and unless there were a succession of persons whose ever-recurring originality prevents the grounds of those beliefs and practices from becoming merely traditional, such dead matter would not resist the smallest shock from anything really alive, and there would be no reason why civilization should not die out, as in the Byzantine Empire. Persons of genius, it is true, are, and are always likely to be, a small minority; but in order to have them, it is necessary to preserve the soil in which they grow. Genius can only breathe freely in an *atmosphere* of freedom. Persons of genius are, *ex vi termini,*[19] *more* individual than any other people — less capable, consequently, of fitting themselves, without hurtful compression, into any of the small number of moulds which society provides in order to save its members the trouble of forming their own character. If from timidity they consent to be forced into one of these moulds, and to let all that part of themselves which cannot expand under the pressure remain unexpanded, society will be little the better for their genius. If they are of a strong character, and break their fetters, they become a mark for the society which has not succeeded in reducing them to commonplace, to point at with solemn warning as "wild," "erratic," and the like; much as if one should complain of the Niagara river for not flowing smoothly between its banks like a Dutch canal.

I insist thus emphatically on the importance of genius, and the necessity of allowing it to unfold itself freely both in thought and in practice, being well aware that no one will deny the position in theory, but knowing also that almost every one, in reality, is totally indifferent to it. People think

19. By the very meaning of the expression.

genius a fine thing if it enables a man to write an exciting poem, or paint a picture. But in its true sense, that of originality in thought and action, though no one says that it is not a thing to be admired, nearly all, at heart, think that they can do very well without it. Unhappily this is too natural to be wondered at. Originality is the one thing which unoriginal minds cannot feel the use of. They cannot see what it is to do for them: how should they? If they could see what it would do for them, it would not be originality. The first service which originality has to render them, is that of opening their eyes: which being once fully done, they would have a chance of being themselves original. Meanwhile, recollecting that nothing was ever yet done which some one was not the first to do, and that all good things which exist are the fruits of originality, let them be modest enough to believe that there is something still left for it to accomplish, and assure themselves that they are more in need of originality, the less they are conscious of the want.

In sober truth, whatever homage may be professed, or even paid, to real or supposed mental superiority, the general tendency of things throughout the world is to render mediocrity the ascendant power among mankind. In ancient history, in the middle ages, and in a diminishing degree through the long transition from feudality to the present time, the individual was a power in himself; and if he had either great talents or a high social position, he was a considerable power. At present individuals are lost in the crowd. In politics it is almost a triviality to say that public opinion now rules the world. The only power deserving the name is that of masses, and of governments while they make themselves the organ of the tendencies and instincts of masses. This is as true in the moral and social relations of private life as in public transactions. Those whose opinions go by the name of public opinion, are not always the same sort of public: in America they are the whole white population; in England, chiefly the middle class. But they are always a mass, that is to say, collective mediocrity. And what is a still greater novelty, the mass do not now take their opinions from dignitaries in Church or State, from ostensible leaders, or from books. Their thinking is done for them by men much like themselves, addressing them or speaking in their name, on the spur of the moment, through the newspapers. I am not complaining of all this. I do not assert that anything better is compatible, as a general rule, with the present low state of the human mind. But that does not hinder the government of mediocrity from being mediocre government. No government by a democracy or a numerous aristocracy, either in its political acts or in the opinions, qualities, and tone of mind which it fosters, ever did or could rise above mediocrity, except in so far as the sovereign Many have let themselves be guided (which in their best times they always have done) by the counsels and influence of a more highly gifted and instructed One or Few. The initiation of all wise or noble things, comes and must come from individuals; generally at first from some one individual. The honour and glory of the average man is that he is capable of following that initiative; that he can respond internally to wise and noble things, and be led to them with his eyes open. I am not countenancing the sort of "hero-worship" which applauds the strong man of genius for forcibly seizing on the government of the world and making it do his bidding in spite of itself. All he can claim is, freedom to point out the way. The power of compelling others into it, is not only inconsistent with the freedom and development of all the rest, but corrupting to the strong man himself. It does seem, however, that when the opinions of masses of merely average men are everywhere become or becoming the dominant power, the counterpoise and corrective to that tendency would be, the more and more pronounced individuality of those who stand on the higher eminences of thought. It is in these circumstances most especially, that exceptional individuals, instead of being deterred, should be encouraged in acting differently from the mass. In other times there was no advantage in their doing so, unless they acted not only differently, but better. In this age the mere example of nonconformity, the mere refusal to bend the knee to custom, is itself a service. Precisely because the tyranny of opinion is such as to make eccentricity a reproach, it is desirable, in order to break through that tyranny, that people should be eccentric. Eccentricity has always abounded when and where strength of character has abounded; and the amount of eccentricity in a society has generally been proportional to the amount of genius, mental vigour, and moral courage which it contained. That so few now dare to be eccentric, marks the chief danger of the time.

I have said that it is important to give the freest scope possible to uncustomary things, in order that it may in time appear which of these are fit to be converted into customs. But independence of action, and disregard of custom are not solely deserving of encouragement for the chance they afford that better modes of action, and customs more worthy of general adoption, may be struck out; nor is it only persons of decided mental superiority who have a just claim to carry on their lives in their own way. There is no reason that all human existences should be constructed on some one, or some small number of patterns. If a person possesses any tolerable amount of common sense and experience, his own mode of laying out his existence is the best, not because it is the best in itself, but because it is his own mode. Human beings are not like sheep; and even sheep are not undistinguishably alike. A man cannot get a coat or a pair of boots to fit him, unless they are either made to his measure, or he has a whole warehouseful to choose from: and is it easier to fit him with a life than with a coat, or are human beings more like one another in their whole physical and spiritual conformation than in the shape of their feet? If it were only that people have diversities of taste, that is reason enough for not attempting to shape them all after one model. But different persons also require different conditions for their spiritual development; and can no more exist healthily in the same moral, than all the variety of plants can in the same physical, atmosphere and climate. The same things which are helps to one person towards the cultivation of his higher nature, are hindrances to another. The same mode of life is a healthy excitement to one, keeping all his faculties of action and enjoyment in their best order, while to another it is a distracting burthen, which suspends or crushes all internal life. Such are the differences among human beings in their sources of pleasure, their susceptibilities of pain, and the operation on them of different physical and moral agencies, that unless there is a corresponding diversity in their modes of life, they neither obtain their fair share of happiness, nor grow up to the mental, moral, and aesthetic stature of which their nature is capable. Why then should tolerance, as far as the public sentiment is concerned, extend only to tastes and modes of life which extort acquiescence by the multitude of their adherents? Nowhere (except in some monastic institutions) is diversity of taste entirely unrecognised; a person may, without blame, either like or dislike rowing, or smoking, or music, or athletic exercises, or chess, or cards, or study, because both those who like each of these things, and those who dislike them, are too numerous to be put down. But the man, and still more the woman, who can be accused either of doing "what nobody does," or of not doing "what everybody does," is the subject of as much depreciatory remark as if he or she had committed some grave moral delinquency. Persons require to posess a title, or some other badge of rank, or of the consideration of people of rank, to be able to indulge somewhat in the luxury of doing as they like without detriment to their estimation. To indulge somewhat, I repeat: for whoever allow themselves much of that indulgence, incur the risk of something worse than disparaging speeches — they are in peril of a commission *de lunatico,*[20] and of having their property taken from them and given to their relations.*

20. Regarding an imputation of insanity.

* There is something both contemptible and frightful in the sort of evidence on which, of late years, any person can be judicially declared unfit for the management of his affairs; and after his death, his disposal of his property can be set aside, if there is enough of it to

There is one characteristic of the present direction of public opinion, peculiarly calculated to make it intolerant of any marked demonstration of individuality. The general average of mankind are not only moderate in intellect, but also moderate in inclinations: they have no tastes or wishes strong enough to incline them to do anything unusual, and they consequently do not understand those who have, and class all such with the wild and intemperate whom they are accustomed to look down upon. Now, in addition to this fact which is general, we have only to suppose that a strong movement has set in towards the improvement of morals, and it is evident what we have to expect. In these days such a movement has set in; much has actually been effected in the way of increased regularity of conduct, and

---

pay the expenses of litigation — which are charged on the property itself. All the minute details of his daily life are pried into, and whatever is found which, seen through the medium of the perceiving and describing faculties of the lowest of the low, bears an appearance unlike absolute commonplace, is laid before the jury as evidence of insanity, and often with success; the jurors being little, if at all, less vulgar and ignorant than the witnesses; while the judges, with that extraordinary want of knowledge of human nature and life which continually astonishes us in English lawyers, often help to mislead them. These trials speak volumes as to the state of feeling and opinion among the vulgar with regard to human liberty. So far from setting any value on individuality — so far from respecting the rights of each individual to act, in things indifferent, as seems good to his own judgment and inclinations, judges and juries cannot even conceive that a person in a state of sanity can desire such freedom. In former days, when it was proposed to burn atheists, charitable people used to suggest putting them in a madhouse instead: it would be nothing surprising now-a-days were we to see this done, and the doers applauding themselves, because, instead of persecuting for religion, they had adopted so humane and Christian a mode of treating these unfortunates, not without a silent satisfaction at their having thereby obtained their deserts.

[A law of 1853 permitted the friends or relatives of a person whom they alleged to be insane simply to apply to a magistrate for an order to commit that person to a lunatic asylum, provided they had obtained the signatures of two medically qualified men (a category that included pharmacists as well as doctors). Mill wrote in a letter to the *Daily News* (July 31, 1858): "A perfectly innocent person can be fraudulently kidnapped, seized, and carried off to a madhouse on the assertion of any two so-called medical men, who may have scarcely seen the victim whom they dismiss to a condition far worse than the penalty which the law inflicts for proved crime. . . . Convicts can appeal against ill treatment; but to the other unfortunates the ordinary use of speech is virtually denied; their sober statements of fact, still more their passionate protests against injustice, are held to be so many instances of insane delusion" (25: 1199). — *Ed.*]

discouragement of excesses; and there is a philanthropic spirit abroad, for the exercise of which there is no more inviting field than the moral and prudential improvement of our fellow-creatures. These tendencies of the times cause the public to be more disposed than at most former periods to prescribe general rules of conduct, and endeavour to make every one conform to the approved standard. And that standard, express or tacit, is to desire nothing strongly. Its ideal of character is to be without any marked character; to maim by compression, like a Chinese lady's foot, every part of human nature which stands out prominently, and tends to make the person markedly dissimilar in outline to commonplace humanity.

As is usually the case with ideals which exclude one-half of what is desirable, the present standard of approbation produces only an inferior imitation of the other half. Instead of great energies guided by vigorous reason, and strong feelings strongly controlled by a conscientious will, its result is weak feelings and weak energies, which therefore can be kept in outward conformity to rule without any strength either of will or of reason. Already energetic characters on any large scale are becoming merely traditional. There is now scarcely any outlet for energy in this country except business. The energy expended in that may still be regarded as considerable. What little is left from that employment, is expended on some hobby; which may be a useful, even a philanthropic hobby, but is always some one thing, and generally a thing of small dimensions. The greatness of England is now all collective: individually small, we only appear capable of anything great by our habit of combining; and with this our moral and religious philanthropists are perfectly contented. But it was men of another stamp than this that made England what it has been; and men of another stamp will be needed to prevent its decline.

The despotism of custom is everywhere the standing hindrance to human advancement, being in unceasing antagonism to that disposition to aim at something better than customary, which is called, according to circumstances, the spirit of liberty, or that of progress or improvement. The spirit of improvement is not always a spirit of liberty, for it may aim at forcing improvements on an unwilling people; and the spirit of liberty, in so far as it resists such attempts, may ally itself locally and temporarily with the opponents of improvement; but the only unfailing and permanent source of improvement is liberty, since by it there are as many possible independent centres of improvement as there are individuals. The progressive principle, however, in either shape, whether as the love of liberty or of improvement, is antagonistic to the sway of Custom, involving at least emancipation from that yoke; and the contest between the two constitutes the chief interest of the history of mankind. The greater part of the world has, properly speaking, no history, because the despotism of Custom is complete. This is the case over the whole East. Custom is there, in all things, the final appeal; justice and right mean conformity to custom; the argument of custom no one, unless some tyrant intoxicated with power, thinks of resisting. And we see the result. Those nations must once have had originality; they did not start out of the ground populous, lettered, and versed in many of the arts of life; they made themselves all this, and were then the greatest and most powerful nations in the world. What are they now? The subjects or dependents of tribes whose forefathers wandered in the forests when theirs had magnificent palaces and gorgeous temples, but over whom custom exercised only a divided rule with liberty and progress. A people, it appears, may be progressive for a certain length of time, and then stop: when does it stop? When it ceases to possess individuality. If a similar change should befall the nations of Europe, it will not be in exactly the same shape: the despotism of custom with which these nations are threatened is not precisely stationariness. It proscribes singularity, but it does not preclude change, provided all change together. We have discarded the fixed costumes of our forefathers; every one must still dress like other people, but the fashion may change once or twice a year. We thus take care that when there is change, it shall be for change's sake, and not from any idea of beauty or convenience; for the same idea of beauty or convenience would not strike all the world at the same moment, and be simultaneously thrown aside by all at another moment. But we are progressive as well as changeable: we continually make new inventions in mechanical things, and keep them until they are again superseded by better; we are eager for improvement in politics, in education, even in morals, though in this last our idea of improvement chiefly consists in persuading or forcing other people to be as good as ourselves. It is not progress that we object to; on the contrary, we flatter ourselves that we are the most progressive people who ever lived. It is individuality that we war against: we should think we had done wonders if we had made ourselves all alike; forgetting that the unlikeness of one person to another is generally the first thing which draws the attention of either to the imperfection of his own type, and the superiority of another, or the possibility, by combining the advantages of both, of producing something better than either. We have a warning example in China — a nation of much talent, and, in some respects, even wisdom, owing to the rare good fortune of having been provided at an early period with a particularly good set of customs, the work, in some measure, of men to whom even the most enlightened European must accord, under certain limitations, the title of sages and philosophers. They are remarkable, too, in the excellence of their apparatus for impressing, as far as possible, the best wisdom they possess upon every mind in the community, and securing that those who have appropriated most of it shall occupy the posts of honour and power. Surely the people who did this have discovered the secret of human progressiveness, and must have kept themselves steadily at the head of the movement of the world. On the contrary, they have become stationary — have remained so for thousands of years; and if they are ever to be farther improved, it must be by foreigners. They have succeeded beyond all hope in what English philanthropists are so industriously working at — in making a people all alike, all governing their thoughts and conduct by the same maxims and rules; and these are the fruits. The modern *régime* of public opinion is, in an unorganized form, what the Chinese educational and political systems are in an organized; and unless individuality shall be able successfully to assert itself against this yoke, Europe, notwithstanding its noble antecedents and its professed Christianity, will tend to become another China.

What is it that has hitherto preserved Europe from this lot? What has made the European family of nations an improving, instead of a stationary portion of mankind? Not any superior excellence in them, which, when it exists, exists as the effect, not as the cause; but their remarkable diversity of character and culture. Individuals, classes, nations, have been extremely unlike one another: they have struck out a great variety of paths, each leading to something valuable; and although at every period those who travelled in different paths have been intolerant of one another, and each would have thought it an excellent thing if all the rest could have been compelled to travel his road, their attempts to thwart each other's development have rarely had any permanent success, and each has in time endured to receive the good which the others have offered. Europe is, in my judgment, wholly indebted to this plurality of paths for its progressive and many-sided development. But it already begins to possess this benefit in a considerably less degree. It is decidedly advancing towards the Chinese ideal of making all people alike. M. de Tocqueville, in his last important work,[21] remarks how much more the Frenchmen of the present day resemble one another, than did those even of the last generation. The same remark might be made of Englishmen in a far greater degree. In a passage already quoted from Wilhelm von Humboldt, he points out two things as necessary conditions of human development, because necessary to render people un-

21. *The Old Regime and the Revolution* (1856).

like one another; namely, freedom, and variety of situations. The second of these two conditions is in this country every day diminishing. The circumstances which surround different classes and individuals, and shape their characters, are daily becoming more assimilated. Formerly, different ranks, different neighbourhoods, different trades and professions, lived in what might be called different worlds; at present, to a great degree in the same. Comparatively speaking, they now read the same things, listen to the same things, see the same things, go to the same places, have their hopes and fears directed to the same objects, have the same rights and liberties, and the same means of asserting them. Great as are the differences of position which remain, they are nothing to those which have ceased. And the assimilation is still proceeding. All the political changes of the age promote it, since they all tend to raise the low and to lower the high. Every extension of education promotes it, because education brings people under common influences, and gives them access to the general stock of facts and sentiments. Improvements in the means of communication promote it, by bringing the inhabitants of distant places into personal contact, and keeping up a rapid flow of changes of residence between one place and another. The increase of commerce and manufactures promotes it, by diffusing more widely the advantages of easy circumstances, and opening all objects of ambition, even the highest, to general competition, whereby the desire of rising becomes no longer the character of a particular class, but of all classes. A more powerful agency than even all these, in bringing about a general similarity among mankind, is the complete establishment, in this and other free countries, of the ascendancy of public opinion in the State. As the various social eminences which enabled persons entrenched on them to disregard the opinion of the multitude, gradually become levelled; as the very idea of resisting the will of the public, when it is positively known that they have a will, disappears more and more from the minds of practical politicians; there ceases to be any social support for non-conformity — any substantive power in society, which, itself opposed to the ascendancy of numbers, is interested in taking under its protection opinions and tendencies at variance with those of the public.

The combination of all these causes forms so great a mass of influences hostile to Individuality, that it is not easy to see how it can stand its ground. It will do so with increasing difficulty, unless the intelligent part of the public can be made to feel its value — to see that it is good there should be differences, even though not for the better, even though, as it may appear to them, some should be for the worse. If the claims of Individuality are ever to be asserted, the time is now, while much is still wanting to complete the enforced assimilation. It is only in the earlier stages that any stand can be successfully made against the encroachment. The demand that all other people shall resemble ourselves, grows by what it feeds on. If resistance waits till life is reduced *nearly* to one uniform type, all derivations from that type will come to be considered impious, immoral, even mostrous and contrary to nature. Mankind speedily become unable to conceive diversity, when they have been for some time unaccustomed to see it.

CHAPTER IV

OF THE LIMITS TO THE AUTHORITY OF

SOCIETY OVER THE INDIVIDUAL

What, then, is the rightful limit to the sovereignty of the individual over himself? Where does the authority of society begin? How much of human life should be assigned to individuality, and how much to society?

Each will receive its proper share, if each has that which more particularly concerns it. To individuality should belong the part of life in which it is chiefly the individual that is interested; to society, the part which chiefly interests society.

Though society is not founded on a contract, and though no good purpose is answered by inventing a contract in order to deduce social obligations from it, every one who receives the protection of society owes a return for the benefit, and the fact of living in society renders it indispensable that each should be bound to observe a certain line of conduct towards the rest. This conduct consists, first, in not injuring the interests of one another; or rather certain interests, which, either by express legal provision or by tacit understanding, ought to be considered as rights; and secondly, in each person's bearing his share (to be fixed on some equitable principle) of the labours and sacrifices incurred for defending the society or its members from injury and molestation. These conditions society is justified in enforcing, at all costs to those who endeavour to withhold fulfilment. Nor is this all that society may do. The acts of an individual may be hurtful to others, or wanting in due consideration for their welfare, without going the length of violating any of their constituted rights. The offender may then be justly punished by opinion, though not by law. As soon as any part of a person's conduct affects prejudicially the interests of others, society has jurisdiction over it, and the question whether the general welfare will or will not be promoted by interfering with it, becomes open to discussion. But there is no room for entertaining any such question when a person's conduct affects the interests of no persons besides himself, or needs not affect them unless they like (all the persons concerned being of full age, and the ordinary amount of understanding). In all such cases there should be perfect freedom, legal and social, to do the action and stand the consequences.

It would be a great misunderstanding of this doctrine, to suppose that it is one of selfish indifference, which pretends that human beings have no business with each other's conduct in life, and that they should not concern themselves about the well-doing or well-being of one another, unless their own interest is involved. Instead of any diminution, there is need of a great increase of disinterested exertion to promote the good of others. But disinterested benevolence can find other instruments to persuade people to their good, than whips and scourges, either of the literal or the metaphorical sort. I am the last person to undervalue the self-regarding virtues; they are only second in importance, if even second, to the social. It is equally the business of education to cultivate both. But even education works by conviction and persuasion as well as by compulsion, and it is by the former only that, when the period of education is past, the self-regarding virtues should be inculcated. Human beings owe to each other help to distinguish the better from the worse, and encouragement to choose the former and avoid the latter. They should be for ever stimulating each other to increased exercise of their higher faculties, and increased direction of their feelings and aims towards wise instead of foolish, elevating instead of degrading, objects and contemplations. But neither one person, nor any number of persons, is warranted in saying to another human creature of ripe years, that he shall not do with his life for his own benefit what he chooses to do with it. He is the person most interested in his own well-being: the interest which any other person, except in cases of strong personal attachment, can have in it, is trifling, compared with that which he himself has; the interest which society has in him individually (except as to his conduct to others) is fractional, and altogether indirect: while, with respect to his own feelings and circumstances, the most ordinary man or woman has means of knowledge immeasurably surpassing those that can be possessed by any one else. The interference of society to overrule his judgment and purposes in what only regards himself, must be grounded on general presumptions; which may be altogether wrong, and even if right, are as likely as not to be misapplied to individual cases, by persons no better acquainted with the circumstances of such cases than those are who look at them merely from without. In this department, therefore, of human affairs, Individuality has its proper field of action. In the conduct of human beings towards one another, it is necessary that general rules should for the most part be observed, in order that people may know what they have to expect; but in each person's own concerns, his individual spontaneity is entitled to free exercise. Considerations to aid his judgment, exhortations to strengthen his will, may be offered to him, even obtruded on him, by others; but he himself is the final judge. All errors which he is likely to commit against advice and warning, are far outweighed by the evil of allowing others to constrain him to what they deem his good.

I do not mean that the feelings with which a person is regarded by others, ought not to be in any way affected by his self-regarding qualities or deficiencies. This is neither possible nor desirable. If he is eminent in any of the qualities which conduce to his own good, he is, so far, a proper object of admiration. He is so much the nearer to the ideal perfection of human nature. If he is grossly deficient in those qualities, a sentiment the opposite of admiration will follow. There is a degree of folly, and a degree of what may be called (thought the phrase is not unobjectionable) lowness or depravation of taste, which, though it cannot justify doing harm to the person who manifests it, renders him necessarily and properly a subject of distaste, or, in extreme cases, even of contempt: a person could not have the opposite qualities in due strength without entertaining these feelings. Though doing no wrong to any one, a person may so act as to compel us to judge him, and feel to him, as a fool, or as a being of an inferior order: and since this judgment and feeling are a fact which he would prefer to avoid, it is doing him a service to warn him of it beforehand, as of any other disagreeable consequence to which he exposes himself. It would be well, indeed, if this good office were much more freely rendered than the common notions of politeness at present permit, and if one person could honestly point out to another that he thinks him in fault, without being considered unmannerly or presuming. We have a right, also, in various ways, to act upon our unfavourable opinion of any one, not to the oppression of his individuality, but in the exercise of ours. We are not bound, for example, to seek his society; we have a right to avoid it (though not to parade the avoidance), for we have a right to choose the society most acceptable to us. We have a right, and it may be our duty, to caution others against him, if we think his example or conversation likely to have a pernicious effect on those with whom he associates. We may give others a preference over him in optional good offices, except those which tend to his improvement. In these various modes a person may suffer very severe penalties at the hands of others, for faults which directly concern only himself; but he suffers these penalties only in so far as they are the natural, and, as it were, the spontaneous consequences of the faults themselves, not because they are purposely inflicted on him for the sake of punishment. A person who shows rashness, obstinacy, self-conceit — who cannot live within moderate means — who cannot restrain himself from hurtful indulgences — who pursues animal pleasures at the expense of those of feeling and intellect — must expect to be lowered in the opinion of others, and to have a less share of their favourable sentiments; but of this he has no right to complain, unless he has merited their favour by special excellence in his social relations, and has thus established a title to their good offices, which is not affected by his demerits towards himself.

What I contend for is, that the inconveniences which are strictly inseparable from the unfavourable judgment of others, are the only ones to which a person should ever be subjected for that portion of his conduct and character which concerns his own good, but which does not affect the interests of others in their relations with him. Acts injurious to others require a totally different treatment. Encroachment on their rights; infliction on them of any loss or damage not justified by his own rights; falsehood or duplicity in dealing with them; unfair or ungenerous use of advantages over them; even selfish abstinence from defending them against injury — these are fit objects of moral reprobation, and, in grave cases, of moral retribution and punishment. And not only these acts, but the dispositions which lead to them, are properly immoral, and fit subjects of disapprobation which may rise to abhorrence. Cruelty of disposition; malice and ill-nature; that most antisocial and odious of all passions, envy; dissimulation and insincerity; irascibility on insufficient cause, and resentment disproportioned to the provocation; the love of domineering over others; the desire to engross more than one's share of advantages (the πλεονεξία of the Greeks);[22] the pride which derives gratification from the abasement of others; the egotism which thinks self and its concerns more important than everything else, and decides all doubtful questions in its own favour; — these are moral vices, and constitute a bad and odious moral character: unlike the self-regarding faults previously mentioned, which are not properly immoralities, and to whatever pitch they may be carried, do not constitute wickedness. They may be proofs of any amount of folly, or want of personal dignity and self-respect; but they are only a subject of moral reprobation when they involve a breach of duty to others, for whose sake the individual is bound to have care for himself. What are called duties to ourselves are not socially obligatory, unless circumstances render them at the same time duties to others. The term duty to onself, when it means anything more than prudence, means self-respect or self-development; and for none of these is any one accountable to his fellow creatures, because for none of them is it for the good of mankind that he be held accountable to them.

The distinction between the loss of consideration which a person may rightly incur by defect of prudence or of personal dignity, and the reproba-

22. Greed.

tion which is due to him for an offence against the rights of others, is not a merely nominal distinction. It makes a vast difference both in our feelings and in our conduct toward him, whether he displeases us in things in which we think we have a right to control him, or in things in which we know that we have not. If he displeases us, we may express our distaste, and we may stand aloof from a person as well as from a thing that displeases us; but we shall not therefore feel called on to make his life uncomfortable. We shall reflect that he already bears, or will bear, the whole penalty of his error; if he spoils his life by mismanagement, we shall not, for that reason, desire to spoil it still further: instead of wishing to punish him, we shall rather endeavour to alleviate his punishment, by showing him how he may avoid or cure the evils his conduct tends to bring upon him. He may be to us an object of pity, perhaps of dislike, but not of anger or resentment; we shall not treat him like an enemy of society: the worst we shall think ourselves justified in doing is leaving him to himself, if we do not interfere benevolently by showing interest or concern for him. It is far otherwise if he has infringed the rules necessary for the protection of his fellow-creatures, individually or collectively. The evil consequences of his acts do not then fall on himself, but on others; and society, as the protector of all its members, must retaliate on him; must inflict pain on him for the express purpose of punishment, and must take care that it be sufficiently severe. In the one case, he is an offender at our bar, and we are called on not only to sit in judgment on him, but, in one shape or another, to execute our own sentence: in the other case, it is not our part to inflict any suffering on him, except what may incidentally follow from our using the same liberty in the regulation of our own affairs, which we allow to him in his.

The distinction here pointed out between the part of a person's life which concerns only himself, and that which concerns others, many persons will refuse to admit. How (it may be asked) can any part of the conduct of a member of society be a matter of indifference to the other members? No person is an entirely isolated being; it is impossible for a person to do anything seriously or permanently hurtful to himself, without mischief reaching at least to his near connexions, and often far beyond them. If he injures his property, he does harm to those who directly or indirectly derived support from it, and usually diminishes, by a greater or less amount, the general resources of the community. If he deteriorates his bodily or mental faculties, he not only brings evil upon all who depended on him for any portion of their happiness, but disqualifies himself for rendering the services which he owes to his fellow creatures generally; perhaps becomes a burthen on their affection or benevolence; and if such conduct were very frequent, hardly any offence that is committed would detract more from the general sum of good. Finally, if by his vices or follies a person does no direct harm to others, he is nevertheless (it may be said) injurious by his example; and ought to be compelled to control himself, for the sake of those whom the sight or knowledge of his conduct might corrupt or mislead.

And even (it will be added) if the consequences of misconduct could be confined to the vicious or thoughtless individual, ought society to abandon to their own guidance those who are manifestly unfit for it? If protection against themselves is confessedly due to children and persons under age, is not society equally bound to afford it to persons of mature years who are equally incapable of self-government? If gambling, or drunkenness, or incontinence, or idleness, or uncleanliness, are as injurious to happiness, and as great a hindrance to improvement, as many or most of the acts prohibited by law, why (it may be asked) should not law, so far as is consistent with practicability and social convenience, endeavour to repress these also? And as a supplement to the unavoidable imperfections of law, ought not opinion at least to organize a powerful police against these vices, and visit rigidly with social penalties those who are known to practise them? There is no question here (it may be said) about restricting individuality, or impeding the trial of new and original experiments in living. The only things it is sought to prevent are things which have been tried and condemned from the beginning of the world until now; things which experience has shown not to be useful or suitable to any person's individuality. There must be some length of time and amount of experience, after which a moral or prudential truth may be regarded as established: and it is merely desired to prevent generation after generation from falling over the same precipice which has been fatal to their predecessors.

I fully admit that the mischief which a person does to himself, may seriously affect, both through their sympathies and their interests, those nearly connected with him, and in a minor degree, society at large. When, by conduct of this sort, a person is led to violate a distinct and assignable obligation to any other person or persons, the case is taken out of the self-regarding class, and becomes amenable to moral disapprobation in the proper sense of the term. If, for example, a man, through intemperance or extravagance, becomes unable to pay his debts, or, having undertaken the moral responsibility of a family, becomes from the same cause incapable of supporting or educating them, he is deservedly reprobated, and might be justly punished; but it is for the breach of duty to his family or creditors, not for the extravagance. If the resources which ought to have been devoted to them, had been diverted from them for the most prudent investment, the moral culpability would have been the same. George Barnwell[23] murdered his uncle to get money for his mistress, but if he had done it to set himself up in business, he would equally have been hanged. Again, in the frequent case of a man who causes grief to his family by addiction to bad habits, he deserves reproach for his unkindness or ingratitude; but so he may for cultivating habits not in themselves vicious, if they are painful to those with whom he passes his life, or who from personal ties are dependent on him for their comfort. Whoever fails in the consideration generally due to the interests and feelings of others, not being compelled by some more imperative duty, or justified by allowable self-preference, is a subject of moral disapprobation for that failure, but not for the cause of it, nor for the errors, merely personal to himself, which may have remotely led to it. In like manner, when a person disables himself, by conduct purely self-regarding, from the performance of some definite duty incumbent on him to the public, he is guilty of a social offence. No person ought to be punished simply for being drunk; but a soldier or a policeman should be punished for being drunk on duty. Whenever, in short, there is a definite damage, or a definite risk of damage, either to an individual or to the public, the case is taken out of the province of liberty, and placed in that of morality or law.

But with regard to the merely contingent, or, as it may be called, constructive injury which a person causes to society, by conduct which neither violates any specific duty to the public, nor occasions perceptible hurt to any assignable individual except himself; the inconvenience is one which society can afford to bear, for the sake of the greater good of human freedom. If grown persons are to be punished for not taking proper care of themselves, I would rather it were for their own sake, than under pretence of preventing them from impairing their capacity of rendering to society benefits which society does not pretend it has a right to exact. But I cannot consent to argue the point as if society had no means of bringing its weaker members up to its ordinary standard of rational conduct, except waiting till they do something irrational, and then punishing them, legally or morally, for it. Society has had absolute power over them during all the early portion of their existence: it has had the whole period of childhood and nonage in which to try whether it could make them capable of rational conduct in life. The existing generation is master both of the training and the entire circumstances of the generation to come; it cannot indeed make them perfectly wise and good, because it is itself so lamentably deficient in goodness and

23. Hero of a well-known tragedy, *The London Merchant* by George Lillo (1693–1739).

wisdom; and its best efforts are not always, in individual cases, its most successful ones; but it is perfectly well able to make the rising generation, as a whole, as good as, and a little better than, itself. If society lets any considerable number of its members grow up mere children, incapable of being acted on by rational consideration of distant motives, society has itself to blame for the consequences. Armed not only with all the powers of education, but with the ascendancy which the authority of a received opinion always exercises over the minds who are least fitted to judge for themselves; and aided by the *natural* penalties which cannot be prevented from falling on those who incur the distaste or the contempt of those who know them; let not society pretend that it needs, besides all this, the power to issue commands and enforce obedience in the personal concerns of individuals, in which, on all principles of justice and policy, the decision ought to rest with those who are to abide the consequences. Nor is there anything which tends more to discredit and frustrate the better means of influencing conduct, then a resort to the worse. If there be among those who it is attempted to coerce into prudence or temperance, any of the material of which vigorous and independent characters are made, they will infallibly rebel against the yoke. No such person will ever feel that others have a right to control him in his concerns, such as they have to prevent him from injuring them in theirs; and it easily comes to be considered a mark of spirit and courage to fly in the face of such usurped authority, and do with ostentation the exact opposite of what it enjoins; as in the fashion of grossness which succeeded, in the time of Charles II, to the fanatical moral intolerance of the Puritans. With respect to what is said of the necessity of protecting society from the bad example set to others by the vicious or the self-indulgent; it is true that bad example may have a pernicious effect, especially the example of doing wrong to others with impunity to the wrong-doer. But we are now speaking of conduct which, while it does no wrong to others, is supposed to do great harm to the agent himself: and I do not see how those who believe this, can think otherwise than that the example, on the whole, must be more salutary than hurtful, since, if it displays the misconduct, it displays also the painful or degrading consequences which, if the conduct is justly censured, must be supposed to be in all or most cases attendant on it.

But the strongest of all the arguments against the interference of the public with purely personal conduct, is that when it does interfere, the odds are that it interferes wrongly, and in the wrong place. On questions of social morality, of duty to others, the opinion of the public, that is, of an overruling majority, though often wrong, is likely to be still oftener right; because on such questions they are only required to judge of their own interests; of the manner in which some mode of conduct, if allowed to be practised, would affect themselves. But the opinion of a similar majority, imposed as a law on the minority, on questions of self-regarding conduct, is quite as likely to be wrong as right; for in these cases public opinion means, at the best, some people's opinion of what is good or bad for other people; while very often it does not even mean that; the public, with the most perfect indifference, passing over the pleasure or convenience of those whose conduct they censure, and considering only their own preference. There are many who consider as an injury to themselves any conduct which they have a distaste for, and resent it as an outrage to their feelings; as a religious bigot, when charged with disregarding the religious feelings of others, has been known to retort that they disregard his feelings, by persisting in their abominable worship or creed. But there is no parity between the feeling of a person for his own opinion, and the feeling of another who is offended at his holding it; no more than between the desire of a thief to take a purse, and the desire of the right owner to keep it. And a person's taste is as much his own peculiar concern as his opinion or his purse. It is easy for any one to imagine an ideal public, which leaves the freedom and choice of individuals in all uncertain matters undisturbed, and only requires them to abstain from modes of conduct which universal experience has condemned. But where has there been seen a public which set any such limit to its censorship? or when does the public trouble itself about universal experience? In its interferences with personal conduct it is seldom thinking of anything but the enormity of acting or feeling differently from itself; and this standard of judgment, thinly disguised, is held up to mankind as the dictate of religion and philosophy, by nine-tenths of all moralists and speculative writers. These teach that things are right because they are right; because we feel them to be so. They tell us to search in our own minds and hearts for laws of conduct binding on ourselves and on all others. What can the poor public do but apply these instructions, and make their own personal feelings of good and evil, if they are tolerably unanimous in them, obligatory on all the world?

The evil here pointed out is not one which exists only in theory; and it may perhaps be expected that I should specify the instances in which the public of this age and country improperly invests its own preferences with the character of moral laws. I am not writing an essay on the aberrations of existing moral feeling. That is too weighty a subject to be discussed parenthetically, and by way of illustration. Yet examples are necessary, to show that the principle I maintain is of serious and practical moment, and that I am not endeavouring to erect a barrier against imaginary evils. And it is not difficult to show, by abundant instances, that to extend the bounds of what may be called moral police, until it encroaches on the most unquestionably legitimate liberty of the individual, is one of the most universal of all human propensities.

As a first instance, consider the antipathies which men cherish on no better grounds than that persons whose religious opinions are different from theirs, do not practise their religious observances, especially their religious abstinences. To cite a rather trivial example, nothing in the creed or practice of Christians does more to envenom the hatred of Mahomedans against them, than the fact of their eating pork. There are few acts which Christians and Europeans regard with more unaffected disgust, than Mussulmans regard this particular mode of satisfying hunger. It is, in the first place, an offence against their religion; but this circumstance by no means explains either the degree or the kind of their repugnance; for wine also is forbidden by their religion, and to partake of it is by all Mussulmans accounted wrong, but not disgusting. Their aversion to the flesh of the "unclean beast" is, on the contrary, of that peculiar character, resembling an instinctive antipathy, which the idea of uncleanness, when once it thoroughly sinks into the feelings, seems always to excite even in those whose personal habits are anything but scrupulously cleanly, and of which the sentiment of religious impurity, so intense in the Hindoos, is a remarkable example. Suppose now that in a people, of whom the majority were Mussulmans, that majority should insist upon not permitting pork to be eaten within the limits of the country. This would be nothing new in Mahomedan countries.* Would it be a legitimate exercise of the moral authority of public opinion? and if not, why not? The practice is really revolting to such a public. They also sincerely think that it is forbidden and abhorred by the Deity. Neither could the prohibition be censured as religious persecution. It might be religious in its origin, but it would not be persecution for religion, since nobody's religion makes it a duty to eat pork. The only tenable ground of condemnation

* The case of the Bombay Parsees is a curious instance in point. When this industrious and enterprising tribe, the descendants of the Persian fire-worshippers, flying from their native country before the Caliphs, arrived in Western India, they were admitted to toleration by the Hindoo sovereigns, on condition of not eating beef. When those regions afterwards fell under the dominion of Mahomedan conquerors, the Parsees obtained from them a continuance of indulgence, on condition of refraining from pork. What was at first obedience to authority became a second nature, and the Parsees to this day abstain both from beef and pork. Though not required by their religion, the double abstinence has had time to grow into a custom of their tribe; and custom, in the East, is a religion.

would be, that with the personal tastes and self-regarding concerns of individuals the public has no business to interfere.

To come somewhat nearer home: the majority of Spaniards consider it a gross impiety, offensive in the highest degree to the Supreme Being, to worship him in any other manner than the Roman Catholic; and no other public worship is lawful on Spanish soil. The people of all Southern Europe look upon a married clergy as not only irreligious, but unchaste, indecent, gross, disgusting. What do Protestants think of these perfectly sincere feelings, and of the attempt to enforce them against non-Catholics? Yet, if mankind are justified in interfering with each other's liberty in things which do not concern the interests of others, on what principle is it possible consistently to exclude these cases? or who can blame people for desiring to suppress what they regard as a scandal in the sight of God and man? No stronger case can be shown for prohibiting anything which is regarded as a personal immorality, than is made out for suppressing these practices in the eyes of those who regard them as impieties; and unless we are willing to adopt the logic of persecutors, and to say that we may persecute others because we are right, and that they must not persecute us because they are wrong, we must beware of admitting a principle of which we should resent as a gross injustice the application to ourselves.

The preceding instances may be objected to, although unreasonably, as drawn from contingencies impossible among us: opinion, in this country, not being likely to enforce abstinence from meats, or to interfere with people for worshipping, and for either marrying or not marrying, according to their creed or inclination. The next example, however, shall be taken from an interference with liberty which we have by no means passed all danger of. Wherever the Puritans have been sufficiently powerful, as in New England, and in Great Britain at the time of the Commonwealth, they have endeavoured, with considerable success, to put down all public, and nearly all private, amusements: especially music, dancing, public games, or other assemblages for purposes of diversion, and the theatre. There are still in this country large bodies of persons by whose notions of morality and religion these recreations are condemned; and those persons belonging chiefly to the middle class, who are the ascendant power in the present social and political condition of the kingdom, it is by no means impossible that persons of these sentiments may at some time or other command a majority in Parliament. How will the remaining portion of the community like to have the amusements that shall be permitted to them regulated by the religious and moral sentiments of the stricter Calvinists and Methodists? Would they not, with considerable peremptoriness, desire these intrusively pious members of society to mind their own business? This is precisely what should be said to every government and every public, who have the pretension that no person shall enjoy any pleasure which they think wrong. But if the principle of the pretension be admitted, no one can reasonably object to its being acted on in the sense of the majority, or other preponderating power in the country; and all persons must be ready to conform to the idea of a Christian commonwealth, as understood by the early settlers in New England, if a religious profession similar to theirs should ever succeed in regaining its lost ground, as religions supposed to be declining have so often been known to do.

To imagine another contingency, perhaps more likely to be realized than the one last mentioned. There is confessedly a strong tendency in the modern world towards a democratic constitution of society, accompanied or not by popular political institutions. It is affirmed that in the country where this tendency is most completely realized — where both society and the government are most democratic — the United States — the feeling of the majority, to whom any appearance of a more showy or costly style of living than they can hope to rival is disagreeable, operates as a tolerably effectual sumptuary law, and that in many parts of the Union it is really difficult for a person possessing a very large income, to find any mode of spending it, which will not incur popular disapprobation. Though such statements as these are doubtless much exaggerated as a representation of existing facts, the state of things they describe is not only a conceivable and possible, but a probable result of democratic feeling, combined with the notion that the public has a right to a veto on the manner in which individuals shall spend their incomes. We have only further to suppose a considerable diffusion of Socialist opinions, and it may become infamous in the eyes of the majority to possess more property than some very small amount, or any income not earned by manual labour. Opinions similar in principle to these, already prevail widely among the artizan class, and weigh oppressively on those who are amenable to the opinion chiefly of that class, namely, its own members. It is known that the bad workmen who form the majority of the operatives in many branches of industry, are decidedly of opinion that bad workmen ought to receive the same wages as good, and that no one ought to be allowed, through piecework or otherwise, to earn by superior skill or industry more than others can without it. And they employ a moral police, which occasionally becomes a physical one, to deter skilful workmen from receiving, and employers from giving, a larger remuneration for a more useful service. If the public have any jurisdiction over private concerns, I cannot see that these people are in fault, or that any individual's particular public can be blamed for asserting the same authority over his individual conduct, which the general public asserts over people in general.

But, without dwelling upon supposititious cases, there are, in our own day, gross usurpations upon the liberty of private life actually practised, and still greater ones threatened with some expectation of success, and opinions proposed which assert an unlimited right in the public not only to prohibit by law everything which it thinks wrong, but in order to get at what it thinks wrong, to prohibit any number of things which it admits to be innocent.

Under the name of preventing intemperance, the people of one English colony, and of nearly half of the United States, have been interdicted by law from making any use whatever of fermented drinks, except for medical purposes: for prohibition of their sale is in fact, as it is intended to be, prohibition of their use. And though the impracticability of executing the law has caused its repeal in several of the States which had adopted it, including the one from which it derives its name, an attempt has notwithstanding been commenced, and is prosecuted with considerable zeal by many of the professed philanthropists, to agitate for a similar law in this country. The association, or "Alliance" as it terms itself, which has been formed for this purpose, has acquired some notoriety through the publicity given to a correspondence between its Secretary and one of the very few English public men who hold that a politician's opinions ought to be founded on principles. Lord Stanley's share in this correspondence is calculated to strengthen the hopes already built on him, by those who know how rare such qualities as are manifested in some of his public appearances, unhappily are among those who figure in political life. The organ of the Alliance, who would "deeply deplore the recognition of any principle which could be wrested to justify bigotry and persecution," undertakes to point out the "broad and impassable barrier" which divides such principles from those of the association. "All matters relating to thought, opinion, conscience, appear to me," he says, "to be without the sphere of legislation; all pertaining to social act, habit, relation, subject only to a discretionary power vested in the State itself, and not in the individual, to be within it." No mention is made of a third class, different from either of these, viz. acts and habits which are not social, but individual; although it is to this class, surely, that the act of drinking fermented liquors belongs. Selling fermented liquors, however, is trading, and trading is a social act. But the infringement complained of is not on the liberty of the seller, but on that of the buyer and consumer; since the State might just as well forbid him to drink wine, as purposely make it impossible for him to obtain it. The Secretary, however, says, "I claim, as a citizen, a right to legislate whenever my social rights are invaded by the social act of another." And now for the definition of these "social rights." "If anything invades my social rights, certainly the traffic in strong drink does. It destroys my primary right of security, by constantly creating and stimulating social disorder. It invades my right of equality, by deriving a profit from the creation of a misery, I am taxed to support. It impedes my right to free moral and intellectual development, by surrounding my path with dangers, and by weakening and demoralizing society, from which I have a right to claim mutual aid and intercourse." A theory of "social rights," the like of which probably never before found its way into distinct language — being nothing short of this — that it is the absolute social right of every individual, that every other individual shall act in every respect exactly as he ought; that whosoever fails thereof in the smallest particular, violates my social right, and entitles me to demand from the legislature the removal of the grievance. So monstrous a principle is far more dangerous than any single interference with liberty; there is no violation of liberty which it would not justify; it acknowledges no right to any freedom whatever, except perhaps to that of holding opinions in secret, without ever disclosing them: for the moment an opinion which I consider noxious, passes any one's lips, it invades all the "social rights" attributed to me by the Alliance. The doctrine ascribes to all mankind a vested interest in each other's moral, intellectual, and even physical perfection, to be defined by each claimant according to his own standard.

Another important example of illegitimate interference with the rightful liberty of the individual, not simply threatened, but long since carried into triumphant effect, is Sabbatarian legislation. Without doubt, abstinence on one day in the week, so far as the exigencies of life permit, from the usual daily occupation, though in no respect religiously binding on any except Jews, is a highly beneficial custom. And inasmuch as this custom cannot be observed without a general consent to that effect among the industrious classes, therefore, in so far as some persons by working may impose the same necessity on others, it may be allowable and right that the law should guarantee to each, the observance by others of the custom, by suspending the greater operations of industry on a particular day. But this justification, grounded on the direct interest which others have in each individual's observance of the practice, does not apply to the self-chosen occupations in which a person may think fit to employ his leisure; nor does it hold good, in the smallest degree, for legal restrictions on amusements. It is true that the amusement of some is the day's work of others; but the pleasure, not to say the useful recreation, of many, is worth the labour of a few, provided the occupation is freely chosen, and can be freely resigned. The operatives are perfectly right in thinking that if all worked on Sunday, seven days' work would have to be given for six days' wages: but so long as the great mass of employments are suspended, the small number who for the enjoyment of others must still work, obtain a proportional increase of earnings; and they are not obliged to follow those occupations, if they prefer leisure to emolument. If a further remedy is sought, it might be found in the establishment by custom of a holiday on some other day of the week for those particular classes of persons. The only ground, therefore, on which restrictions on Sunday amusements can be defended, must be that they are religiously wrong; a motive of legislation which never can be too earnestly protested against. "Deorum injuriæ Diis curæ."[24] It remains to be proved that society or any of its officers holds a commission from on high to avenge any supposed offence to Omnipotence, which is not also a wrong to our fellow creatures. The notion that it is one man's duty that another should be religious, was the foundation of all the religious persecutions ever perpetrated, and if admitted, would fully justify them. Though the feeling which breaks out in the repeated attempts to stop railway travelling on Sunday, in the resistance to the opening of Museums, and the like, has not the cruelty of the old persecutors, the state of mind indicated by it is fundamentally the same. It is a determination not to tolerate others in doing what is permitted by their religion, because it is not permitted by the persecutor's religion. It is a belief that God not only abominates the act of the misbeliever, but will not hold us guiltless if we leave him unmolested.

I cannot refrain from adding to these examples of the little account commonly made of human liberty, the language of downright persecution which breaks out from the press of this country, whenever it feels called on to notice the remarkable phenomenon of Mormonism. Much might be said on the unexpected and instructive fact, that an alleged new revelation, and a religion founded on it, the product of palpable imposture, not even supported by the *prestige* of extraordinary qualities in its founder, is believed by hundreds of thousands, and has been made the foundation of a society, in the age of newspapers, railways, and the electric telegraph. What here concerns us is, that this religion, like other and better religions, has its martyrs; that its prophet and founder was, for his teaching, put to death by a mob; that others of its adherents lost their lives by the same lawless violence; that they were forcibly expelled, in a body, from the country in which they first grew up; while, now that they have been chased into a solitary recess in the midst of a desert, many in this country openly declare that it

24. "Harm to the gods is the concern of the gods"; see Tacitus, *Annals* I.73.

would be right (only that it is not convenient) to send an expedition against them, and compel them by force to conform to the opinions of other people. The article of the Mormonite doctrine which is the chief provocative to the antipathy which thus breaks through the ordinary restraints of religious tolerance, is its sanction of polygamy; which, though permitted to Mahomedans, and Hindoos, and Chinese, seems to excite unquenchable animosity when practised by persons who speak English, and profess to be a kind of Christians. No one has a deeper disapprobation than I have of this Mormon institution; both for other reasons, and because, far from being in any way countenanced by the principle of liberty, it is a direct infraction of that principle, being a mere rivetting of the chains of one half of the community, and an emancipation of the other from reciprocity of obligation towards them. Still, it must be remembered that this relation is as much voluntary on the part of the women concerned in it, and who may be deemed the sufferers by it, as is the case with any other form of the marriage institution; and however surprising this fact may appear, it has its explanation in the common ideas and customs of the world, which teaching women to think marriage the one thing needful, make it intelligible that many a woman should prefer being one of several wives, to not being a wife at all. Other countries are not asked to recognise such unions, or release any portion of their inhabitants from their own laws on the score of Mormonite opinions. But when the dissentients have conceded to the hostile sentiments of others, far more than could justly be demanded; when they have left the countries to which their doctrines were unacceptable, and established themselves in a remote corner of the earth, which they have been the first to render habitable to human beings; it is difficult to see on what principles but those of tyranny they can be prevented from living there under what laws they please, provided they commit no aggression on other nations, and allow perfect freedom of departure to those who are dissatisfied with their ways. A recent writer, in some respects of considerable merit, proposes (to use his own words,) not a crusade, but a *civilizade,* against this polygamous community, to put an end to what seems to him a retrograde step in civilization. It also appears so to me, but I am not aware that any community has a right to force another to be civilized. So long as the sufferers by the bad law do not invoke assistance from other communities, I cannot admit that persons entirely unconnected with them ought to step in and require that a condition of things with which all who are directly interested appear to be satisfied, should be put an end to because it is a scandal to persons some thousands of miles distant, who have no part or concern in it. Let them send missionaries, if they please, to preach against it; and let them, by any fair means (of which silencing the teachers is not one,) oppose the progress of similar doctrines among their own people. If civilization has got the better of barbarism when barbarism had the world to itself, it is too much to profess to be afraid lest barbarism, after having been fairly got under, should revive and conquer civilization. A civilization that can thus succumb to its vanquished enemy, must first have become so degenerate, that neither its appointed priests and teachers, nor anybody else, has the capacity, or will take the trouble, to stand up for it. If this be so, the sooner such a civilization receives notice to quit, the better. It can only go on from bad to worse, until destroyed and regenerated (like the Western Empire) by energetic barbarians.

CHAPTER V

APPLICATIONS

The principles asserted in these pages must be more generally admitted as the basis for discussion of details, before a consistent application of them to all the various departments of government and morals can be attempted with any prospect of advantage. The few observations I propose to make on questions of detail, are designed to illustrate the principles, rather than to follow them out to their consequences. I offer, not so much applications, as specimens of application; which may serve to bring into greater clearness the meaning and limits of the two maxims which together form the entire doctrine of this Essay, and to assist the judgment in holding the balance between them, in the cases where it appears doubtful which of them is applicable to the case.

The maxims are, first, that the individual is not accountable to society for his actions, in so far as these concern the interests of no person but himself. Advice, instruction, persuasion, and avoidance by other people if thought necessary by them for their own good, are the only measures by which society can justifiably express its dislike or disapprobation of his conduct. Secondly, that for such actions as are prejudicial to the interests of others, the individual is accountable, and may be subjected either to social or to legal punishments, if society is of opinion that the one or the other is requisite for its protection.

In the first place, it must by no means be supposed, because damage, or probability of damage, to the interests of others, can alone justify the interference of society, that therefore it always does justify such interference. In many cases, an individual, in pursuing a legitimate object, necessarily and therefore legitimately causes pain or loss to others, or intercepts a good which they had a reasonable hope of obtaining. Such oppositions of interest between individuals often arise from bad social institutions, but are unavoidable while those institutions last; and some would be unavoidable under any institutions. Whoever succeeds in an overcrowded profession, or in a competitive examination; whoever is preferred to another in any contest for an object which both desire, reaps benefit from the loss of others, from their wasted exertion and their disappointment. But it is, by common admission, better for the general interest of mankind, that persons should pursue their objects undeterred by this sort of consequences. In other words, society admits no right, either legal or moral, in the disappointed competitors, to immunity from this kind of suffering; and feels called on to interfere, only when means of success have been employed which it is contrary to the general interest to permit — namely, fraud or treachery, and force.

Again, trade is a social act. Whoever undertakes to sell any description of goods to the public, does what affects the interest of other persons, and of society in general; and thus his conduct, in principle, comes within the jurisdiction of society: accordingly, it was once held to be the duty of governments, in all cases which were considered of importance, to fix prices, and regulate the processes of manufacture. But it is now recognised, though not till after a long struggle, that both the cheapness and the good quality of commodities are most effectually provided for by leaving the producers and sellers perfectly free, under the sole check of equal freedom to the buyers for supplying themselves elsewhere. This is the so-called doctrine of Free Trade, which rests on grounds different from, though equally solid with, the principle of individual liberty asserted in this Essay. Restrictions on trade, or on production for purposes of trade, are indeed restraints; and all restraint, *quâ* restraint, is an evil: but the restraints in question affect only that part of conduct which society is competent to restrain, and are wrong solely because they do not really produce the results which it is desired to produce by them. As the principle of individual liberty is not involved in the doctrine of Free Trade, so neither is it in most of the questions which arise respecting the limits of that doctrine: as for example, what amount of public control is admissible for the prevention of fraud by adulteration; how far sanitary precautions, or arrangements to protect workpeople employed in dangerous occupations, should be enforced on employers. Such questions involve considerations of liberty, only in so far as leaving people to themselves is always better, *cateris paribus,*[25] than controlling them: but that they may be legitimately controlled for these ends, is in principle undeniable. On the other hand, there are questions relating to interference with trade, which are essentially questions of liberty; such as the Maine Law, already touched upon; the prohibition of the importation of opium into China; the restriction of the sale of poisons; all cases, in short, where the object of the interference is to make it impossible or difficult to obtain a particular commodity. These interferences are objectionable, not as

25. Other things being equal.

infringements on the liberty of the producer or seller, but on that of the buyer.

One of these examples, that of the sale of poisons, opens a new question; the proper limits of what may be called the functions of police; how far liberty may legitimately be invaded for the prevention of crime, or of accident. It is one of the undisputed functions of government to take precautions against crime before it has been committed, as well as to detect and punish it afterwards. The preventive function of government, however, is far more liable to be abused, to the prejudice of liberty, than the punitory function; for there is hardly any part of the legitimate freedom of action of a human being which would not admit of being represented, and fairly too, as increasing the facilities for some form or other of delinquency. Nevertheless, if a public authority, or even a private person, sees any one evidently preparing to commit a crime, they are not bound to look on inactive until the crime is committed, but may interfere to prevent it. If poisons were never bought or used for any purpose except the commission of murder, it would be right to prohibit their manufacture and sale. They may, however, be wanted not only for innocent but for useful purposes, and restrictions cannot be imposed in the one case without operating in the other. Again, it is a proper office of public authority to guard against accidents. If either a public officer or any one else saw a person attempting to cross a bridge which had been ascertained to be unsafe, and there were no time to warn him of his danger, they might seize him and turn him back, without any real infringement of his liberty; for liberty consists in doing what one desires, and he does not desire to fall into the river. Nevertheless, when there is not a certainty, but only a danger of mischief, no one but the person himself can judge of the sufficiency of the motive which may prompt him to incur the risk: in this case, therefore, (unless he is a child, or delirious, or in some state of excitement or absorption incompatible with the full use of the reflecting faculty), he ought, I conceive, to be only warned of the danger; not forcibly prevented from exposing himself to it. Similar considerations, applied to such a question as the sale of poisons, may enable us to decide which among the possible modes of regulation are or are not contrary to principle. Such a precaution, for example, as that of labelling the drug with some word expressive of its dangerous character, may be enforced without violation of liberty: the buyer cannot wish not to know that the thing he possesses has poisonous qualities. But to require in all cases the certificate of a medical practitioner, would make it sometimes impossible, always expensive, to obtain the article for legitimate uses. The only mode apparent to me, in which difficulties may be thrown in the way of crime committed through this means, without any infringement, worth taking into account, upon the liberty of those who desire the poisonous substance for other purposes, consists in providing what, in the apt language of Bentham, is called "preappointed evidence." This provision is familiar to every one in the case of contracts. It is usual and right that the law, when a contract is entered into, should require as the condition of its enforcing performance, that certain formalities should be observed, such as signatures, attestation of witnesses, and the like, in order that in case of subsequent dispute, there may be evidence to prove that the contract was really entered into, and that there was nothing in the circumstances to render it legally invalid: the effect being, to throw great obstacles in the way of fictitious contracts, or contracts made in circumstances which, if known, would destroy their validity. Precautions of a similar nature might be enforced in the sale of articles adapted to be instruments of crime. The seller, for example, might be required to enter in a register the exact time of the transaction, the name and address of the buyer, the precise quality and quantity sold; to ask the purpose for which it was wanted, and record the answer he received. When there was no medical prescription, the presence of some third person might be required, to bring home the fact to the purchaser, in case there should afterwards be reason to believe that the article had been applied to criminal purposes. Such regulations would in general be no material impediment to obtaining the article, but a very considerable one to making an improper use of it without detection.

The right inherent in society, to ward off crimes against itself by antecedent precautions, suggests the obvious limitations to the maxim, that purely self-regarding misconduct cannot properly be meddled with in the way of prevention or punishment. Drunkenness, for example, in ordinary cases, is not a fit subject for legislative interference; but I should deem it perfectly legitimate that a person, who had once been convicted of any act of violence to others under the influence of drink, should be placed under a special legal restriction, personal to himself; that if he were afterwards found drunk, he should be liable to a penalty, and that if when in that state he committed another offence, the punishment to which he would be liable for that other offence should be increased in severity. The making himself drunk, in a person whom drunkenness excites to do harm to others, is a crime against others. So, again, idleness, except in a person receiving support from the public, or except when it constitutes a breach of contract, cannot without tyranny be made a subject of legal punishment; but if either from idleness or from any other avoidable cause, a man fails to perform his legal duties to others, as for instance to support his children, it is no tyranny to force him to fulfil that obligation, by compulsory labour, if no other means are available.

Again, there are many acts which, being directly injurious only to the agents themselves, ought not to be legally interdicted, but which, if done publicly, are a violation of good manners, and coming thus within the category of offences against others, may rightfully be prohibited. Of this kind are offences against decency; on which it is unnecessary to dwell, the rather as they are only connected indirectly with our subject, the objection to publicity being equally strong in the case of many actions not in themselves condemnable, nor supposed to be so.

There is another question to which an answer must be found, consistent with the principles which have been laid down. In cases of personal conduct supposed to be blameable, but which respect for liberty precludes society from preventing or punishing, because the evil directly resulting falls wholly on the agent; what the agent is free to do, ought other persons to be equally free to counsel or instigate? This question is not free from difficulty. The case of a person who solicits another to do an act, is not strictly a case of self-regarding conduct. To give advice or offer inducements to any one, is a social act, and may therefore, like actions in general which affect others, be supposed amenable to social control. But a little reflection corrects the first impression, by showing that if the case is not strictly within the definition of individual liberty, yet the reasons on which the principle of individual liberty is grounded, are applicable to it. If people must be allowed, in whatever concerns only themselves, to act as seems best to themselves at their own peril, they must equally be free to consult with one another about what is fit to be so done; to exchange opinions, and give and receive suggestions. Whatever it is permitted to do, it must be permitted to advise to do. The question is doubtful, only when the instigator derives a personal benefit from his advice; when he makes it his occupation, for subsistence or pecuniary gain, to promote what society and the state consider to be an evil. Then, indeed, a new element of complication is introduced; namely, the existence of classes of persons with an interest opposed to what is considered as the public weal, and whose mode of living is grounded on the counteraction of it. Ought this to be interfered with, or not? Fornication, for example, must be tolerated, and so must gambling; but should a person be free to be a pimp, or to keep a gambling-house? The case is one of those which lie on the exact boundary line between two principles, and it is not at once apparent to which of the two it properly belongs. There are arguments on both sides. On the side of toleration it may be said, that the fact of following anything as an occupation, and living or profiting by the practice of it, cannot make that criminal which would otherwise be admissible; that the act should either be consistently permitted or consistently prohibited; that if the principles which we have hitherto defended are true, society has no business, *as* society, to decide anything to be wrong which concerns only the individual; that it cannot go beyond dissuasion, and that one person should be as free to persuade, as another to dissuade. In opposition to this it may be contended, that although the public, or the State, are not warranted in authoritatively deciding, for purposes of repression or punishment, that such or such conduct affecting only the interests of the individual is good or bad, they are fully justified in assuming, if they regard it as bad, that its being so or not is at least a disputable question: That, this being supposed, they cannot be acting wrongly in endeavouring to exclude the influence of solicitations which are not disinterested, of instigators who cannot possibly be impartial — who have a direct personal interest on one side, and that side the one which the State believes to be wrong, and who confessedly promote it for personal objects only. There can surely, it may be urged, be nothing lost, no sacrifice of good, by so ordering matters that persons shall make their election, either wisely or foolishly, on their own prompting, as free as possible from the arts of persons who stimulate their inclinations for interested purposes of their own. Thus (it may be said) though the statutes respecting unlawful games are utterly indefensible — though all persons should be free to gamble in their own or each other's houses, or in any place of meeting established by their own subscriptions, and open only to the members and their visitors — yet public gambling-houses should not be permitted. It is true that the prohibition is never effectual, and that whatever amount of tyrannical power is given to the police, gambling-houses can always be maintained under other pretences; but they may be compelled to conduct their operations with a certain degree of secrecy and mystery, so that nobody knows anything about them but those who seek them; and more than this, society ought not to aim at. There is considerable force in these arguments; I will not venture to decide whether they are sufficient to justify the moral anomaly of punishing the accessary, when the principal is (and must be) allowed to go free; of fining or imprisoning the procurer, but not the fornicator, the gambling-house keeper, but not the gambler. Still less ought the common operations of buying and selling to be interfered with on analogous grounds. Almost every article which is bought and sold may be used in excess, and the sellers have a pecuniary interest in encouraging that excess; but no argument can be founded on this, in favour, for instance, of the Maine Law; because the class of dealers in strong drinks, though interested in their abuse, are indispensably required for the sake of their legitimate use. The interest, however, of these dealers in promoting intemperance is a real evil, and justifies the State in imposing restrictions and requiring guarantees, which but for that justification would be infringements of legitimate liberty.

A further question is, whether the State, while it permits, should nevertheless indirectly discourage conduct which it deems contrary to the best interests of the agent; whether, for example, it should take measures to render the means of drunkenness more costly, or add to the difficulty of procuring them, by limiting the number of the places of sale. On this as on most other practical questions, many distinctions require to be made. To tax stimulants for the sole purpose of making them more difficult to be obtained, is a measure differing only in degree from their entire prohibition; and would be justifiable only if that were justifiable. Every increase of cost is a prohibition, to those whose means do not come up to the augmented price; and to those who do, it is a penalty laid on them for gratifying a particular taste. Their choice of pleasures, and their mode of expending their income, after satisfying their legal and moral obligations to the State and to individuals, are their own concern, and must rest with their own judgment. These considerations may seem at first sight to condemn the selection of stimulants as special subjects of taxation for purposes of revenue. But it must be remembered that taxation for fiscal purposes is absolutely inevitable; that in most countries it is necessary that a considerable part of that taxation should be indirect; that the State, therefore, cannot help imposing penalties, which to some persons may be prohibitory, on the use of some articles of consumption. It is hence the duty of the State to consider, in the imposition of taxes, what commodities the consumers can best spare; and *à fortiori*,[26] to select in preference those of which it deems the use, beyond a very moderate quantity, to be positively injurious. Taxation, therefore, of stimulants, up to the point which produces the largest amount of revenue (supposing that the State needs all the revenue which it yields) is not only admissible, but to be approved of.

The question of making the sale of these commodities a more or less exclusive privilege, must be answered differently, according to the purposes to which the restriction is intended to be subservient. All places of public resort require the restraint of a police, and places of this kind peculiarly, because offences against society are especially apt to originate there. It is, therefore, fit to confine the power of selling these commodities (at least for consumption on the spot) to persons of known or vouched-for respectability

26. Accordingly with still stronger cause.

of conduct; to make such regulations respecting hours of opening and clos-
ing as may be requisite for public surveillance, and to withdraw the licence
if breaches of the peace repeatedly take place through the connivance or
incapacity of the keeper of the house, or if it becomes a rendezvous for
concocting and preparing offences against the law. Any further restriction I
do not conceive to be, in principle, justifiable. The limitation in number, for
instance, of beer and spirit-houses, for the express purpose of rendering
them more difficult of access, and diminishing the occasions of temptation,
not only exposes all to an inconvenience because there are some by whom
the facility would be abused, but is suited only to a state of society in which
the labouring classes are avowedly treated as children or savages, and
placed under an education of restraint, to fit them for future admission to the
privileges of freedom. This is not the principle on which the labouring
classes are professedly governed in any free country; and no person who
sets due value on freedom will give his adhesion to their being so governed,
unless after all efforts have been exhausted to educate them for freedom and
govern them as freemen, and it has been definitively proved that they can
only be governed as children. The bare statement of the alternative shows
the absurdity of supposing that such efforts have been made in any case
which needs be considered here. It is only because the institutions of this
country are a mass of inconsistencies, that things find admittance, into our
practice which belong to the system of despotic, or what is called paternal,
government, while the general freedom of our institutions precludes the
exercise of the amount of control necessary to render the restraint of any
real efficacy as a moral education.

It was pointed out in an early part of this Essay, that the liberty of the
individual, in things wherein the individual is alone concerned, implies a
corresponding liberty in any number of individuals to regulate by mutual
agreement such things as regard them jointly, and regard no persons but
themselves. This question presents no difficulty, so long as the will of all the
persons implicated remains unaltered; but since that will may change, it is
often necessary, even in things in which they alone are concerned, that they
should enter into engagements with one another; and when they do, it is fit,
as a general rule, that those engagements should be kept. Yet in the laws,
probably, of every country, this general rule has some exceptions. Not only
persons are not held to engagements which violate the rights of third parties, but it is sometimes considered a sufficient reason for releasing them
from an engagement, that it is injurious to themselves. In this and most
other civilized countries, for example, an engagement by which a person
should sell himself, or allow himself to be sold, as a slave, would be null

and void; neither enforced by law nor by opinion. The ground for thus limiting his power of voluntarily disposing of his own lot in life, is apparent, and is very clearly seen in this extreme case. The reason for not interfering, unless for the sake of others, with a person's voluntary acts, is consideration for his liberty. His voluntary choice is evidence that what he so chooses is desirable, or at the least endurable, to him, and his good is on the whole best provided for by allowing him to take his own means of pursuing it. But by selling himself for a slave, he abdicates his liberty; he foregoes any future use of it, beyond that single act. He therefore defeats, in his own case, the very purpose which is the justification of allowing him to dispose of himself. He is no longer free; but is thenceforth in a position which has no longer the presumption in its favour, that would be afforded by his voluntarily remaining in it. The principle of freedom cannot require that he should be free not to be free. It is not freedom, to be allowed to alienate his freedom. These reasons, the force of which is so conspicuous in this peculiar case, are evidently of far wider application; yet a limit is everywhere set to them by the necessities of life, which continually require, not indeed that we should resign our freedom, but that we should consent to this and the other limitation of it. The principle, however, which demands uncontrolled freedom of action in all that concerns only the agents themselves, requires that those who have become bound to one another, in things which concern no third party, should be able to release one another from the engagement: and even without such voluntary release, there are perhaps no contracts or engagements, except those that relate to money or money's worth, of which one can venture to say that there ought to be no liberty whatever of retraction. Baron Wilhelm von Humboldt, in the excellent essay from which I have already quoted, states it as his conviction, that engagements which involve personal relations or services, should never be legally binding beyond a limited duration of time; and that the most important of these engagements, marriage, having the peculiarity that its objects are frustrated unless the feelings of both the parties are in harmony with it, should require nothing more than the declared will of either party to dissolve it. This subject is too important, and too complicated, to be discussed in a parenthesis, and I touch on it only so far as is necessary for purposes of illustration. If the conciseness and generality of Baron Humboldt's dissertation had not obliged him in this instance to content himself with enunciating his conclusion without discussing the premises, he would doubtless have recognised that the question cannot be decided on grounds so simple as those to which he confines himself. When a person, either by express promise or by conduct, has encouraged another to rely upon his continuing to act in a certain way — to build expectations and calculations, and stake any part of his plan of life upon that supposition, a new series of moral obligations arises on his part towards that person, which may possibly be overruled, but cannot be ignored. And again, if the relation between two contracting parties has been followed by consequences to others; if it has placed third parties in any peculiar position, or, as in the case of marriage, has even called third parties into existence, obligations arise on the part of both the contracting parties towards those third persons, the fulfilment of which, or at all events the mode of fulfilment, must be greatly affected by the continuance or disruption of the relation between the original parties to the contract. It does not follow, nor can I admit, that these obligations extend to requiring the fulfilment of the contract at all costs to the happiness of the reluctant party; but they are a necessary element in the question; and even if, as Von Humboldt maintains, they ought to make no difference in the *legal* freedom of the parties to release themselves from the engagement (and I also hold that they ought not to make *much* difference), they necessarily make a great difference in the *moral* freedom. A person is bound to take all these circumstances into account, before resolving on a step which may affect such important interests of others; and if he does not allow proper weight to those interests, he is morally responsible for the wrong. I have made these obvious remarks for the better illustration of the general principle of liberty, and not because they are at all needed on the particular question, which, on the contrary, is usually discussed as if the interest of children was everything, and that of grown persons nothing.

I have already observed that, owing to the absence of any recognised general principles, liberty is often granted where it should be withheld, as well as withheld where it should be granted; and one of the cases in which, in the modern European world, the sentiment of liberty is the strongest, is a case where, in my view, it is altogether misplaced. A person should be free to do as he likes in his own concerns; but he ought not to be free to do as he likes in acting for another, under the pretext that the affairs of another are his own affairs. The State, while it respects the liberty of each in what specially regards himself, is bound to maintain a vigilant control over his exercise of any power which it allows him to possess over others. This obligation is almost entirely disregarded in the case of the family relations, a case, in its direct influence on human happiness, more important than all others taken together. The almost despotic power of husbands over wives needs not be enlarged upon here, because nothing more is needed for the complete removal of the evil, than that wives should have the same rights, and should receive the protection of law in the same manner, as all other persons; and because, on this subject, the defenders of established injustice do not avail themselves of the plea of liberty, but stand forth openly as the champions of power. It is in the case of children, that misapplied notions of liberty are a real obstacle to the fulfilment by the State of its duties. One would almost think that a man's children were supposed to be literally, and not metaphorically, a part of himself, so jealous is opinion of the smallest interference of law with his absolute and exclusive control over them; more jealous than of almost any interference with his own freedom of action: so much less do the generality of mankind value liberty than power. Consider, for example, the case of education. Is it not almost a self-evident axiom, that the State should require and compel the education, up to a certain standard, of every human being who is born its citizen? Yet who is there that is not afraid to recognise and assert this truth? Hardly any one indeed will deny that it is one of the most sacred duties of the parents (or, as law and usage now stand, the father), after summoning a human being into the world, to give to that being an education fitting him to perform his part well in life towards others and towards himself. But while this is unanimously declared to be the father's duty, scarcely anybody, in this country, will bear to hear of obliging him to perform it. Instead of his being required to make any exertion or sacrifice for securing education to the child, it is left to his choice to accept it or not when it is provided gratis! It still remains unrecognised, that to bring a child into existence without a fair prospect of being able, not only to provide food for its body, but instruction and training for its mind, is a moral crime, both against the unfortunate offspring and against society; and that if the parent does not fulfil this obligation, the State ought to see it fulfilled, at the charge, as far as possible, of the parent.

Were the duty of enforcing universal education once admitted, there would be an end to the difficulties about what the State should teach, and how it should teach, which now convert the subject into a mere battle-field for sects and parties, causing the time and labour which should have been spent in educating, to be wasted in quarrelling about education. If the government would make up its mind to *require* for every child a good education, it might save itself the trouble of *providing* one. It might leave to parents to obtain the education where and how they pleased, and content itself with helping to pay the school fees of the poorer class of children, and defraying the entire school expenses of those who have no one else to pay for them. The objections which are urged with reason against State education, do not apply to the enforcement of education by the State, but to the State's taking upon itself to direct that education; which is a totally different thing. That the whole or any large part of the education of the people should be in State hands, I go as far as any one in deprecating. All that has been said of the importance of individuality of character, and diversity in opinions and modes of conduct, involves, as of the same unspeakable importance, diversity of education. A general State education is a mere contrivance for moulding people to be exactly like one another; and as the mould in which it casts them is that which pleases the predominant power in the government, whether this be a monarch, a priesthood, an aristocracy, or the majority of the existing generation, in proportion as it is efficient and successful, it establishes a despotism over the mind, leading by natural tendency to one over the body. An education established and controlled by the State, should only exist, if it exist at all, as one among many competing experiments, carried on for the purpose of example and stimulus, to keep the others up to a certain standard of excellence. Unless, indeed, when society in general is in so backward a state that it could not or would not provide for itself any proper institutions of education, unless the government undertook the task; then, indeed, the government may, as the less of two great evils, take upon itself the business of schools and universities, as it may that of joint stock companies, when private enterprise, in a shape fitted for undertaking great works of industry, does not exist in the country. But in general, if the country contains a sufficient number of persons qualified to provide education under government auspices, the same persons would be able and willing to give an equally good education on the voluntary principle, under the assurance of remuneration afforded by a law rendering education compulsory, combined with State aid to those unable to defray the expense.

The instrument for enforcing the law could be no other than public examinations, extending to all children, and beginning at an early age. An age might be fixed at which every child must be examined, to ascertain if he (or she) is able to read. If a child proves unable, the father, unless he has some sufficient ground of excuse, might be subjected to a moderate fine, to be worked out, if necessary, by his labour, and the child might be put to school at his expense. Once in every year the examination should be renewed, with a gradually extending range of subjects, so as to make the universal acquisition, and what is more, retention, of a certain minimum of general knowledge, virtually compulsory. Beyond that minimum, there should be voluntary examinations on all subjects, at which all who come up to a certain standard of proficiency might claim a certificate. To prevent the State from exercising, through these arrangements, an improper influence over opinion, the knowledge required for passing an examination (beyond the merely instrumental parts of knowledge, such as languages and their use) should, even in the higher class of examinations, be confined to facts and positive science exclusively. The examinations on religion, politics, or other disputed topics, should not turn on the truth or falsehood of opinions, but on the matter of fact that such and such an opinion is held, on such grounds, by such authors, or schools, or churches. Under this system, the rising generation would be no worse off in regard to all disputed truths, than they are at present; they would be brought up either churchmen or dissenters as they now are, the state merely taking care that they should be instructed churchmen, or instructed dissenters. There would be nothing to hinder them from being taught religion, if their parents chose, at the same schools where they were taught other things. All attempts by the state to bias the conclusions of its citizens on disputed subjects, are evil; but it may very properly offer to ascertain and certify that a person possesses the knowledge, requisite to make his conclusions, on any given subject, worth attending to. A student of philosophy would be the better for being able to stand an examination both in Locke and in Kant, whichever of the two he takes up with, or even if with neither: and there is no reasonable objection to examining an atheist in the evidences of Christianity, provided he is not required to profess a belief in them. The examinations, however, in the higher branches of knowledge should, I conceive, be entirely voluntary. It would be giving too dangerous a power to governments, were they allowed to exclude any one from professions, even from the profession of teacher, for alleged deficiency of qualifications: and I think, with Wilhelm von Humboldt, that degrees, or other public certificates of scientific or professional acquirements, should be given to all who present themselves for examination, and stand the test; but that such certificates should confer no advantage over competitors, other than the weight which may be attached to their testimony by public opinion.

It is not in the matter of education only, that misplaced notions of liberty prevent moral obligations on the part of parents from being recognised, and legal obligations from being imposed, where there are the strongest grounds for the former always, and in many cases for the latter also. The fact itself, of causing the existence of a human being, is one of the most responsible actions in the range of human life. To undertake this responsibility — to bestow a life which may be either a curse or a blessing — unless the being on whom it is to be bestowed will have at least the ordinary chances of a desirable existence, is a crime against that being. And in a country either over-peopled, or threatened with being so, to produce children, beyond a very small number, with the effect of reducing the reward of labour by their competition, is a serious offence against all who live by the remuneration of their labour. The laws which, in many countries on the Continent, forbid marriage unless the parties can show that they have the means of supporting a family, do not exceed the legitimate powers of the state: and whether such laws be expedient or not (a question mainly dependent on local circumstances and feelings), they are not objectionable as violations of liberty. Such laws are interferences of the state to prohibit a mischievous act — an act injurious to others, which ought to be a subject of reprobation, and social stigma, even when it is not deemed expedient to superadd legal punishment. Yet the current ideas of liberty, which bend so easily to real infringements of the freedom of the individual, in things which concern only himself, would repel the attempt to put any restraint upon his inclinations when the consequence of their indulgence is a life, or lives, of wretchedness and depravity to the off-spring, with manifold evils to those sufficiently within reach to be in any way affected by their actions. When we compare the strange respect of mankind for liberty, with their strange want of respect for it, we might imagine that a man had an indispensable right to do harm to others, and no right at all to please himself without giving pain to any one.

I have reserved for the last place a large class of questions respecting the limits of government interference, which, though closely connected with the subject of this Essay, do not, in strictness, belong to it. These are cases in which the reasons against interference do not turn upon the principle of liberty: the question is not about restraining the actions of individuals, but about helping them: it is asked whether the government should do, or cause to be done, something for their benefit, instead of leaving it to be done by themselves, individually, or in voluntary combination.

The objections to government interference, when it is not such as to involve infringement of liberty, may be of three kinds.

The first is when the thing to be done is likely to be better done by individuals than by the government. Speaking generally, there is no one so fit to conduct any business, or to determine how or by whom it shall be conducted, as those who are personally interested in it. This principle condemns the interferences, once so common, of the legislature, or the officers of government, with the ordinary processes of industry. But this part of the subject has been sufficiently enlarged upon by political economists, and is not particularly related to the principles of this Essay.

The second objection is more nearly allied to our subject. In many cases, though individuals may not do the particular thing so well, on the average, as the officers of government, it is nevertheless desirable that it should be done by them, rather than by the government, as a means to their own mental education — a mode of strengthening their active faculties, exercising their judgment, and giving them a familiar knowledge of the subjects with which they are thus left to deal. This is a principal, though not the sole, recommendation of jury trial (in cases not political); of free and popular local and municipal institutions; of the conduct of industrial and philanthropic enterprises by voluntary associations. These are not questions of liberty, and are connected with that subject only by remote tendencies; but they are questions of development. It belongs to a different occasion from the present to dwell on these things as parts of national education; as being, in truth, the peculiar training of a citizen, the practical part of the political education of a free people, taking them out of the narrow circle of personal and family selfishness, and accustoming them to the comprehension of joint interests, the management of joint concerns — habituating them to act from public or semi-public motives, and guide their conduct by aims which unite instead of isolating them from one another. Without these habits and powers, a free constitution can neither be worked nor preserved, as is exemplified by the too-often transitory nature of political freedom in countries where it does not rest upon a sufficient basis of local liberties. The management of purely local business by the localities, and of the great enterprises of industry by the union of those who voluntarily supply the pecuniary means, is further recommended by all the advantages which have been set forth in this Essay as belonging to individuality of development, and diversity of modes of action. Government operations tend to be everywhere alike. With individuals and voluntary associations, on the contrary, there are varied experiments, and endless diversity of experience. What the State can usefully do, is to make itself a central depository, and active circulator and diffuser, of the experience resulting from many trials. Its business is to enable each experimentalist to benefit by the experiments of others, instead of tolerating no experiments but its own.

The third, and most cogent reason for restricting the interference of government, is the great evil of adding unnecessarily to its power. Every function superadded to those already exercised by the government, causes its influence over hopes and fears to be more widely diffused, and converts, more and more, the active and ambitious part of the public into hangers-on of the government, or of some party which aims at becoming the government. If the roads, the railways, the banks, the insurance offices, the great joint-stock companies, the universities, and the public charities, were all of them branches of the government; if, in addition, the municipal corporations and local boards, with all that now devolves on them, became departments of the central administration; if the employés of all these different enterprises were appointed and paid by the government, and looked to the government for every rise in life; not all the freedom of the press and popular constitution of the legislature would make this or any other country free otherwise than in name. And the evil would be greater, the more efficiently and scientifically the administrative machinery was constructed — the more skilful the arrangements for obtaining the best qualified hands and heads with which to work it. In England it has of late been proposed that all the members of the civil service of government should be selected by competitive examination, to obtain for those employments the most intelligent and instructed persons procurable; and much has been said and written for and against this proposal. One of the arguments most insisted on by its opponents, is that the occupation of a permanent official servant of the State does not hold out sufficient prospects of emolument and importance to attract the highest talents, which will always be able to find a more inviting career in the professions, or in the service of companies and other public bodies. One would not have been surprised if this argument had been used by the friends of the proposition, as an answer to its principal difficulty. Coming from the opponents it is strange enough. What is urged as an objection is the safety-valve of the proposed system. If indeed all the high talent of the country *could* be drawn into the service of the government, a proposal tending to bring about that result might well inspire uneasiness. If every part of the business of society which required organized concert, or large and comprehensive views, were in the hands of the government, and if government offices were universally filled by the ablest men, all the enlarged culture and practised intelligence in the country, except the purely speculative, would be concentrated in a numerous bureaucracy, to whom alone the rest of the community would look for all things: the multitude for direction and dictation in all they had to do; the able and aspiring for personal advancement. To be admitted into the ranks of this bureaucracy, and when admitted, to rise therein, would be the sole objects of ambition. Under this régime, not only is the outside public ill-qualified, for want of practical experience, to criticize or check the mode of operation of the bureaucracy, but even if the accidents of despotic or the natural working of popular institutions occasionally raise to the summit a ruler or rulers of reforming inclinations, no reform can be effected which is contrary to the interest of the bureaucracy. Such is the melancholy condition of the Russian empire, as is shown in the accounts of those who have had sufficient opportunity of observation. The Czar himself is powerless against the bureaucratic body; he can send any one of them to Siberia, but he cannot govern without them, or against their will. On every decree of his they have a tacit veto, by merely refraining from carrying it into effect. In countries of more advanced civilization and of a more insurrectionary spirit, the public, accustomed to expect everything to be done for them by the State, or at least to do nothing for themselves without asking from the State not only leave to do it, but even how it is to be done, naturally hold the State responsible for all evil which befals them, and when the evil exceeds their amount of patience, they rise against the government and make what is called a revolution; whereupon somebody else, with or without legitimate authority from the nation, vaults into the seat, issues his orders to the bureaucracy, and everything goes on much as it did before; the bureaucracy being unchanged, and nobody else being capable of taking their place.

A very different spectacle is exhibited among a people accustomed to transact their own business. In France, a large part of the people having been engaged in military service, many of whom have held at least the rank of non-commissioned officers, there are in every popular insurrection several persons competent to take the lead, and improvise some tolerable plan of action. What the French are in military affairs, the Americans are in every kind of civil business; let them be left without a government, every body of Americans is able to improvise one, and to carry on that or any other public business with a sufficient amount of intelligence, order, and decision. This is what every free people ought to be: and a people capable of this is certain to be free; it will never let itself be enslaved by any man or body of men because these are able to seize and pull the reins of the central administration. No bureaucracy can hope to make such a people as this do or undergo anything that they do not like. But where everything is done through the bureaucracy, nothing to which the bureaucracy is really adverse can be done at all. The constitution of such countries is an organization of the experience and practical ability of the nation, into a disciplined body for the purpose of governing the rest; and the more perfect that organization is in itself, the more successful in drawing to itself and educating for itself the persons of greatest capacity from all ranks of the community, the more complete is the bondage of all, the members of the bureaucracy included. For the governors are as much the slaves of their organization and discipline, as the governed are of the governors. A Chinese mandarin is as much the tool and creature of a despotism as the humblest cultivator. An individual Jesuit is to the utmost degree of abasement the slave of his order, though the order itself exists for the collective power and importance of its members.

It is not, also, to be forgotten, that the absorption of all the principal ability of the country into the governing body is fatal, sooner or later, to the mental activity and progressiveness of the body itself. Banded together as they are — working a system which, like all systems, necessarily proceeds in a great measure by fixed rules — the official body are under the constant temptation of sinking into indolent routine, or, if they now and then desert that mill-horse round, of rushing into some half-examined crudity which has struck the fancy of some leading member of the corps: and the sole check to these closely allied, though seemingly opposite, tendencies, the only stimulus which can keep the ability of the body itself up to a high standard, is liability to the watchful criticism of equal ability outside the body. It is indispensable, therefore, that the means should exist, independently of the government, of forming such ability, and furnishing it with the opportunities and experience necessary for a correct judgment of great practical affairs. If we would possess permanently a skilful and efficient body of functionaries — above all, a body able to originate and willing to adopt improvements; if we would not have our bureaucracy degenerate into a pedantocracy, this body must not engross all the occupations which form and cultivate the faculties required for the government of mankind.

To determine the point at which evils, so formidable to human freedom and advancement, begin, or rather at which they begin to predominate over the benefits attending the collective application of the force of society, under its recognised chiefs, for the removal of the obstacles which stand in the way of its well-being; to secure as much of the advantages of centralized power and intelligence, as can be had without turning into governmental channels too great a proportion of the general activity, is one of the most difficult and complicated questions in the art of government. It is, in a great measure, a question of detail, in which many and various considerations must be kept in view, and no absolute rule can be laid down. But I believe that the practical principle in which safety resides, the ideal to be kept in view, the standard by which to test all arrangements intended for overcoming the difficulty, may be conveyed in these words: the greatest dissemination of power consistent with efficiency; but the greatest possible centralization of information, and diffusion of it from the centre. Thus, in municipal administration, there would be, as in the New England States, a very minute division among separate officers, chosen by the localities, of all business which is not better left to the persons directly interested; but besides this, there would be, in each department of local affairs, a central superintendence, forming a branch of the general government. The organ of this superintendence would concentrate, as in a focus, the variety of information and experience derived from the conduct of that branch of public business in all the localities, from everything analogous which is done in foreign countries, and from the general principles of political science. This central organ should have a right to know all that is done, and its special duty should be that of making the knowledge acquired in one place available for others. Emancipated from the petty prejudices and narrow views of a locality by its elevated position and comprehensive sphere of observation, its advice would naturally carry much authority; but its actual power, as a permanent institution, should, I conceive, be limited to compelling the local officers to obey the laws laid down for their guidance. In all things not provided for by general rules, those officers should be left to their own judgment, under responsibility to their constituents. For the violation of rules, they should be responsible to law, and the rules themselves should be laid down by the legislature; the central administrative authority only watching over their execution, and if they were not properly carried into effect, appealing, according to the nature of the case, to the tribunal to enforce the law, or to the constituencies to dismiss the functionaries who had not executed it according to its spirit. Such, in its general conception, is the central superintendence which the Poor Law Board is intended to exercise over the administrators of the Poor Rate throughout the country. Whatever powers the Board exercises beyond this limit, were right and necessary in that peculiar case, for the cure of rooted habits of maladministration in matters deeply affecting not the localities merely, but the whole community; since no locality has a moral right to make itself by mismanagement a nest of pauperism, necessarily overflowing into other localities, and impairing the moral and physical condition of the whole labouring community. The powers of administrative coercion and subordinate legislation possessed by the Poor Law Board (but which, owing to the state of opinion on the subject, are very scantily exercised by them), though perfectly justifiable in a case of first-rate national interest, would be wholly out of place in the superintendence of interests purely local. But a central organ of information and instruction for all the localities, would be equally valuable in all departments of administration. A government cannot have too much of the kind of activity which does not impede, but aids and stimulates, individual exertion and development. The mischief begins when, instead of calling forth the activity and powers of individuals and bodies, it substitutes its own activity for theirs; when, instead of informing, advising, and, upon occasion, denouncing, it makes them work in fetters, or bids them stand aside and does their work instead of them. The worth of a State, in the long run, is the worth of the individuals composing it; and a State which postpones the interests of *their* mental expansion and elevation, to a little more of administrative skill, or of that semblance of it which practice gives, in the details of business; a State which dwarfs its men, in order that they may be more docile instruments in its hands even for beneficial purposes, will find that with small men no great thing can really be accomplished; and that the perfection of machinery to which it has sacrificed everything, will in the end avail it nothing, for want of the vital power which, in order that the machine might work more smoothly, it has preferred to banish.

THE END

Rethinking
On Liberty

A Freedom Both Personal and Political

OWEN FISS

The plurality of the human condition and the capacity of each individual to create a distinctive life for himself lie at the core of John Stuart Mill's worldview. Mill wrote *On Liberty* to foster our individuality, even to the point of eccentricity, and to attack the forces that drive us to conformity. "That so few now dare to be eccentric," Mill warned, "marks the chief danger of the time" (p. 131).

Mill sought such diversity not for its own sake but rather to fulfill a larger vision of human development. He defended individuality, and even eccentricity, on the theory that they reflect the fullest development of our personalities. Such development, he argued, would promote both the happiness of each individual and the well-being of society. As Mill saw it, "In proportion to the development of his individuality, each person becomes more valuable to himself, and is therefore capable of being more valuable to others" (pp. 127–28).

With these purposes in mind, Mill formulated his principle of individual liberty. In modern times this principle has come to be known as the harm principle, but it still better might be called the harm-to-others principle.[1] It provides that interferences with an individual's liberty can be justified only to prevent him from harming others, never merely for his own good.

Implicit in the harm-to-others principle is the view that all social coercion must be justified, and that such interference can be justified only if it prevents an individual from harming others. In effect, it gives each individual the freedom to decide what is best for himself. Mill assumed that this freedom would lead to the fullest development of each individual and thus enable "human beings [to] become a noble and beautiful object of contemplation" (p. 127).

The harm-to-others principle is the overarching theme of *On Liberty* and arguably its most distinctive contribution. Mill's essay, however, is also a stirring affirmation of the importance of freedom of speech and thus often is read, especially in legal circles, as the theoretical foundation for the protection of free speech — the focus of my concern.

Although modern lawyers tend to separate Mill's discussion of free speech from his more general defense of individual liberty, we must first determine whether Mill actually embraced two distinct principles, as I argue he did, or whether the free speech principle is simply a special application of the harm-to-others principle. As a special application, speech could be protected on the theory, sometimes invoked, that it causes no harm to others. Conceiving freedom of speech more broadly, indeed as an independent principle, would allow for the protection of speech even if it causes harm to others.

In the first chapter of *On Liberty,* Mill introduced the harm-to-others principle. Rather than further develop that principle in the second chapter, though, he launched into a defense of free speech — not with the rather limp argument that it causes no harm to others, but because it is a necessary means for testing one's belief. Only through free and open discussion can we learn whether our views are true or false. No one is infallible, and if even after free and open discussion an individual adheres to the same beliefs, that individual will do so with a new appreciation and even firmer conviction in their truth.

In the third chapter of *On Liberty,* Mill resumed the discussion of the harm-to-others principle and invoked the distinction between speech and action to define the jurisdiction of that principle. The harm-to-others principle applies only to action, he argued, not to speech. Men should be free to form their opinions and to express them "without reserve" (p. 121). A different question arises, according to Mill, when people act upon those opinions. In the domain of action, the harm-to-others principle operates and secures a freedom more limited than the one afforded to speech.

Speech for Mill was not a solipsistic activity. Speech occurs in the presence of others, and Mill argued for a freedom to receive opinions as well as to express them. The freedom he insisted upon was, in a phrase he used repeatedly, a "freedom of discussion." In emphasizing the social dimensions of speech, Mill necessarily acknowledged that speech may contribute to a sequence of events that harms others. Still, he insisted upon a measure of freedom for the expression of opinion that transcends the freedom for action provided by the harm-to-others principle. As Mill put it, "No one pretends that actions should be as free as opinions" (p. 121).

At the beginning of Chapter III, Mill acknowledged that speech might be "a positive instigation" to some action that harms others. In a passage that has become a standard part of the lawyer's repertory, Mill wrote, "An opinion that corn-dealers are starvers of the poor, or that private property is robbery, ought to be unmolested when simply circulated through the press, but may justly incur punishment when delivered orally to an excited mob assembled before the house of a corn-dealer, or when handed about among the same mob in the form of a placard" (p. 121).

The purpose of this passage is to establish society's authority to restrain those who incite an excited mob. Because of this focus, Mill did not pause to explain why those who express the same view as the instigator of the mob, but who do so through the press, should be let alone. Is it because they cause no harm to others, or is it because they enjoy a freedom to express that opinion — "corn-dealers are starvers of the poor," "private property is robbery" — in spite of the harm to others? Only if we ignore the importance of culture — or, more pointedly, the cumulative effects of public discourse on action, some of which may transgress the law — might we say that systematic attacks in the press upon private property or the propertied classes will not weaken the attachment or respect afforded to private property and thus not affect or harm others. There is no reason to believe Mill was of that view.

It is thus fair to say that in affirming the right of the press to carry or even advance attacks on private property, Mill was either prepared to protect speech even when it affects or harms others or, alternatively, that he would require very special kinds of harms in order to justify the restraint on speech. Not only must the action that inflicts the harm be unlawful, but the relation between that action and the speech must be direct and immediate, and the harm inflicted must be nearly calamitous, as when the excited mob storms the house of the corn-dealer. Under either alternative, Mill may be read as treating free speech as an independent principle that imposes limits on society's authority to interfere with our liberty, limits greater than those imposed by the general harm-to-others principle.[2]

Although Mill did not fully identify freedom of speech as a principle independent of harm-to-others, in another context altogether — the market for goods and services — he explicitly acknowledged that harm to others is not always a sufficient basis for restraints on liberty. In the fifth and last chapter of *On Liberty,* "Applications," Mill acknowledged that in ordinary competitive activities, the person who wins out "reaps benefit from the loss of others" and that "trade is a social act" (pp. 156–57). Under the harm-to-others principle, therefore, restraints on trade would seem justified. But he denied or avoided that conclusion, and thereby gave life to what he referred to as "the so-called doctrine of Free Trade." He argued that restraints on trade are "wrong solely because they do not really produce the results which it is desired to produce by them" (p. 157).

In one respect, Mill justifies free trade somewhat differently than he does free speech. Whereas the reasoning underlying his defense of free speech — the fullest development of each individual — is primarily moral or humanistic, his defense of free trade appears largely pragmatic: restraints on trade are likely to be counterproductive. Notwithstanding this difference, however, the free trade principle operates in much the same fashion as the one guaranteeing free speech. Both invalidate restraints that otherwise might be justified under the harm-to-others principle.

Over the course of the twentieth century, free speech has become the property of lawyers more than of philosophers. The contours of this freedom have been crafted largely by courts, most notably the Supreme Court of the United States. Starting in the New Deal era, the Supreme Court became increasingly generous in protecting freedom of speech, and did so even as it sustained the government's regulatory authority in the face of generalized claims of individual liberty of the type that might be thought to be protected by Mill's harm-to-others principle. In legal terms, free speech triumphed as substantive due process collapsed. Freedom of speech was protected even though the Supreme Court acknowledged that, absent a free speech issue, there was sufficient basis for public authorities to regulate.

Substantive due process received its most dramatic and forceful statement in the late nineteenth and early twentieth centuries, when the Due Process Clause of the Fourteenth Amendment ("nor shall any state deprive any person of life, liberty, or property, without due process of law") was used to strike down legislation on the ground that it interfered with individual liberty. Sometimes, Mill's harm-to-others principle was invoked in support of this attack on legislation.[3] The most venerable due process ruling of this period was the Supreme Court's 1905 decision in *Lochner v. New York,* setting aside a New York law that established a sixty-hour ceiling on the work week in bakeries.[4] The Court reasoned that the statute was an unconstitutional infringement on individual liberty, specifically the freedom of employees and employers to enter into contracts determining work conditions.

During the New Deal, as the Court began to give real life to freedom of speech, it also repudiated *Lochner* and its progeny on the ground that legislation like the New York bakers rule furthered the general welfare.[5] Freedom of speech gained as substantive due process began to lose. This shift first became visible in the 1931 decision of *Near v. Minnesota,* in which the Supreme Court invoked principles of free speech to set aside a broad injunction that arguably served public purposes and thus could be understood as preventing harm to others.[6]

The injunction in question was aimed at a local newspaper (the *Saturday Press*) that had published a series of articles about crime in Minneapolis.

The series claimed that a Jewish gangster was in control of gambling and bootlegging in the city and accused law enforcement officers, particularly the chief of police, with dereliction of duty and maintaining a cozy relation with the gangster. Acting under a Minnesota statute that allowed abatement or suppression of "a malicious, scandalous and defamatory" newspaper, the state court issued an order against further publication of the *Saturday Press* or any other malicious, scandalous, and defamatory newspaper. The Supreme Court did not dispute the defamatory character of the articles that triggered the injunctive proceeding. The Court did not deny the harm that the articles may have caused public officials, but it invalidated the Minnesota statute and the order to which it gave rise on the ground that it was an unacceptable prior restraint on publication. "This," Chief Justice Hughes said of the mode of state regulation, "is of the essence of censorship."[7]

In the period since *Near v. Minnesota,* during which the juridical tradition of protecting speech has grown in scope and depth, Mill's passionate defense of free speech in *On Liberty* has often been invoked in support of the Court's stance. From one perspective, such references seem entirely appropriate because they are premised on the view that Mill advanced two distinct principles — freedom of speech and harm-to-others — and further that he allowed a greater freedom to speech than to action. The juridical distinction between substantive due process and freedom of speech may be said to have made explicit what was only implicit in Mill.

On the other hand, using Mill in this way to support the growing tradition of protecting free speech in the courts is misleading because it obscures the primarily personal, as opposed to political, character of the freedom that Mill sought. Although Mill's free speech and harm-to-others are distinct principles, in the sense that the former may prohibit social restraints that the latter tolerates, invoking one without regard to the other obscures the theoretical ground that they both share: a desire to promote the fullest development of each individual.

As I have said, personal development lies at the heart of *On Liberty.* Mill hoped for social progress but saw it as a natural, almost inevitable, consequence of the full development of the talent and personality of every individual. He defended both the harm-to-others principle and freedom of speech on this ground. Mill valued freedom of speech because it created the necessary environment in which conventional views about how to live one's life may be openly criticized and evaluated. Free discussion does not ensure that the individual knows what course to follow in charting his life, let alone that he will choose it. But without listening to diverse opinions and testing one's inclination through open discussion, the individual has little hope of ever gaining such understanding. Freedom of speech fosters individuality through the process of self-examination.

In the American constitutional domain, by contrast, freedom of speech is not like Mill's a philosophic principle but rather a rule of law articulated in the process of creating a structure of government. It thus has a more political than personal character. Although the United States Constitution makes some assumptions about human nature and may ultimately seek to ensure the fullest development of citizens and of society in general, its immediate purpose was more limited. The framers did not seek to create the conditions needed for the individual to flourish, nor did they ever declare such a right; rather, they sought to bring into being a government and endow it with democratic legitimacy. The framing of the Constitution was essentially an eighteenth-century enterprise of state building, and the First Amendment emerged as part of this specific enterprise. It seeks not to foster the kind of individuality Mill sought but rather to ensure the proper functioning of the system of governance that the Constitution establishes.

Whereas for Mill freedom of speech was essential for the full development of the individual personality, from the perspective of the Constitution freedom of speech is valued for the contribution it makes to the working of the democratic system. Freedom of speech fosters democracy through the process of public deliberation. Free and open debate may, as Mill argued, help individuals determine how they should live their lives, but from the viewpoint of the First Amendment that benefit is incidental to the pursuit of the more political end: providing citizens with the information and knowledge that they need in order to exercise their democratic prerogative effectively and wisely.[8] Free speech is needed to enable citizens to decide which of their beliefs are false and which are true — or, put differently, who is the best candidate or which policy is the soundest for the polity to pursue.

The censorship that Mill feared was primarily social. He raised his voice against the informal sanctions that an individual who spoke his mind might experience. The deliberate snub was of more concern than a prison sentence. Of course, Mill condemned state suppression, but he saw this threat to freedom as secondary. The state was nothing more than the agent of society and, in his world, less a threat to personal freedom than society itself. The tools at the state's disposal may well be harsher and more brutal than those available to social acquaintances or than the instruments of popular opinion, such as the newspapers, schools, and churches. But from freedom's perspective, social sanctions could restrain liberty as much as those imposed by law. Indeed, there was reason to be especially fearful of social sanctions, for they were likely to be more pervasive than those exercised by the state. Mill presented *On Liberty* as a protest against "the despotism of custom" (p. 134).

Mill discussed the idea of the social sanction largely in the context of the harm-to-others principle rather than the free speech principle. He was worried about the forces that compel people to live conventional lives. This feature of his discussion is not at all surprising—that people should be free to do whatever they wish provided that it does not harm others is, after all, the principal subject of *On Liberty*. Yet it does not distort Mill's purposes to extend the concept of social censorship to the domain of speech as well. A social sanction can be as much a restraint on the liberty to speak as it is on the freedom to act.

Mill was careful to distinguish the social sanction from the legitimate reactions on the part of others to what one does or professes. He was not calling for suppression of judgment—far from it. "We have a right," Mill insisted, "to act upon our unfavourable opinion of any one, not to the oppression of his individuality, but in the exercise of ours" (p. 141). We have a right to shun anyone of whom we have an unfavorable opinion, and even to caution others against that individual. He was for judgment, though against sanction. Mill acknowledged the hurtful consequence of judgment on the nonconforming individual, but used the idea of intentionality (with all its weaknesses) to mark the boundary between judgment and sanction or between legitimate and illegitimate response. He wrote, "In these various modes a person may suffer very severe penalties at the hands of others, for faults which directly concern only himself; but he suffers these penalties only in so far as they are the natural, and, as it were, the spontaneous consequences of the faults themselves, not because they are purposely inflicted on him for the sake of punishment" (p. 141).

In identifying social as opposed to formal legal sanctions as his principal concern, Mill's views may well reflect the historical milieu in which he found himself—the polite society of the mid-Victorian generation. His views also may have been influenced by his own particular life circumstances—specifically, his relationship with Harriet Taylor, a relationship, described more fully in David Bromwich's essay in this volume, that defied all conventions.[9] The two first met in 1830, when Harriet Taylor, wife of John Taylor, felt restless in her marriage and sought Mill's companionship. Over the next twenty years, Mill and Mrs. Taylor saw each other almost daily and sometimes even traveled together. All of this occurred with the acquiescence of John Taylor, who facilitated the relationship and remained on good terms with Mill, but it scandalized London society, and the two were forced to keep to themselves. Mr. Taylor died in 1849; Mill and Mrs.

Taylor observed the traditional two-year mourning period and married in 1851. Mrs. Taylor died the year before *On Liberty* was published, and with a moving inscription Mill dedicated to her this deeply felt protest against the tyranny of custom.

Aside from such historical contingencies, Mill's emphasis upon social, as opposed to state, censorship may follow from the value he ascribed to freedom in the process of individual self-development. Mill saw freedom of speech as a means of examining the validity of established conventions, and thus he needed to guard against the kind of sanctions that were most likely to be enlisted in the protection of those conventions. A theory of free expression that condemned state censorship while permitting social censorship would do little to provide the individual with the freedom needed to examine prevailing ethical doctrines and religious creeds or, more generally, to determine how best to live his life.

The political conception of free speech has a different orientation. Although it also values free and open debate — what Mill described as "the collision of adverse opinions" (p. 118) — the understanding it seeks to promote is not that of the individual but of the democratic citizen. The issue the citizen confronts is not how to live his life — Mill's concern — but how to make public officials responsive to his desires and needs. Accordingly, the animating concern is that public officials will manipulate or control citizens, and thus compromise the sovereignty of the people, by suppressing criticism of state policies or interfering with the choice of candidates for public office. No wonder, then, that the First Amendment of the United States Constitution is worded as a restraint on a branch of government: "Congress shall make no law abridging the freedom of speech, or of the press."

This line between political and personal freedom is not always drawn with pristine clarity. In fact, it has become blurred as judicial doctrine has expanded its recognition of the possible agents of censorship. In one well-known American case decided in the late 1940s, Justice Hugo Black maintained that the state had a constitutional duty to protect a street-corner speaker from the threat of violence by a heckler.[10] He voiced this view in dissent, but his position later became majority doctrine[11] and served as the foundation for a wide variety of arguments that sought to broaden our understanding of the forces, including some more social in nature, that might threaten free speech.

Black's rule denying the heckler a veto was applied, for example, to prevent shopping center owners from excluding political activists from their property, and to require broadcasters to air views that otherwise might be slighted.[12] Those who subscribed to this position were able to satisfy the technical legal requirement of "state action" — the fact that the First Amendment consists of a prohibition on a state agency — by treating state inaction as a form of action. The state abridges the freedom of speech, they argued, when it fails to protect a speaker from the heckler, or from the shopping center owner, or from the broadcaster.

As lawyers and courts voiced constitutional concern over the censorial practices of such private actors, one important practical distinction between political and personal freedom began to disappear. The law moved closer to Mill's position that restraints exercised by the state are the qualitative equivalent of those exercised by private agents. Indeed, in his elucidation of the harm-to-others principle, Mill explicitly acknowledged that in exceptional cases, inaction is a form of action (p. 82). Still, an important difference persists between Mill and the direction of constitution law I have described. A recognition that social censorship might be tantamount to state censorship when the state fails to curb private actors who threaten free speech is not the same as condemnation of social censorship outright. The constitutional focus remains on the state. Most forms of social censorship remain beyond the reach of the Constitution and courts.

The distinctive character of political, as opposed to personal, freedom is also reflected in the scope of expressive activities protected. Although the Supreme Court has been generous in its use of the First Amendment to protect speech, it has largely confined that protection to speech essentially public or political in nature, whereas Mill imposed no such limitation on the categories of speech protected by his principle. This difference between the two theories is illustrated by reference to the law of libel and one of the Supreme Court's most emphatic endorsements of the idea of political freedom: *New York Times v. Sullivan.*[13]

The *Sullivan* case arose during the civil rights era of the early 1960s, when a number of Alabama officials had brought a successful libel action in state court against the *New York Times* for carrying an advertisement in support of Martin Luther King, Jr., and his followers. Entitled "Heed Their Rising Voices," the advertisement charged local Alabama officials, in some instances falsely, with harassing civil rights activists. In an opinion rooted in the idea that "debate on public issues should be uninhibited, robust, and wide-open,"[14] the Supreme Court reversed the state court judgment and construed the First Amendment to require that in order to sustain a libel judgment for public officials, the allegedly false statements of fact in the advertisement had to have been made with "actual malice" — that is, with knowledge that they were false or with reckless disregard for their falsity.[15] A careless error was not enough.

The Justices were fully aware of the larger political significance of the *Sullivan* case and rested their decision on the premise that "the central meaning"[16] of the First Amendment was to prohibit criminal sedition laws that punished criticism of government. Accordingly, the Court has been reluctant to extend the forceful protection of speech manifest in *Sullivan* to matters unrelated to politics. In subsequent cases, for example, the Court ruled that a private party, as opposed to a public official, could recover for libel even if the speaker was merely careless about the falsity of his statement.[17] Actual malice is not required.

A plurality of the Justices also expressly declined to apply the actual malice requirement to allegedly defamatory statements that did not touch on politics but instead involved a false credit report on a business enterprise. Speaking for himself and for Justices Rehnquist and O'Connor, Justice Powell explained that "not all speech is of equal First Amendment importance." He went on to dispense with the actual malice requirement in that case because of "the reduced constitutional value of speech involving no matters of public concern."[18]

Sometimes a whole category of speech — for example, commercial advertising — has been placed beyond constitutional protection because it is not sufficiently related to politics. A commercial advertisement seeks to persuade its audience to buy some good or service, and thus arguably does not raise a matter of concern to the public or organized political community. As a result, the Supreme Court had traditionally placed commercial advertising beyond the protection of the First Amendment.[19]

The Court broke from this tradition in the mid-1970s, but did so in a case that had clear political and public ramifications. The advertising in question concerned the availability of abortions; it therefore implicated a claim of equal rights for women, and the principle affirmed in 1973 that allowed women to control their reproductive destinies. The advertisement appeared in 1971 in a Virginia newspaper. It urged those wanting an abortion to contact the Women's Pavilion in New York "for immediate placement in accredited hospitals and clinics at low cost." The state court held that the advertisement was a commercial one and thus was not protected by the First Amendment. The Supreme Court reversed.[20] The advertisement did more than simply propose a commercial transaction; it reported, for example, that abortions are now legal in New York, which was, in the Court's eyes, factual material of clear public interest. The Court also declared, however, that speech is not automatically stripped of its First Amendment protection merely because it proposes a commercial transaction or involves sales or solicitations.

Soon thereafter the Court extended its ruling and used the First Amendment to protect pharmacists who advertised the prices of prescription drugs.[21] Still later First Amendment protection was extended to other kinds of advertisements, including those intended to promote electricity sales.[22] By 1996 the doctrine had evolved to the point that the Supreme Court used the First Amendment to invalidate a Rhode Island statute that prohibited off-premise advertisements about the price of alcoholic beverages.[23] Two high-volume discount liquor retailers had brought the constitutional challenge to the law.

In all these case the Justices were sharply divided. Those who disfavored using the free speech guarantee of the First Amendment to protect advertising reminded their colleagues of the essentially political character of the guaranteed freedom. That group remained a minority, but even the prevailing majority scrutinized the regulations in question with considerably less force or enthusiasm than it applied to regulations of more political speech. This difference in the degree of scrutiny itself also reflects the distinction between political and personal conceptions of free speech.

Quite possibly, the majority's willingness to intervene at all may derive less from an appreciation for the value of commercial speech than from a desire to affirm the limits of state authority, or from a skepticism about the public purposes served by the ban on advertising, especially if the state was, as in the case of liquor, unwilling to ban or ration the advertised product or activity. In that respect, the majority may be less concerned with freedom of speech than with the old substantive due process, which, like Mill's harm-to-others principle, limits government interference with individual liberty regardless of whether speech is involved.

In this dispute over the protection afforded by the First Amendment to commercial advertising, Mill lends support to neither group. Because he embraced a personal conception of free speech, the argument of the dissenting bloc about the nonpolitical character of commercial advertising would not register with him at all. But he was also reluctant to defend the protection of commercial advertising under either his free speech or his harm-to-others principle. On this issue, Mill was fairly explicit.

Late in *On Liberty*, Mill considered the case of a person who gives advice, counsels, or instigates another to engage in an act that harms no one other than the person engaging in the action. He acknowledged that these communicative activities are social inasmuch as they may cause someone to harm himself, and thus are not strictly within the protection of his principle guaranteeing a freedom to each individual to do as he wishes provided it does not harm others. Mill concluded, however, that the reasons underlying that principle require that these actions be protected. Most notably, Mill did not invoke the free speech principle to reach that conclusion. He wrote, "If people must be allowed, in whatever concerns only themselves, to act as seems best to themselves at their own peril, they must equally be free to consult with one another about what is fit to be so done; to exchange opinions, and give and receive suggestions. Whatever it is permitted to do, it must be permitted to advise to do" (p. 160).

Yet Mill entertained the possibility of making an exception to this general rule in cases in which "the instigator derives a personal benefit from his advice" (p. 160) and society justifiably believes that the action might harm the person engaging in it. Mill was clear that the mere risk that liquor may be used intemperately is not a sufficient justification for a law prohibiting its sale, for every article bought or sold may be used in excess. Still, he insisted that we might well acknowledge that "the interest . . . of these dealers in promoting intemperance is a real evil, and justifies the State in imposing restrictions" (p. 162). With considerable disdain for the advertising industry, even as it existed in his time, Mill contemplated a world in which people decide to engage in some self-regarding action "on their own prompting, as free as possible from the arts of persons who stimulate their inclinations for interested purposes of their own" (p. 161).

For these reasons, it seems difficult to read Mill's general defense of individual liberty as yielding a protection of commercial advertising. The same is true for his free speech principle, because it is so personal in nature and linked to the process of self-examination. *On Liberty* lends no support to the prevailing majority on the United States Supreme Court regarding this issue.

On the other hand, Mill's idea of personal freedom might yield support for protecting yet another category of speech — art — that has proved problematic for a constitutional regime devoted primarily to the protection of speech relating to politics. To find support for protecting art in Mill, we would have to imagine a fusion of the political and the personal — or, expressed differently, to appreciate that political freedom may well depend on a healthy measure of personal freedom.

American society has not attempted to restrain artistic production in general, and for the most part has confined itself to regulating the sale or distribution of sexually provocative books, magazines, and films. Such censorship has been defended on the grounds that widespread dissemination of sexually explicit material increases the risk of violence against women and may disrupt the normal developmental pattern of children by exposing them to sexual themes at too early an age. More recently, some have defended the regulation of pornography on the ground that pornography transforms women into sexual objects and thereby contributes to their subordination.

In the 1930s and 1940s, as speech began to win expanded protection in the courts, state censorship of sexually explicit works of art was unrestrained, and even in such cases as *Near v. Minnesota* was assumed to be unquestionably valid. In the second half of the twentieth century, however, beginning most notably in the 1960s, the Supreme Court broke from this tradition and became increasingly hostile to censorship of works deemed to be obscene or pornographic. The Court has not denied the state power to censor sexually explicit literature and art altogether, but in the name of freedom of speech it has established tight bounds on this particular jurisdiction of the censor.

The result has been a body of decisions that seems much admired and secure as part of the constitutional tradition of protecting free speech.[24] It is hard to imagine our law without it. Starting, though, from the premise that the Constitution is devoted to protecting political speech, a question of how to justify these decisions naturally arises. Democracy may require periodic elections, competition among rival candidates, and free and open debate about the merits of each candidate and his performance in office. But does it also require that we be free to read *Lady Chatterley's Lover?*

Mill defended freedom of speech because it enables people to critically evaluate the social conventions that govern their lives. It permits us to question religious dogma and prevailing ethical tenets. Mill saw free speech as part of a process of self-examination and conceived of that process in essentially rationalistic terms. As such, he was less concerned with freedom of speech than with "freedom of discussion," "freedom of opinions," and "freedom of thought." Art that does not express an opinion but rather appeals to the imagination might find it hard to secure a place in such a rationalistic scheme. But once we acknowledge the importance of art in the development of the human personality — that it has a crucial role, for example, in challenging conventions by picturing the lives of others and helping us to experience them — we can understand that art, too, may claim protection under Mill's free speech principle. What would be protected under that principle is not the act of artistic creation — the expression of the artist — but rather the freedom to view and experience art, which, much like free and open debate about religion and ethics, is essential for the critical evaluation of conventions and thus for the full development of the human personality.

This adjustment to Mill's theory is rather minor and thus we can readily understand why a personal conception of freedom would protect art. To bring art within a free speech principle conceived in political terms, however, we must take yet another step and further acknowledge that healthy functioning of the democratic system depends upon an independent-minded, critical, and imaginative citizenry. In a word, a vibrant democracy requires the kind of individuality Mill sought to protect. Citizens not only need to hear arguments concerning public issues but must be capable of evaluating them. Democracy is a form of self-government and thus requires citizens capable of governing themselves.

In 1948 Alexander Meiklejohn, also a philosopher, published a series of lectures he had given earlier at the University of Chicago. The book was entitled *Free Speech and Its Relation to Self-Government.*[25] In it Meiklejohn set forth a theory of political freedom as bold and demanding as Mill's theory of personal freedom. Over the next several decades, as the Court curtailed the anticommunist crusade spearheaded by Senator Joseph McCarthy, protected civil rights activists, and limited the censorship of art, Meiklejohn's work became increasingly important as a key to understanding constitutional doctrine, including such cases as *New York Times v. Sullivan.*[26]

Meiklejohn saw that freedom of speech serves democracy by maintaining the vitality of public debate, but keenly understood that democracy's well-being also depends on the capacity of citizens to evaluate what they are being told. He grasped the connection between personal and political freedom. Accordingly, although Meiklejohn believed that the function of freedom of speech is to enhance the responsiveness of the political system to the needs and interests of citizens, he defended the Court's effort to curb the censorship of art on the ground that political freedom requires the independence of judgment and thus the freedom that Mill valued. As Meiklejohn put it in 1961, just as the Supreme Court's doctrine on obscenity was taking shape, "I believe, as a teacher, that the people do need novels and dramas and paintings and poems, 'because they will be called upon to vote.' "[27]

Some of those who, much like Meiklejohn, view the First Amendment as a protection of political freedom have rejected this line of reasoning. The most notable example is Robert Bork. In his now-famous 1971 article in the *Indiana Law Journal,* Bork argued that if the First Amendment required the protection of art on the theory that political freedom depends on personal freedom, it would lead to "an analogical stampede," with virtually no limit to the scope of the First Amendment.[28] Anything needed for creating an alert citizenry would be protected. Accordingly, Bork insisted upon a very tight connection between political content and speech properly protected under the First Amendment: only speech that was explicitly about government, such as criticizing a candidate or favoring one government policy over another, would be protected. Such a principle would, of course, leave most art outside the protection of the First Amendment and thus call into question the entire body of law through which Supreme Court doctrine has placed limits on the state's ability to censor sexually explicit literature and films.

The full implications of Bork's position became clear in 1987, when he was nominated to become a Justice of the Supreme Court. After a prolonged and acrimonious debate, the Senate rejected his nomination.[29] Many factors accounted for this decision, including partisan politics, as well as Bork's views on a number of issues unrelated to his stance on art. (In the same 1971 law review article, for example, Bork denounced the privacy doctrine that later led the Supreme Court to strike down statutes criminalizing abortion. Even before that, he argued against the enactment of the Civil Rights Act of 1964.) But Bork's criticism of the Supreme Court's decisions curbing the censorship of obscenity also played an important role in the opposition to him, and we thus might find in the Senate's rejection of his nomination, as well in the evolution and studied persistence of the judicial doctrine itself, a public recognition of the view that political freedom rests on the kind of personal freedom that lies at the heart of *On Liberty*. This is not to claim a priority of one type of freedom over the other on some metaphysical scale, but only to underscore their interdependence. Had Mill not written his essay under conditions of political freedom that he took for granted, he surely would have acknowledged that the personal freedom so essential to individuality depends upon freedom from state oppression.

An appreciation of the connections between political and personal freedom renders intelligible, indeed secure, an important branch of First Amendment doctrine. It does, however, leave two challenges for the constitutional lawyer. The first consists of the one Bork posed — of stopping the "analogical stampede" that may well follow from using the First Amendment to protect art. In the decades ahead, we need to formulate principles that distinguish art from the many activities, some of a communicative character, that may be essential for personal development but which, as an initial matter, seem to lie outside of the protection of the First Amendment. Work? Education? Dancing?

The second challenge arises from Mill's emphasis on social, as distinct from state, censorship, which, as I have said, derives from his personal conception of freedom. Recognizing the dependence of political freedom on personal freedom may have allowed the Supreme Court to be firm in its protection of art, but we should note that the Court has limited its protection of art to occasions when the threat of censorship comes from the state. For Mill, such protection against "the tyranny of the magistrate" would not have been enough; "there needs [to be] protection also," he said, "against the tyranny of the prevailing opinion and feeling" (p. 76).

Although by many measures the tyranny of custom that Mill feared has certainly diminished since the time that he wrote, the need persists to develop bold and independent citizens, and thus to defend and protect individuality. To meet this need, however, we will have to confront afresh the dilemma posed by the fact that the constitutional guarantee of free speech is a prohibition against censorship by the state. True, the doctrine denying the heckler a veto teaches how that limitation might be finessed as a purely technical matter, insofar as the inaction of the state may be characterized as a form of action. But the issue is more substantive than technical. The First Amendment can be extended in this way only on rare and exceptional occasions, still to be defined, for otherwise we would subvert the structure of the law itself, which derives from the political character of the freedom guaranteed therein.

NOTES

The author wishes to acknowledge the generous assistance of William Fick, Matthew Lindsay, and Tali Farimah Farhadian and the comments of Robert Post and Samuel Sheffler and the members of their seminar at the University of California, Berkeley.

1. The usage can be traced to Joel Feinberg, *Harm to Others* (New York, 1984).

2. For a recent review of the literature and an analysis coming to a similar conclusion, see Daniel Jacobson, "Mill on Liberty, Speech, and the Free Society," *Philosophy and Public Affairs* 29 (2000): 276–309.

3. For example, see *Mugler v. Kansas,* 123 U.S. 623, 632 (1887) (Statement of Counsel for Plaintiff). Asking the Court to overturn his client's conviction for violating state prohibition laws, counsel argued: "There has never been, and can never be, any question more important or more vital to the existence of civil liberty than that involved in this case. It is the question of the centuries, over and about which men have fought and suffered and

died, until out of the dark and dreary struggle the great truth has been established that 'the only freedom which deserves the name is that of pursuing our own good in our own way, so long as we do not attempt to deprive others, or impede their efforts to obtain it. Each is the proper guardian of his own health, whether bodily, mental, or spiritual. Mankind are greater gainers by suffering each other to live as seems good to themselves, than by compelling each to live as seems good to the rest.' John Stuart Mill 'On Liberty.' "

4. 198 U.S. 45 (1905).

5. *West Coast Hotel Co. v. Parrish,* 300 U.S. 379 (1937); *NLRB v. Jones and Laughlin Steel Corp.,* 301 U.S. 1 (1937). See generally Owen Fiss, *Troubled Beginnings of the Modern State, 1888–1910* (New York, 1993), pp. 7–8.

6. 283 U.S. 697 (1931).

7. 283 U.S. at 713.

8. See Owen Fiss, "The Idea of Political Freedom," in *Looking Back at Law's Century,* ed. Austin Sarat, Bryant Garth, and Robert A. Kagan (New York, 2002), pp. 35–58.

9. See Phyllis Rose, *Parallel Lives: Five Victorian Marriages* (New York, 1983), pp. 101–40.

10. *Feiner v. New York,* 340 U.S. 315 (1951) (Black, J., dissenting). Also see generally Harry Kalven, Jr., *The Negro and the First Amendment* (Chicago, 1966).

11. See, for example, *Reno v. ACLU,* 521 U.S. 844 (1997).

12. *Amalgamated Food Employers v. Logan Valley Plaza,* 391 U.S. 308 (1968); *Red Lion Broadcasting Co. v. FCC,* 395 U.S. 367 (1969). Also see generally Owen Fiss, "The Censorship of Television," in *Eternally Vigilant: Free Speech in the Modern Era,* ed. Lee C. Bollinger and Geoffrey Stone (Chicago, 2002), pp. 257–83.

13. 376 U.S. 254 (1964).

14. 376 U.S. at 270.

15. Justice Brennan, the author of the Court's opinion, quoted *On Liberty* in a footnote for support. The footnote reads: "Even a false statement may be deemed to make a valuable contribution to public debate, since it brings about 'the clearer perception and livelier impression of truth, produced by its collision with error.' " 376 U.S. at 279 n. 19.

16. 376 U.S. at 273.

17. *Gertz v. Robert Welch Inc.,* 418 U.S. 323 (1974).

18. *Dun & Bradstreet, Inc. v. Greenmoss Builders, Inc.,* 472 U.S. 749, 758, 761 (1985).

19. *Valentine v. Chrestensen,* 316 U.S. 52 (1942).

20. *Bigelow v. Virginia,* 421 U.S. 809 (1975).

21. *Virginia State Board of Pharmacy v. Virginia Citizens Consumer Council,* 425 U.S. 748 (1976).

22. *Central Hudson Gas v. Public Service Commission,* 447 U.S. 557 (1980).

23. *44 Liquormart v. Rhode Island,* 517 U.S. 484 (1996).

24. Harry Kalven, Jr., *A Worthy Tradition: Freedom of Speech in America,* ed. Jaime Kalven (New York, 1988), pp. 33–53.

25. Alexander Meiklejohn, *Free Speech and Its Relation to Self-Government* (New York, 1948), rpt. as Alexander Meiklejohn, *Political Freedom: The Constitutional Powers of the People* (Westport, Conn., 1965).

26. See, for example, William J. Brennan, Jr., "The Supreme Court and the Meiklejohn Interpretation of the First Amendment," *Harvard Law Review* 79 (1965): 1–20. As noted earlier, Justice Brennan wrote the majority opinion in *New York Times v. Sullivan.*

27. Alexander Meiklejohn, "The First Amendment Is an Absolute," *Supreme Court Review* (1961): 263 (quoting Harry Kalven, Jr., "Metaphysics of the Law of Obscenity," *1960 Supreme Court Review,* p. 16).

28. Robert H. Bork, "Neutral Principles and Some First Amendment Problems," *Indiana Law Journal* 47 (1971): 27.

29. Committee on the Judiciary, Nomination of Robert H. Bork to be an Associate Justice of the U.S. Supreme Court, *S. Executive Rep. No.* 100–7 (1987), *S. Hrg.* 100–1011 (1987).

On Liberty

A REVALUATION

RICHARD A. POSNER

On Liberty is the best, as well as the best-known, statement of what I consider to be my own political philosophy (using *political* in a very broad sense, given Mill's belief that public opinion is an even bigger threat to liberty than government is). I do not mean that it is the source of that philosophy. I became a libertarian in approximately Mill's sense before I read *On Liberty* for the first time about a decade ago, though I cannot deny the possibility of indirect influence. Nor do I mean to imply agreement with every particular of Mill's thesis, or even that I think it adequately argued in all respects or even fully consistent; none of these statements would be accurate either. But *On Liberty* is the most powerful, eloquent, and imaginative defense known to me of the libertarian principle, though the principle itself, as I shall point out, may not have been altogether clear in Mill's mind.

The principle is simple, though the application is often difficult: "The sole end for which mankind are warranted, individually or collectively, in interfering with the liberty of action of any of their number, is self-protection," that is, "to prevent harm to others" (p. 80). In other words, my rights end where your nose begins. Neither law (government regulation) nor morality (condemnation by public opinion) has any business with my "self-regarding" acts, only with my "other-regarding" acts — that is, acts that, like a punch in the nose, inflict temporal harm without consent or justification. (Unfortunately, this terminology has become somewhat obscure as a result of a shift in the connotation of *regarding*. We are likely today to think of *self-regarding* as meaning selfish and *other-regarding* as altruistic.) The qualification *temporal* is key. The harm must be tangible, secular, material — physical or financial, or, if emotional, focused and direct — rather than moral or spiritual. The line that separates what is the business of others from what is no one's business but one's own runs between slander and giving offense, between dynamiting a competitor's plant and competing with him by means of lower prices or better service or product quality, between rape and engaging in private consensual homosexual activities, between stopping a person from harming another and stopping him from harming himself, and, at its narrowest, between "offences against decency," such as drunkenness, committed in private and the same offenses committed in public (p. 160).

Mill's concept of liberty is thus intended to protect the individual from both well-meaning and hostile interferences with his autonomy. You are not to coerce him because you think you have a superior conception of how he should live (because, for example, you think that he has false consciousness or adaptive preferences or fails to worship the true God); and you are not to force him to abandon his opinions or behavior simply because you find them or it offensive. It is the antithesis of Robert Bork's thesis that "no activity that society thinks immoral is victimless. Knowledge that an activity is taking place is a harm to those who find it profoundly immoral." The modern Millian thus combines the antipaternalism and affection for the free market that constitute the ideology of the Republican Party with the tolerance of "deviant" personal behavior that is characteristic of the Democratic Party.

To explain and defend the principle of liberty, Mill's essay moves from freedom of thought to freedom of expression to freedom of action (liberty of conduct). The order is significant — and at first glance odd. Especially when viewed from a utilitarian standpoint, freedom of thought and freedom of expression are most naturally conceived of as just aspects of liberty of conduct (which is not to deny the expressive function of some conduct), or perhaps both freedom of expression and liberty of conduct are aspects of a more encompassing notion of liberty. Some libertarians chafe at the primacy that modern liberals accord to freedom of expression over economic freedom. That primacy is indeed one of the legacies of *On Liberty*. Mill, departing in the direction of Aristotle from the nonjudgmental "gratification" utilitarianism of Bentham ("pushpin is as good as poetry") and of Mill's father, thought that the right goal for human beings was not simple happiness or contentment but rather the fullest expression of our distinctive powers. These powers are mental in a broad sense that encompasses the artistic and ethical imagination as well as scientific and logical thought. They are essential to individuality as a project rather than as a given. For Mill, "to be an individual involves finding adequate language and imagery to bring forth and define the embryonic sense of who one actually is." Mill's concept of liberty is designed to create the social environment most conducive to fostering individuality in that sense.

Freedom of thought, and freedom to communicate one's thoughts to others, may seem so obviously conducive to the fullest expression of a person's distinctive powers as to require no elaboration. Yet one of the most interesting and distinctive points made in *On Liberty* is an argument for freedom of expression that is *not* intuitive. It is the fallibilist argument (a foreshadowing of arguments made by such later philosophers of science as Charles Sanders Peirce and Karl Popper, and by Oliver Wendell Holmes, Jr.) that the validity of a hypothesis cannot be determined without making the hypothesis run the gauntlet of hostile challenge: "The beliefs which we have most warrant for have no safeguard to rest on but a standing invitation to the whole world to prove them unfounded. If the challenge is not accepted, or is accepted and the attempt fails, we are far enough from certainty still; but we have done the best that the existing state of human reason admits of; we have neglected nothing that could give the truth a chance of reaching us. . . . This is the amount of certainty attainable by a fallible being, and this the sole way of attaining it" (p. 91).

Turning from intellectual liberty to liberty of conduct, Mill makes an argument that at first glance may seem to owe nothing to his distinctive version of utilitarianism: it is the economist's working assumption that people are better judges of their own self-interest than strangers are. Mill calls this the "strongest" argument against public interference with personal conduct (p. 146). It may seem purely prudential, the sort of argument any utilitarian, perhaps any sensible person, would make. But it is linked to Mill's particular concerns through the idea that "he who lets the world, or his own portion of it, choose his plan of life for him, has no need of any other faculty than the ape-like one of imitation. He who chooses his plan for himself, employs all his faculties" (p. 124). If other people are allowed to determine our choices of how to live, they are not really our choices, and we are not employing all our faculties.

Undergirding both freedom of expression and liberty of conduct is the idea that intellectual and social progress is impossible without experimentation, including, in the realm of conduct, "experiments in living" (p. 144), which in turn presuppose diversity of taste and outlook. What made "the European family of nations an improving, instead of a stationary portion of mankind" was "not any superior excellence in them . . . but their remarkable diversity of character and culture. Individuals, classes, nations, have been extremely unlike one another: they have struck out a great variety of paths, each leading to something valuable" (p. 136). If Mill appealed to diversity to provide the variation necessary for a process of selection to validate or refute social experiments, his argument would be Darwinian; but in the clause "each leading to something valuable" is implied a syncretic rather than selective concept of the enriching effect of cultural diversity. There is no sense that experiments in living produce adaptation to the social environment in the way that natural selection produces adaptation to the natural environment.

I mentioned the economic flavor of one of Mill's arguments for liberty of conduct. Mill was, of course, a distinguished economist as well as a distinguished philosopher, and it is natural to equate his conception of liberty of contract with the economics of laissez-faire. But it is erroneous, at least without careful qualification. As usually understood, laissez-faire in the economic sense of the term means that government is not to intervene in the market except to internalize externalities. The externalities can be positive (benefits) or negative (costs). National defense is an example of a positive externality; if I set up an antimissile defense in my backyard, it will benefit my neighbors as much as myself, and so national defense will be underproduced unless all are coerced to contribute to it. Pollution is an example of a negative externality. Because it is a cost not borne by the producer of the goods whose manufacture generates pollution as a by-product or by his customers, the government must force them to bear the cost if there is to be the economically optimal output of the goods. Properly speaking, the existence of an externality is a necessary rather than sufficient condition for government intervention, because the cost of that intervention must be considered, along with the actual and not merely the potential benefits. But that refinement is not important to my discussion.

Mill's conception of liberty of conduct was broader than the conventional economic conception that I have just outlined in several respects. It was broader first because it was intended to limit not only government interventions in self-regarding conduct (that is, conduct that does not produce external effects) but also the coercive operation of public opinion; indeed, Mill seems to have been more concerned about the coercive effect of public opinion than about governmental coercion. Mill's conception of liberty of conduct was also broader in excluding intangible externalities, notably offensiveness, from the domain of permissible infringements of liberty of contract. From an economic standpoint (though perhaps a superficial one, as I'll argue), there is no difference in principle between incurring higher laundry costs because of air pollution and being offended by knowing that people are blaspheming one's God, engaging in deviant sex acts, visiting prostitutes, or reading pornography. But Mill thought that while it was proper to express disapproval of such behavior, it was wrong for public opinion to condemn it as immoral, let alone for government to suppress it. "The individual is not accountable to society for his actions, in so far as these concern the interests of no person but himself" (p. 156). This is a startlingly narrow conception of morality. Moral duties to oneself are a conspicuous feature of many religious moral codes (thou shalt not commit suicide, be a glutton, masturbate). Moreover, Mill's concept of self-regarding conduct extends to consensual conduct between adults, the sort of thing that morality is commonly thought concerned in (for example, homosexual relations, fornication, gambling).

It is easy to relate the distinction Mill draws between temporal and moral externalities to his underlying concern with encouraging the fullest realization of mankind's potential. If people were prevented by the stigmatizing force of public condemnation, even though it was not backed up by legal sanctions, from engaging in "deviant" behavior, the necessary diversity of thought and action, the necessary experiments in living — diversity and experimentation necessary for both personal realization and social progress — would be stifled.

These two goals that Mill emphasizes, personal realization and social progress, are distinct but related. Insofar as the first rejects, while the second in its ordinary economic interpretation accepts, the givenness of the individual's preexisting desires, *On Liberty* may be thought to break sharply with the conventional economic conception of value. But that takes too static a view. Mill is surely right that progress in the most elementary economic sense (a rising standard of living, for example) requires that there be people who will "commence new practices" (p. 129). These are the people, he explains, who are genuine individualists in a sea of conformist mediocrity. It is through the project of self-realization of these geniuses that "new practices" come about which are then adopted by the ordinary people, to the latter's benefit. And so self-realization is the motor of social progress.

Most of Mill's other departures from a conventional economic model can also be understood and defended in economic terms, most easily in the case of education. *On Liberty* advocates universal education of children, at the cost of the state if the parents can't afford to pay for their children's education. Education facilitates a person's attaining his or her mental potential, but it also produces substantial positive externalities by increasing productivity and fostering political stability.

Even Mill's distinction, at first glance arbitrary from an economic standpoint, between temporal and moralistic externalities can be defended in economic terms. It introduces a dynamic element into the analysis of externalities that is missing from the orthodox economic version. (*Dynamic* here refers just to considering future as well as present consequences; its opposite is *static.*) Suppressing offensive conduct may be efficient in the short run, provided the costs in offensiveness outweigh the benefits to the offenders, but, for the sake of the long run, consideration must also be given to the benefits of allowing experiments with deviant modes of life. Incurring net costs of offense today may produce more than offsetting future benefits. If the benefits of social and intellectual experimentation are weighted heavily, as I would be inclined to do for the reasons given by Mill, and if the coercive effect of public opinion is believed to be substantial, Mill's conception of liberty of conduct becomes the economic optimum: the costs of offending people are outweighed by the long-term benefits from encouraging a degree of freedom and individuality that generate such costs as a by-product. But this is not to suggest that Mill himself would have thought that offensive behavior could properly be repressed if it happened not to create offsetting social benefits.

This analysis helps to answer one of the traditional objections to Mill's liberty principle, that it depends on a theory of people's interests which Mill does not supply. If I have an interest in being spared the mental suffering that I will experience if someone ridicules my religious beliefs, then the ridiculer is guilty of an other-regarding act and can be punished. Put more broadly, Mill fails to explain whether insult is a part of liberty or an infringement of right. But the answer is implicit in his analysis. The answer is that it depends on whether privileging some class of insults promotes social and economic progress by encouraging free thinking and experiments in living, or more precisely whether the long-term benefits from such a degree of liberty exceed the costs.

The answer is too general to be very helpful, however — which underscores the fact that I have thus far limited my discussion of liberty of conduct largely to the conceptual. Descent to the level of application brings a number of questionable features of Mill's analysis into view. I connect these in part to the character of *On Liberty* as a "public-intellectual work" rather than a philosophical treatise. A public intellectual in the sense in which I use the term is an intellectual who writes on public matters for the general educated public. Today, though not in Mill's era, he or she is likely to be an academic. Mill was a strong believer in as well as practitioner of the "higher journalism," which could serve as a pretty good description of most public-intellectual work today. Often the public intellectual is someone who has established a scholarly reputation that gives his or her public-intellectual work credibility and enables the advancement of ideas that would be rejected out of hand from someone who lacked such a reputation. And so it was in Mill's case. Although he was not an academic, he turned to public-intellectual work, most notably in *On Liberty* and *The Subjection of Women,* after establishing a sterling scholarly reputation with his treatises on logic and on economics. Successfully carrying this reputation to his public-intellectual work, Mill received a respectful though critical hearing for views that were radical and even heretical at the time and might have been dismissed as crackpot had he not been so respected for his scholarly contributions.

What marks *On Liberty* as a public-intellectual work is its brevity, concreteness, and lucidity. It is written for, and even today accessible to, the educated nonspecialist, something that cannot be said of even so distinguished a modern treatise of political philosophy as John Rawls's *A Theory of Justice.* These are great strengths. But *On Liberty* has also the weaknesses of its strengths. Mill did not escape the standard pitfalls of public-intellectual work. Mistaken prophecy, for one. He thought that Europe was being crushed by a spirit of conformity. "At present individuals are lost in the crowd" (p. 130). "The modern *régime* of public opinion is, in an unorganised form, what the Chinese educational and political systems are in an organised" form. Europe was "decidedly advancing towards the Chinese ideal of making all people alike" (p. 136). Mill thought that the spread of education, of communications, and of trade, and above all a trend toward greater social equality, were pushing Europe in that direction, seemingly inexorably (p. 137). We now realize that these trends undermine rather than promote conformity. People who are well informed, well traveled, affluent, socially mobile, urban, and not intimidated by their social betters are more likely to think for themselves than people cosseted in a web of local, traditional, and familial networks and hierarchies.

Mill was largely unworried about government's role in these (to him) ominous trends. He seems to have thought the days of governmental coercion of the citizenry largely over — another mistake — and that the real danger to be feared was the tyranny of public opinion. "It is desirable, in order to break through that tyranny, that people should be eccentric. . . . That so few now dare to be eccentric marks the chief danger of the time" (p. 131). This will strike Americans as odd, both because of their own tradition of nonconformism and because of the reputation of the English for cultivating eccentricity. Mill's reasoning, for what it's worth, is that law enforces only an outward conformity, whereas public opinion "leaves fewer means of escape, penetrating much more deeply into the details of life, and enslaving the soul itself" (p. 76). He seems to have thought that the possibility of being merely accused of immorality, even when no temporal sanction was attached, was a tremendous deterrent. That may be why he defined morality so narrowly that self-regarding acts, however distasteful, could not be labeled immoral.

The public opinion he particularly had in mind was belief in the tenets of Christianity. *On Liberty* fairly breathes hostility to organized Christianity, which he describes as "essentially a doctrine of passive obedience" (p. 115). His conception of morality implicitly rejects Christian doctrine, which is concerned with many of the practices that he considered self-regarding and, for that reason, placed outside the domain of morality altogether. He seems to have exaggerated Christianity's actual grip on English thought, but he may have had in mind something rather different — its hold over public rhetoric and the obstacle thus created to social experimentation. The distinction can be grasped by noting that an avowed atheist could not win a major election in the United States, even though most Americans are either casual or heterodox in their religious faith.

Also like much public-intellectual work, *On Liberty* is superficial, perhaps owing to its brevity in relation to the breadth of the ground that it covers. To call a work both great and superficial is a paradox easily dispelled. *On Liberty* is great because of the force and eloquence with which it expounds the libertarian position and because of the distinctive arguments that it makes in support of the position. It is superficial in its account of the scope, the limits, of the position. The most interesting questions about freedom of speech concern its limitations, which Mill does not discuss, apart from the obvious one that it is does not extend to incitements to crime. About libel and slander; about copyright; about sedition; about the theater — about all these he is silent, even though these were conspicuous examples of areas in which freedom of speech was limited in his society.

The most interesting questions about liberty of conduct also concern its limitations. Here Mill makes a number of arguments and proposals that are in tension with the principle that he is expounding, such as that voluntarily to enslave oneself is inconsistent with liberty of conduct, though we "enslave" ourselves every time we sign an employment contract; that suicide is also inconsistent with that liberty, though the decision whether to live or die would seem to be the ultimate self-regarding act; that while it is improper to interfere with Mormon polygamy in Utah, it is proper for England to refuse to recognize the validity of a polygamous marriage of Mormons who have come to England, let alone to permit English people to make such marriages, because polygamy is a form of female slavery even when desired by women; that the state should be free to prescribe safe working conditions for employees of private firms; and that people should be forbidden to marry unless they can show they have the financial means to support any children they may produce. Mill makes a very curious argument for taxing liquor: that because government has to raise revenue by means of taxation, it might as well tax goods of which "it deems the use, beyond some very moderate quantity, to be positively injurious" (p. 162). But to the extent that the tax deters the consumption of the good, the revenue raised by it will be reduced. Hence the fact that the government must tax does not justify a tax intended to interfere with people's self-regarding acts, as distinct from a revenue-maximizing tax that might have such an unintended side-effect.

I do not say that these and other interferences with liberty of conduct of which Mill approves can't be reconciled with Mill's ruling principles; but he makes no efforts, or only perfunctory and unpersuasive ones, to do so. Take the proposition that people should be forbidden to marry if they lack the means to support any children that the marriage may produce. Because the production of children is not a self-regarding act (children are not property), the proposition is not strictly inconsistent with this theory of liberty. But it makes one wonder whether the theory is libertarian enough, as it is difficult to imagine a more obnoxious interference with private conduct than requiring prospective spouses to prove their solvency to the state's satisfaction.

Mill's discussion of polygamy is particularly unsatisfactory. An emphatic supporter of equal rights for women, he might have been expected to argue that once women were liberated from the restrictions that law and custom imposed on them, the terms of the marriage would be the free choice of the marrying couple. Instead he said without qualification that polygamy was "a mere riveting of the chains of one half of the community" (p. 154). But if so, why would it be improper, as he believed, for the U.S. government to seek to extirpate the practice?

Mill stresses that a policy of noninterference with Mormon polygamy in Utah is proper only if people in Utah who don't want to live under a polygamous regime are free to leave. This point sits oddly with a modern sensibility. It implies that it was wrong for the Supreme Court (in its 1954 decision in *Brown v. Board of Education*) to outlaw public school segregation in the South, for blacks who didn't want their children to attend segregated schools could move to the North, where the public schools were not segregated (not officially, anyway, but the Court has never held purely de facto segregation to violate the Constitution). Segregation was a vestige and reminder of slavery, but remember that the fact polygamy was "a mere riveting of the chains of one half of the community" did not in Mill's view warrant government interference with it, as long as the people affected by it were free to leave.

The point is not that Mill, had he been living in 1954, would have approved of segregation any more than he approved of polygamy in 1859.

The point is that his theory would have required the U.S. government to allow segregated schools in the South, because southern blacks were free to move to the North if they didn't like southern customs. Millions did move to the North.

And speaking of schools, Mill failed to explore the tension between the principle of liberty and the notion that the overarching social goal is enabling people to exercise their rational faculties. That goal is the basis for his argument for universal education at no cost to the poor — but taxation is a form of coercion and thus a prima facie infringement of liberty, and in the case of education is not justified by the harm principle, for the inability of a person to finance his children's education will not ordinarily be the result of culpable conduct by the well-to-do. If failure to assist strangers is a form of doing harm to them (a very strained sense of harm), the principle of liberty disintegrates.

The largest objection to Mill's analysis, the one forcefully put by his early antagonist James Fitzjames Stephen, is that he considered people too unconnected. The objection exposes a deep tension in *On Liberty*. On the one hand, Mill thought people extraordinarily submissive to the force of public opinion, to the point where, as I have said, just being accused of immorality was likely to have the same coercive force as the law. On the other hand, he thought it feasible to dissuade them from condemning even deeply offensive behavior, such as gambling, drunkenness, and prostitution, if it caused them no direct physical or financial harm. This raises the question whether he had a consistent picture of human psychology. If people are imitative and conformist, the bad example provided by, say, drunkenness (even if private) might by encouraging public drunkenness lead to widespread "other-regarding" harms, such as, to take a modern example, drunken driving. To put this differently, if people are robustly individualistic, they are unlikely to be as swayed by public opinion as Mill thought, while if he is correct about their susceptibility to the pressure of public opinion, they may be incapable of responsibly exercising the broad liberties that he wanted conferred on them. But this is to treat the population as a uniform mass, and Mill may have thought, realistically, that what was wanted of the common man was not individuality but a tolerance for the eccentricity of an intellectual vanguard.

Notwithstanding the criticisms that I have been making, there is much more right than wrong with *On Liberty,* as we can see by contrasting its vision of social progress with that of Mill's contemporary critic Stephen. Stephen thought that people could not be kept in line unless government supported religion; specifically, law had to be founded on the moral doctrines of Christianity. He thought that the result of giving women equal rights with men would be "that women would become men's slaves and drudges, that they would be made to feel their weakness and to accept its consequences to the very utmost. Submission and protection are correlative. Withdraw the one and the other is lost, and force will assert itself a hundred times more harshly through the law of contract than ever it did through the law of status." He also thought it "a question . . . whether the enormous development of equality in America, the rapid production of an immense multitude of commonplace, self-satisfied, and essentially slight people is an exploit which the whole world need fall down [before] and worship."

Stephen was wrong in all these respects. Americans are not an "essentially slight people." Equal rights for women have not made women slaves and drudges compared with what they were before, although it has made some of them worse off. Above all, the "old time" religion that Stephen favored (he dismissed the Sermon on the Mount as "a pathetic overstatement of duties") has not proved necessary to maintain social order. Europe has lost the religion but retained the order.

In Mill and Stephen we have prototypes of the two main versions of what can loosely be called "modern conservatism" in contrast to "modern liberalism," which is to say welfare or egalitarian liberalism ("social democracy" would be the more apt term). One version of modern conservatism is social conservatism, a term that includes both the religious conservatism of a William Buckley and the neoconservatism of an Irving Kristol or a Norman Podhoretz. The other version is libertarianism — and *On Liberty* remains its bible. This is so even though a degree of welfarism is implicit in *On Liberty*. The undogmatic libertarianism of *On Liberty* may help close the gap between libertarianism and welfare liberalism by helping us to see the gap as the result of a disagreement not over principle but over the best policies for realizing the principle. Mill's goal was liberty, but he believed that the means to the goal included such measures of active government as the guaranty of universal education.

Mill's Liberty and the
Problem of Authority

JEAN BETHKE ELSHTAIN

I can still recall my reaction on reading radical feminist tomes in the 1970s that attacked liberalism and the vocabulary of liberal political thought, together with extant political regimes constituted by liberal principles. I, too, believed that there were many things wrong with "the System," but it was news to me that the whole thing was rotten: root, tree, and branch. What was rotten about it seemed to be encapsulated in *bourgeois liberalism,* with liberalism always preceded by the modifier that indicted it as the tool of a dominant class. Bourgeois liberalism was sometimes transmogrified into *patriarchal liberalism* or *liberal patriarchal capitalism.* In these designations, liberalism was proclaimed rhetorically to be a tool deployed by the dominant male or capitalist classes — a decoy to throw women off the track and to trap them in false consciousness as they embraced an anemic version of bourgeois right and lost sight of a transformative revolutionary consciousness.

I never quite understood what held this radical rhetoric together. It seemed less an analysis than an assault. The ire of many of my age-cohort against "the liberal establishment" often meant reserving the harshest invectives for "bourgeois liberals." When a bourgeois liberal pushed rights or economic justice or anything else, that advocacy was taken to task for having the sinister aim of giving the "oppressed" a few crumbs in order to keep the working class, or African Americans, or women, or somebody somewhere from revolting and overthrowing the whole system.

I had, and have, my own quarrels with the liberal tradition, but it is important to go on record as a critic who seeks to engage the liberal tradition and not to overthrow it, even assuming such a thing were possible. There is, of course, a real question just how accommodating liberalism can be and remain liberalism. There are so many liberalisms, and there is so much elasticity in central liberal categories — liberty, rights, freedom, equality (understood a certain way or ways), limited government, and the like — that extension, emendation, expansion, even restriction are always possibilities. But then what remains?

The liberalism that I endorse is one that urgently seeks balance between unacceptable extremes; that ranks freedom for individual persons as a good but holds that that freedom is limited in complex ways; that believes in rights first and foremost as immunities — ways to protect persons from the overreach of power — but also in a positive sense, as a way to promote some vision of human flourishing within, not in opposition to, community. This liberalism is aware of the ironies of history, the pervasiveness of moral conflict, and our inability to perfect either the human person or human societies but our responsibility, nonetheless, to see to it that the least harm is done to persons. Is this liberalism? Yes, insofar as, one way or another, all contemporary American political thinkers are liberals of one sort or another, given the way liberal categories course through the groundwater of our culture. But the vision in brief that I have just sketched bears little relationship to the austere liberalism enshrined in John Stuart Mill's classic essay *On Liberty*. Clearly, one can resist the fusion of Millianism and liberalism and go on to defend a more complex, less constricted liberalism than Mill musters. To this end, I will take up three problematic features of Mill's vision of liberty: his collapse of all authority into tyranny and domination; his epistemological muddle; and his thin view of the human person.

The Collapse of Authority into Tyranny

Mill is slippery with language, especially where his key categories are concerned. Let one example here at the outset stand for the whole. In *On Liberty*, Mill adumbrates his famous "harm" principle, which holds that actions that are entirely self-regarding are of no concern to anyone save the individual who acts. His "very simple principle" of liberty holds that no one's liberty can be restricted unless his actions harm, or threaten to harm, the interests of others. That this is by no means a simple claim is clear as Mill proceeds. What is self-regarding? What does it mean to prevent harm to another, the only legitimate reason for interfering with the liberty of action of anyone? When one tries to derive a coherent understanding of what is self-regarding and what is not, the "simple" principle escapes one's grasp. Mill offers at least nine definitions of a self-regarding act and what counts as a violation of the principle. He is by no means saying the same thing each time. To wit: a self-regarding act: (1) "merely concerns" oneself, (2) concerns only oneself, (3) concerns the interest of oneself, (4) affects oneself, (5) chiefly interests oneself. This means that one cannot act in ways that (6) "are prejudicial" to another, or (7) molest another, or (8) makes "a nuisance" of oneself, although one can (9) prevent harm.

Juggling core concepts and introducing caveats that appear rhetorically to be minor emendations but, in fact, constitute significant alterations of basic categories, are practices rather typical of Mill's conduct of argument in this essay. If anything approaches a sacred principle for Mill, it is that the individual is entirely *sovereign:* "Over himself, over his own body and mind, the individual is sovereign" (p. 81). But this does not apply to children, nor to "backward states of society in which the race itself may be considered as in its nonage" (p. 81). Wherever the [human] race is in its nonage, despotism is a legitimate mode of government — so long as the end of this despotic rule is "their improvement, and the means justified by actually effecting that end" (p. 81). However, liberty has *no* application if people are incapable of being improved; instead, there is obedience to "an Akbar or a Charlemagne" if the barbarians are "so fortunate as to find one." Mill's oppositions are harsh: *either* individualistic self-sovereignty *or* despotism. This sidesteps the question of how persons emerge out of what Mill calls "backward states of society" and, even more basically, what counts as backward. Presumably, there is a historical telos that presses in this direction, at least for the West and areas ruled "despotically" by the West until they reach politically adulthood.

So, in addition to Mill's fuzziness, I am concerned about the dubious clarity he attains on certain central questions by trafficking in stark antinomies, the most important being his insistence in the second paragraph of *On Liberty* that the "struggle between liberty and authority" is the primordial battle that liberty can and must win and is winning, at least among the most advanced and intelligent portions of the human race. Mill goes on to explore various derivations of the term *liberty;* but authority he simply collapses into power, and power walks hand-in-hand with tyranny. In light of this collapse, what happens to the issue of *political legitimacy,* to which the question of authority is inexorably linked? A primary distinction marked in Western political thought is the fissure between rule that is legitimate, that bears a defensible warrant, and rule that is illegitimate. In our lifetimes, we have witnessed the remarkable phenomenon of authoritarian regimes, having been stripped of their authority, their tyranny having been revealed and exposed, caving in and making way for constitutional orders newly authorized and hence legitimate in their right to govern. One thinks of President Vaclav Havel of the Czech (then Czechoslovakian) Republic proclaiming to his countrymen and countrywomen on his inauguration in 1990 as their elected president, "Your government, my people, is restored to you." Havel could never have made such a claim had he not been working with the distinction that Mill disdains — that between authority on the one hand and tyranny or despotism on the other.

In her famous essay "What Is Authority?" Hannah Arendt laments the modern tendency to perpetuate the mistake of conflating power, coercion, even violence with moral authority.[1] Mao did this most famously when he said, "Morality grows out of the barrel of a gun." No niceties about authority here. Arendt castigates Mao for this. What grows out of the barrel of a gun is violence, not that authentic power Arendt associates with authority. Arendt understood that being bound in particular ways — by law, by tradition, by the force of past example and experience — helps to guarantee frameworks for action and to sustain particular public spaces. The bound authority figure is never free to do just anything and to make it stick as legitimate. *That* is the illegitimate seizure of unbounded freedom to act of a king who, having become a tyrant, might be killed as a scourge to his people and a rebel against God — if one follows John of Salisbury's twelfth-century *Policraticus.*

The twentieth century knew altogether too many tyrants, whether Hitler, Stalin, or Pol Pot, who recognized the laws neither of God, nor of nature, nor of human decency (a "common sense," in Arendt's formulation), nor of rights, and made themselves laws unto themselves, hence enactors of capricious terror and violence. To see this sort of thing as one end of a continuum of authority is, for Arendt, to do violence to the truth. It is a political world constituted by authority that rejects despots as unfit to rule. Mill would certainly agree that despots are unfit to rule, save when a people is in its nonage. But he makes it more difficult — if one stays within the either/or he sets up — to establish criteria that help to distinguish the one, the despot, from the other, the legitimate representative, prime minister, president, or other figure. Perhaps what lies behind Mill's lack of subtlety is his assault against traditional religious authority — whether it inheres in Scripture or in religious leaders who are not elected but who can by no means be said to be in their positions of authority simply by virtue of arbitrariness or caprice or as emanations of the dark shadow of authoritarianism. That much is clear. But it seems to me that the logical extension of Mill's position is liberal monism.

By *liberal monism* I mean the view that all institutions internal to a democratic society must conform to a single principle of representation (roughly, one person one vote) and that a single standard can be applied to determine what counts as reason and deliberation. Mill's fusion of authority and tyranny is instructive in this regard. He associates tradition, or invocations of tradition, with a lack of enlightened reason (with superstition and a weak-kneed tendency to defer to authority), as well as a tendency to seek power rather than liberty.

His argument comes through most clearly in another of his classic essays, *The Subjection of Women*.[2] Here Mill helps to lay the basis for liberal monism by counterposing, in another of his famous either/ors, reason and instinct. Reason, he insists, "speaks in one voice" and that which is not reason is instinct, being "the worse rather than the better parts of human nature" (p. 18). He assumes a unity of moral and political beliefs among those individuals who are dominated by reason. His ideal is to attain an "apotheosis of Reason" and to reject utterly the "idolatry" of instinct, an idolatry "infinitely more degrading than any other, and the most pernicious of the false worships of the present day" (p. 18). Thus authority and the idolatry of instinct are on one side of a great divide, reason and liberty on the other.

The lack of nuance involved in posing power vs. liberty and reason vs. instinct implicates Mill in another muddle generated by his thinking on authority. For authority situates the question of power differently, adding nuance that is lost by conceiving of power as something people have or do not have in calculable degrees. Mill helped to set in motion the current tendency to see power hidden in the interstices of every moment, every exchange, every relationship. Authority, in this scheme of things, becomes a cynical ploy used by those who have power to pull the wool over the eyes of those who have none, claiming divine or popular legitimation as they do so. That there is some truth to this charge no one can doubt. But this is not and cannot be the whole truth, for it misses entirely the constitutive role of authority in creating and sustaining diverse relationships in various settings. You cannot sustain parent-child relationships, teacher-student relationships, pastor-communicant relationships, legislator-constituent relationships, and so on, without a complex sense of authority.

Admittedly, male-female relationships are a different case, presuming the coexistence of two adults, one of whom should not be deemed prima facie the lesser partner in an authority-constituted relationship. Mill's drive to confine this discussion to liberty vs. power, however, places women in an impossible bind. Here's how it works. Mill writes: "Where liberty cannot be hoped for, and power can, power becomes the grand object of human desire; those to whom others will not leave the undisturbed management of their own affairs, will compensate themselves, if they can, by meddling for their own purposes with the affairs of others. . . . The love of power and the love of liberty are in eternal antagonism. Where there is least liberty, the passion for power is the most ardent and unscrupulous."[3]

As one unravels the presumptions imbedded in this claim, something like the following emerges — and, remember, power is condemned in Mill's account: (1) if liberty is denied, power is pursued; (2) where there is least liberty, the urge for power is most forceful and least controllable; (3) women, confined to domesticity, turn the domestic arena into a field of force in which they play the unscrupulous game of private power over others; (4) if women received public liberty (not power), their quest for private power would cease, having lost its raison d'être. Does this make sense? In addition to the contestable presumptions concerning the opposition of power to liberty, there are hidden premises in Mill's argument that further undercut his case. These covert views have to do with male motivation. Mill here is inconsistent. He has already claimed that those individuals who have long held public liberty — males — continue to be driven by a desire for private power. Yet on his view concerning women and the vectors of power and liberty, the female drive for private power will cease once the arena of public liberty is achieved. One way or another, a quest for power is illegitimate, and, as Mill equates power to authority, it, too, goes out the window.

Yet women's resistance to second-class status and their historic fight for equity was, in large part, what the American social theorist and reformer Jane Addams called an ever-elusive quest for *auctoritas,* the right of the speaker to be make herself heard in a public arena.[4] Addams associated authority with a search for truths that might be taken as authoritative and contribute thereby to what, in her more soaring moments, she called the "cathedral of humanity." More down to earth, she associated the forcefulness of legitimate authority with the search for both morals and justice. In Mill's account, women are on a quest for liberty, but both power and authority are either problematic or even anathematized as standing in eternal opposition to liberty.

Mill is unwilling or unable to conjure with the possibility that authority and autonomy not only need not be put into opposition but might, instead, be mutually constitutive. Mill issues a clarion call for liberty that provides no intelligible account of how authority in a liberal society is to be exercised in a way that a Millian can defend. It is no surprise that citizens of the quintessential liberal society, the United States, are so quick on the trigger when it comes to claiming that someone is stifling them or threatening their "free expression" and at the same time so perplexed about authority and about the complexity of authority relationships. If we are to think seriously about authority, hence legitimacy, we will not find Mill to be much help; indeed, stuck with his either/ors, we will be driven to the unhappy implications of a liberal monist position.

That is why it is important at every turn to be reminded of just how complex authority is, involving everything from warrants for political rule to warrants for authorized interpretations and claims to truth. These question are part of a complex epistemological inquiry, and it is to this I next turn.

Epistemological Muddles

We are all familiar with Mill's argument that liberty of thought is the most important and fundamental right for human beings. Silencing an expression is evil because it deprives us of the opportunity to get to the truth.[5] Mill holds to a fallibilistic understanding of truth. So far, so good. The problem lies not in his insistence that one can never claim the whole truth, good for all time and never subject to emendation. Anyone who understands the limits of human reason understands that. The problem lies elsewhere — in Mill's presumption that reason, to be reason, always moves one direction, away from anything labeled *tradition* and toward everything labeled *reason*. Tautologically, reason is what is reasonable. Reason, remember, speaks in one voice for Mill.

Truth, for Mill, emerges through a free play of opinion: it is consensual, always open to correction. Mill is optimistic that truth will win in a collision with error — *if* the proper conditions for the full airing of opinion pertain:

> If all mankind minus one, were of one opinion, and only one person were of the contrary opinion, mankind would be no more justified in silencing that one person, than he, if he had the power, would be justified in silencing mankind. Were an opinion a personal possession of no value except to the owner; if to be obstructed in the enjoyment of it were simply a private injury, it would make some difference whether the injury was inflicted only on a few persons or on many. But the peculiar evil of silencing the expression of an opinion is, that it is robbing the human race; posterity as well as the existing generation; those who dissent from the opinion, still more than those who hold it. If the opinion is right, they are deprived of the opportunity of exchanging error for truth: if wrong, they lose, what is almost as great a benefit, the clearer perception and livelier impression of truth, produced by its collision with error. (p. 87)

Here is the problem: Mill assumes that those who would suppress a view or deny it full airing must be assuming their own infallibility; it is, he says, to proclaim that "*their* certainty is the same thing as *absolute* certainty" (p. 88). But does this follow? Surely there are opinions that simply cannot be taken seriously. One may not deny them an airing, but it is altogether too much to ask that one "consider" each and every view seriously and assume that each expression of opinion, at least at its first voicing, is rationally equal to every other. Any appeal to tradition is ruled out and thus cannot even enter the lists as part of the contestation. The only way to judge a true opinion is to look at what is reached after a full opportunity to challenge and to defend opinions has taken place. Even the most obnoxious views should have a hearing. Given the long story of what Mill calls "falsehood" before his own time — intolerance, bad doctrines — his narrative aims to protect people from error even as it blasts what he considers intolerant ideas of true and false. Mill will admit only certain sorts of rationalized accounts to justify an opinion.

What this means is that over time the number of "doctrines which are no longer disputed or doubted will be constantly on the increase: and the well-being of mankind may almost be measured by the number and gravity of the truths which have reached the point of being uncontested. The cessation, on one question after another, of serious controversy, is one of the necessary incidents of the consolidation of opinion; a consolidation as salutary in the case of true opinions, as it is dangerous and noxious when the opinions are erroneous" (p. 110). So progress is measured by the consolidation of true opinion, which means a narrowing of the range of that which is contested. But as the process by which humankind has arrived at truths up to the point (still unachieved) of absolute freedom of opinion, has been flawed and even noxious, no truth whose origin lies in a past that was tainted can be appealed to as part of an authentic process of rational contestation.

Even if desirable, this seems an impossible criterion to meet, especially in light of the fact that Mill further claims that it is self-evident that there are ninety-nine persons "totally incapable of judging of it [the history of opinion and process of discerning truth] for one who is capable" (p. 90). It is a reasonable implication that those who have a superior power of discernment may discount the views of those whose track record seems lamentable in their eyes, perhaps because they are making moves in the process Mill has already declared illegitimate by appealing to past example or tradition. But how, in actual practice, do we counterpose one opinion to another without first settling the usefulness of an opinion; and that, as Mill puts it, is itself a "matter of opinion," as disputable as any other (p. 92). In practice this yields a radical skepticism that is skeptical about everything save itself. Mill would resist this conclusion by putting opinion to the test in light of his overarching telos of what counts as humankind's improvement: the increase of liberty over authority/power.[6]

It is important to note as well that all moral reasoning not utilitarian in nature — romanticism, myth, and religion, especially — are illegitimate on Mill's view. Whatever may be good or beneficent lurking in such appeals could, he claims, be absorbed without remainder into his empiricist, procedural method of arriving at provisional truths. A true opinion, to be true, cannot abide in the mind as a matter of prejudgment: "This is not the way in which truth ought to be held by a rational being" (p. 103). Otherwise truth would be just one superstition among others.

There are several rejoinders to Mill's epistemological claims. One is that there are, in the words of James Fitzjames Stephen, "innumerable propositions on which a man may have a rational assurance that he is right whether others are or are not at liberty to contradict him, and that although he does not claim infallibility. . . . There are plenty of reasons for not forbidding people to deny the existence of London Bridge and the river Thames, but the fear that the proof of those propositions would be weakened or that the person making the law would claim infallibility is not among the number."[7]

Freud, too, approaches the matter of truth in probabilistic terms, and to do justice to his point a long quotation is necessary:

Let us suppose that the question at issue is the constitution of the interior of the earth. We have, as you are aware, no certain knowledge about it. We suspect that it consists of heavy metals in an incandescent state. Then let us imagine that someone puts forward an assertion that the interior of the earth consists of water saturated with carbonic acid — that is to say, with a kind of soda-water. We shall no doubt say that this is most improbable, that it contradicts all our expectations and pays no attention to the known facts which have led us to adopt the metal hypothesis. Nevertheless it is not inconceivable; if someone were to show us a way of testing the soda-water hypothesis we should follow it without objecting. But suppose now that someone else comes along and seriously asserts that the core of the earth consists of jam. Our reaction to this will be quite different. We shall tell ourselves that jam does not occur in nature, that it is a product of human cooking, that, moreover, the existence of this material presupposes the presence of fruit-trees and their fruit, and that we cannot see how we can locate vegetation and human cookery in the interior of the earth. The result of these intellectual objections will be a switching of our interest: instead of starting upon an investigation of whether the core of the earth really consists of jam, we shall ask ourselves what sort of person this must be who can arrive at such a notion, or at most we shall ask him where he got it from. The unlucky inventor of the jam theory will be very much insulted and will complain that we are refusing to make an objective investigation of his assertion on the ground of a pretendly scientific prejudice. But this will be of no help to him. *We perceive that prejudices are not always to be reprobated, but that they are sometimes justified and expedient because they save us useless labour. In fact they are only conclusions based on an analogy with other well-founded judgements.*[8]

Freud's defense of prejudices might be taken as analogous to Mill's view of the consolidation of truthful opinions, hence not applicable as a rejoinder to Mill at all. But Mill has posed the problem of truth as one of absolute freedom of opinion necessary to the procedure — the only procedure — for arriving at truth. Mill recognizes the bind but has no way out of it — especially not if one puts into the mix his fretting about the tyranny of the majority. It is not clear how his consolidation of truths, hence the diminution of the number of matters open to serious dispute, comports with his assault on society's overweening and overbearing drive against liberty for the individual. He suggests that ways be found to simulate the contestation of opinion even after a truth has been settled because otherwise the matter might settle into a prejudice — a pre-judgment — and that is forbidden or illegitimate for Mill.

Another formidable defender of taking certain views on trust as part of an authoritative tradition is Alexis de Tocqueville, a thinker much admired by Mill. A central feature of Tocqueville's worst-case scenario about the prospects of the American democracy is that democratic authority cannot be sustained by a radically skeptical epistemology. For Tocqueville religious belief "was inseparable from free government and free public life because it was the channel of a self-imposed moral restraint that shaped and, in so doing, liberated the individual for participation in the republic."[9] Tocqueville, in other words, puts together that which Mill drives apart — liberty *and* authority; truth *and* prejudgments. He worries that the collapse of religious authority necessary to sustain those institutions that engage in ethical formation may foment in turn a political crisis. Over time, the horizon of democracy recedes as complex authoritative traditions erode or collapse. People refuse to take anything on trust. Why is this a problem? Because, in Tocqueville's words, "If a man had to prove for himself all the truths of which he makes use every day, he would never come to an end of it. He would wear himself out proving preliminary points and make no progress. . . . Some beliefs must be accepted without discussion so that it is possible to go deeply into a few selected ones for examination. It is true that any man accepting any opinion on trust from another puts his mind in bondage. But it is a salutary bondage, which allows him to make good use of freedom. So somewhere and somehow authority is always bound to play a part in intellectual and moral life." [10]

Mill could never speak of salutary bondage, by which, of course, Tocqueville means not unthinking enthrallment but the acceptance on the basis of well-earned trust of certain perduring truths. Even if one tries to downplay Mill's simultaneous insistence that all opinions have the same right to a public airing and that 99 percent of people haven't the where-withal to engage in truth-finding disputation, it is more difficult to square the circle when it comes to his refusal to grant any warrant to views derived from tradition. This is especially so, for Mill, if the truth claims involved are associated with an authoritative warrant of some sort, which means, for Mill that the origin of the claim lies in the "odious" source of illegitimate power.

Mill offers us no way to adjudicate true from false opinion save to assess its utility. But assessments of utility are always from a point of view — utility is not an impersonal yardstick, an epistemological deus ex machina dropping down into the scene. And that point of view, to be consistent with Mill's argument, is itself essentially contested. We are, it seems, doomed to wear ourselves out in refusing to take certain preliminaries for granted. Unless — and it is a rather big unless — the views mesh with Mill's precon-ditions for authentic contestation, which means authority can play no role in determining the truth of the matter. This leads me to my final colloquy with Mill, regarding his understanding of the human person.

Mill's Thin Subject

Mill's subject is sovereign. We are the sole judges of our own good. There are all sorts of ways Mill finds to interfere with individual liberty that, he insists, do not contravene his basic principle: for example, imposing taxes on and restricting drinking houses, because infringement on good manners is actionable (p. 152). He also entertains the idea of forbidding marriage to those who cannot demonstrate that they have the means of supporting a family, a rule that, in practice, would prohibit marriage to persons falling below a certain socioeconomic level (p. 169). But my primary concern here is Mill's general understanding of the human person. Twentieth-century philosophy is, in part, a flight from and subsequent rediscovery of, what at one time was called human nature but is more compellingly referred to as *anthropos-logos,* knowledge of that creature we call human.

Consigned to the graveyard of pernicious appeals, for Mill, is nature. Nature joins company with authority, tradition, instinct. Indeed, he often equates nature and instinct. Mill denies that "nature participates in a human moral order."[11] Nature for Mill stands in opposition to rationally justified morality. Nature is animalistic desire. This animalistic desire is opposed to a relationship of "perfect equality" between men and women. Reason and Instinct (hypostasized in capitals by Mill) are eternally counterposed. Instinct embodies the worst of us. It is an idolatry he characterizes as more "degrading" than any other; indeed, the "most pernicious" in a list of "false worships." To back up this dire conclusion, Mill paints an unflattering portrait of his contemporaries, male and female. Both have succumbed to sensation with its concomitant rule of force.[12] A split between reason and desire (desire representing nature unvarnished) undergirds Mill's argument. The triumph of reason alone, with desire brought to heel, guarantees that human relations will be uplifted to the sphere of understanding and drained of the disintegrating and degenerative force of passion. This is part of the increasing rationalization of human society.[13]

The full force of Mill's defense of reason severed from desire becomes intelligible only if one appreciates Mill's overall repudiation of desire as an enslavement to passions: obedience to the body, not the mind. Lowly lust is one problem that flows from bodily desires insofar as they are not rationalized. But there is also a perverting "desire of power" displayed by women who, lacking public and civic identity, seek manipulative power in the private realm, even as men hold public power, something Mill also criticizes with great severity. Why men, who have public liberty, have not been cleansed of the distortions of power, is unclear. Presumably the answer lies in the fact that their liberty turns on their power — over women. Even as men "cling to the theories that justify their passions," women cleave to the passions that justify their power. Men want not only women's obedience but their sentiments. The woman must be not only a slave but an agreeable and pliant one at that. As a result, her degradation is the "lowest" possible, for she is "the instrument of an animal function contrary to her inclinations."[14] Presumably, this means that women are less desiring creatures than men; that sexuality is something largely forced upon women by men. Given Mill's devotion to rigid bifurcations, passion is bad even as reason is good. One gets no sense from Mill that desires themselves are laced with complex thought and emotion, and not just an automatic excrescence in response to a crude stimulus.

At the same time as he launches this brief against slavish and enslaving passions, Mill extols what the family of an ideal future is to become: a school of equality. He presses this notion without much discussion of love and familial attachment. He uses the word *love* in a positive sense once in his entire essay on *The Subjection of Women*. The other two uses point to a degradation — woman's yearning "to be loved" and her "loving submission." Eschewing appeals to love as a loaded term and a trap, his picture of an ideal future is curiously arid. Mill cannot permit any appeal to "intense attachments," for these are used only to justify slavery of one sort or another. Attachments in his rational future society are curiously flattened. Mill here cuts against the grain of our most basic moral intuitions, namely that "intense attachments" and an appeal to such may be the basis of the moral life rather than a degradation. He not only lifts reason or mind up as the better part of human nature, he severs reason and mind from nature. Just as an appeal to tradition is illegitimate — and this would, presumably, include an appeal to a long tradition of argument (like that of natural law) — so is an appeal to powerful emotion and intense attachment. We see that Mill's arguments concerning warrants for truth claims are internally connected to his bleak anthropology. We wind up with a variation on the theme of men-as-brutes and women-as-victims.[15]

An "original" law of the jungle pertains in relations between the sexes because this law refuses to proclaim itself as originating in sheer force absent any intelligible embodied imperative. Were the "true character" of male-female relations to be proclaimed, it would be seen immediately that these are incompatible with modern civilization. A Millian version of an argument from false consciousness surfaces, insofar as women are men's "willing slaves," active colluders in their own "degradation." The *only* way to change this degrading situation is to adopt "in the family the same moral rule which is adapted to the normal constitution of human society." Women must be admitted "to all the functions and occupations hitherto retained as the monopoly of the stronger sex," although how they are to do this and not fall into the degradations associated with wielding such power is unclear.[16] Only under the terms of perfect equality will woman's true nature (here Mill slips and appeals to nature, but it is a nature vetted by full rationality, hence legitimate) be revealed. Cleansed of brute instinct, cleansed of passion and what now passes for love, an alternative and rather impersonal sensibility will emerge as the basis of intimate relationships.

The mistake made by Mill and inherited by one powerful strain in liberalism is to assume that, stripped of the passion and complexity of particular ties and loyalties, a more general and sustainable order of benevolence is made possible. There is no evidence at all that this is the case. That we are necessarily prejudiced in favor of our own — our own lovers, mates, children, friends — is a constant and consistent feature of all known human societies, past and present. That we are capable of reaching out to others in ties of friendship and concern is also undeniably true. This requires moral formation, our growth into ethical selves, and such a transformation turns on authoritative relationships between parents and children, teachers and learners. Mill's analysis lacks a recognition of the deep human, and moral, emotions at work in our most intimate relationships. What begins as passion, we may hope will prove susceptible to ethical and moral restraint. But it is futile to try to drain the passion from it. We simply know too much about the potent interaction of body and mind to claim that you could alter the interactions of complex physiological responses and a body-subject; that you could leapfrog over the "particular," as it were, in favor of a generalized "universal" norm that is then applied to all particular relationships.

Mill's anthropology is a dualism of a particular kind. Its origins seem Manichaean. Within Manichaeanism, matter, including the human body, is polluted by definition. That which is pure is spirit. Only one who distances himself or herself from the pollution of matter is uplifted to a higher realm. The philosopher James Eli Adams has observed that Mill's personification of Nature as a horror and a tyranny may account for his pessimistic assessment of human moral psychology.[17] Whatever its source, Mill's picture of the almost entirely degraded present condition of the vast majority of humankind that will make way for a future condition in which a small elite has battled the brutality of natural forces and emerged victorious is finally unconvincing and would, in practice, be undemocratic insofar as it involves restricting marriage to a certain class. His future condition is also impossible to attain insofar as his ideal for a marriage cleansed of lowly desire is of "two persons of cultivated faculties, *identical in opinions and purposes,* between whom there exists the best kind of equality, similarity of powers and capacities with reciprocal superiority in them. . . . This, and this only, is the ideal of marriage."[18] We come full circle. His marriage ideal, flowing from his anthropological presuppositions, is here wedded to his epistemological conviction that a rational and egalitarian marriage requires that husband and wife have identical opinions and purposes, but that these be arrived at through robust self-sovereignty. His liberal monism is here displayed once again. It is for that reason that I conclude as I began in the conviction that a compelling liberalism cannot be a Millian liberalism taken neat.

NOTES

1. Hannah Arendt, "What Is Authority?" in *Between Past and Future* (Baltimore, 1980).

2. *The Subjection of Women* (Greenwich, Conn., 1970). Here I rely in part on portions of my discussion of Mill in my *Public Man, Private Woman: Women in Social and Political Thought* (Princeton, 1981; 2d ed., 1993), pp. 132–46.

3. *Subjection of Women,* pp. 123–24.

4. Jane Addams, "Cassandra," valedictory, *Rockford Seminary Magazine* (July 1881). She used the Latin — somewhat incorrectly, calling it *authoritas.* On the right of a speaker to be heard, the ancient meaning of freedom of speech associated with auctoritas, see Peter Brown's monograph on antique rhetoric, *Power and Persuasion in Late Antiquity: Towards a Christian Empire* (Madison, Wisc., 1992).

5. Truth, of course, contributes to utility. I am not going to discuss utilitarianism here, but I agree in general with Bernard Williams that utilitarianism, in its paradigmatic form, is a great simple-mindedness with "too few thoughts and feelings to match the world as it really is." See J. J. C. Smart and Bernard Williams, *Utilitarianism: For and Against* (Cambridge, 1973), p. 95.

6. I cannot here elaborate on another epistemological matter, namely Mill's romantic view of the lone possessor of truth who might be stymied if all views are not assured an equal hearing. It may be the case that certain scientific truths begin as lonely possessions — although even that is doubtful. But I submit that no political truth can ever be conjured up in isolation through the ratiocination of a single, solitary self. Mill's argument holds that it is only after submitting the view which "for all we know" may be true to the crucible of contestation that the view will be known as true or false. The dialogical nature of truth, however, goes all the way down to its formulation in the first place.

7. James Fitzjames Stephen, *Liberty, Equality, Fraternity* (Chicago, 1991 [1873]), p. 76.

8. Sigmund Freud, "Dreams and Occultism," chapter 30 of *New Introductory Lectures on Psychoanalysis,* in *The Standard Edition of the Complete Psychological Works of Sigmund Freud,* vol. 22, trans. and ed. James Strachey (London, 1964), p. 32 [emphasis added].

9. George Armstrong Kelly, *Politics and Religious Consciousness in America* (New Brunswick, N.J., 1974), p. 103.

10. Alexis de Tocqueville, *Democracy in America* (New York, 1988 [1835]), p. 434.

11. James Eli Adams, "Philosophical Forgetfulness: John Stuart Mill's 'Nature,' " *Journal of the History of Ideas* 53 (1992): 437–54, quotation at 438.

12. *Subjection of Women,* p. 22.

13. Here I draw upon both *Public Man, Private Woman* and an essay entitled, "What's Love Got to Do With It?" *Salmagundi,* nos. 114–15 (Spring–Summer 1997), pp. 166–81.

14. *Subjection of Women,* pp. 27, 49.

15. See *Subjection of Women,* pp. 21–22, 85.

16. Ibid., pp. 64, 68.

17. Adams, "Philosophical Forgetfulness," pp. 445–46.

18. *Subjection of Women,* p. 121 [emphasis added].

Mill as a Critic of Culture and Society

JEREMY WALDRON

Suppose we take seriously Mill's insistence that *On Liberty* should be understood as an argument about social and cultural coercion rather than as an argument about the limits of the criminal law. I don't think that it is necessary to spend much time establishing the *fact* of this insistence. It forms much of the argument of Chapter I of the essay, a chapter in which Mill traces the dominant source of tyranny in society from rule by the few, through democratic rule by the many (the "tyranny of the majority"), to the informal tyranny of society.[1] The whole argument in *On Liberty* proceeds from the premise that the tyranny of society is not necessarily, and indeed nowadays not even commonly, exercised through legal or political channels:

> When society itself is the tyrant — society collectively over the separate individuals who compose it — its means of tyrannizing are not restricted to the acts which it may do by the hands of its political functionaries. Society can and does execute its own mandates: and if it issues wrong mandates instead of right, or any mandates at all in things with which it ought not to meddle, it practices a social tyranny more formidable than many kinds of political oppression, since, though not usually upheld by such extreme penalties, it leaves fewer means of escape, penetrating much more deeply into the details of life, and enslaving the soul itself. (p. 76)

With this kind of oppression in its sights, the aim of *On Liberty* is to raise "a strong barrier of moral conviction" against "the engines of moral repression" (p. 83) that threaten individuality in the modern world. "There is," Mill writes, "a limit to the legitimate interference of collective *opinion* with individual independence; and to find that limit, and maintain it against encroachment, is as indispensable to a good condition of human affairs, as protection against political despotism" (p. 76).

And suppose we take this seriously, not just by conceding that Mill's argument applies to social pressure as well as legal coercion, but by acknowledging that social pressure is the main topic, and not in any way a derivative or secondary application, of the argument in the book. Law is actually the secondary subject matter of *On Liberty*. The laws that worry Mill—provisions prohibiting atheists from giving evidence in court (p. 98) and legal rules governing the committal of English eccentrics to mental institutions (p. 132)—are no more than "the rags and remnants of persecution" (p. 99): "For a long time past, the chief mischief of the legal penalties is that they strengthen the social stigma. It is that stigma which is really effective, and so effective is it, that the profession of opinions which are under the ban of society is much less common in England, than is, in many other countries, the avowal of those which incur risk of judicial punishment" (p. 100).

Suppose we take all this seriously. How different will our understanding of the argument of *On Liberty* be as a result? I think the approach that I am suggesting will enrich our understanding of Mill. It means that we can present him as a participant in the great movements of nineteenth-century social theory rather than as a forerunner of our own rather flat and formalistic debates about liberalism in twentieth-century political philosophy. Mill as analytic forerunner is often criticized for being sociologically naive, and those who follow in his footsteps are sometimes accused of being unhealthily preoccupied with laws and constitutions, and unduly neglectful of social structure and the grounds of social change. It is often thought that they ought to be compelled to read books by such sociological theorists as Alexis de Tocqueville, Karl Marx, Friedrich Engels, Emile Durkheim, and Max Weber as a corrective.[2] Well, if we read Mill in the way that I am suggesting, we can begin to see him as engaged in the same enterprise as Tocqueville, Marx, Engels, Durkheim, and Weber.

All these writers were concerned about the emergence of a new phenomenon in human affairs — not a new kind of state, but a new kind of society. They watched with fascination the emergence of mass society and the emancipation of public opinion that attended urbanization, industrialization, bureaucracy, and democratization. What they saw was a source of both exhilaration and dismay. They could see the progress that was being made in material conditions, and in respect of social equality, too. At the same time, they were alarmed by the way mass opinion tended to flatten out all differences and impose a new sort of uniformity, a new sort of dullness and mean-spiritedness in human affairs.[3] Modern Western society, they knew, was progressive; but they had no reason to suppose that its progressiveness would endure, that it would not slip gently into a flat, stationary, or degenerative condition, characteristic — in many of their writings — of China after its most progressive phase.[4] Theirs were not timeless social philosophies; they were theoretical constructions tuned exquisitely to social change. The thinkers I have mentioned — Mill among them — had begun to figure out the relation between ideas and social change, and they were well aware that ideas which seemed urgently relevant in one era might seem anodyne or irrelevant in another. England, France, and America may have seemed progressive in the middle of the nineteenth century, and fear about individuality might have seemed overblown. But these thinkers feared that, as time went on, people who were at the time well-off, well-fed, and responsive to progress and innovation might proceed through various degrees of complacency to new forms of social repression — becoming timorous, diffident, and socially subservient in their character — so that the spurs to progress would be attenuated, and people would live their lives in comfortable but desperate quietude, never daring or attempting the shock of a new or unreceived idea or an unconventional way of life. So, then: what does Mill look like if we read him in this company?

Mill's Social Critique

To begin with, he can be read as much less of an atomist. Mill's social and political philosophy is sometimes described as excessively individualistic, with the distinction between self- and other-regarding actions (pp. 80–81) and his apparent privileging of the former regarded as prime evidence of this. In fact, *On Liberty* is focused very much on the social side of human nature. Mill recognizes that humans feel an intense need to be part of a social whole; and actually it is this need that generates many of the essay's main concerns. For example, when Mill worries that the modern individual is incapable of paying attention to his own self-development in his social and cultural decision making, he understands that it is the individual's sociability that threatens his individuality. Instead of thinking like individuals, people look all the time to what everyone else is doing: "It does not occur to them to have any inclination, except for what is customary. . . . Even in what people do for pleasure, conformity is the first thing thought of; they like in crowds; they exercise choice only among things commonly done: peculiarity of taste, eccentricity of conduct, are shunned equally with crimes" (p. 126). Now, Mill's response to this social conformism is not simply a normative individualism. He cannot simply say, "People *are* social; but they *ought* to behave more individualistically." For Mill respects and treasures human sociability. His moral philosophy assigns an important role to "the social feelings of mankind" — "the desire to be in unity with our fellow creatures."

> The social state is at once so natural, so necessary, and so habitual to man, that, except in some unusual circumstances or by an effort of voluntary abstraction, he never conceives himself otherwise than as a member of a body; and this association is riveted more and more, as mankind are further removed from the state of savage independence. . . . The deeply rooted conception which every individual even now has of himself as a social being, tends to make him feel it one of his natural wants that there should be harmony between his feelings and aims and those of his fellow creatures.

On this basis, Mill entertained in *Utilitarianism* the sunny hypothesis that people cannot help feeling concern for the interests of others, and that therefore the utilitarian creed does not need much support from external sanctions.[5]

Sociability plays an important role, too, in the argument of *On Liberty*. Mill says that it would be "a great misunderstanding" of his argument in the essay to suppose that he is prescribing "selfish indifference, which pretends that human beings have no business with each other's conduct in life" (p. 140). Even descriptively, the essay reveals a subtle understanding of human sociability. On the one hand, as we have just seen, it is the psychological basis of the social conformism that troubles Mill. On the other hand, it constitutes a dreadful vulnerability on the part of the individual to social pressure and social coercion. As social beings, we are much more vulnerable than atomistic individuals would be to one another's disapproval, particularly when it is expressed en masse. To the extent that we anticipate the prospect of the mass of our neighbors withholding their company from anyone with unorthodox views or unorthodox lifestyle, to that extent we all live "from the highest class of society down to the lowest, . . . as under the eye of a hostile and dreaded censorship" (p. 126). A society of atomists would not be vulnerable in this way; and if Mill's philosophy were simply one of normative atomism, he might just tell us to buck up and brace ourselves against the pain of this social isolation.[6] But such advocacy is not enough: if individuality is valued, it is a something that society must be taught to value. We are social beings, and the best way to protect us against social coercion is to warn others to be careful about the impact of their actions and judgments on our social vulnerabilities.

Another way in which this reading of *On Liberty* might affect our estimation of Mill as a social thinker has to do with the generation of preferences. Utilitarians and liberals are commonly supposed to profess indifference about the way in which individual preferences are generated. They take preferences as given, we are told, responding to them as mere data: they refuse to look behind the individual's preferences; they are interested only in tolerating and aggregating the satisfaction of such wants as actually exist.

Well, applied to the Mill that I am reading, in *On Liberty* and elsewhere, this is a slander. Mill is intensely interested in the social processes whereby preferences, opinions, and plans of life are generated. I have already cited the relevant passages from Chapter III of *On Liberty:* the point about people failing to ever ask themselves, "What do I prefer? or, what would suit my character and disposition? or, what would allow the best and highest in me to have fair play, and enable it to grow and thrive?"

> They ask themselves, what is suitable to my position? what is usually done by persons of my station and pecuniary circumstances? or (worse still) what is usually done by persons of a station and circumstances superior to mine? I do not mean that they choose what is customary, in preference to what suits their own inclination. It does not occur to them to have any inclination, except for what is customary. (p. 126)[7]

Moreover, Mill's interest in this is not just descriptive or sociological; he *evaluates* the processes by which preferences are generated. Large parts of his ethics — for example, the distinction between higher and lower pleasures — are unintelligible apart from the assumption that the generation of preferences is a proper subject for ethical scrutiny.[8]

Again, Mill is commonly taken to have believed that the truth will always emerge in modern society in "the marketplace of ideas."[9] Such an interpretation cannot possibly survive acquaintance with his pessimism about the current state of popular opinion in England, in regard to precisely those aspects of it that were most marketlike. For example:

> This is a reading age; and precisely because it is so reading an age, any book which is the result of profound meditation is perhaps less likely to be duly and profitably read than at a former period. The world reads too much and too quickly to read well. . . . It is difficult to know what to read, except by reading every thing; and so much of the world's business is now transacted through the press, that it is necessary to know what is printed, if we desire to know what is going on. Opinion weighs with so vast a weight in the balance of events, that ideas of no value in themselves are of importance from the mere circumstance that they *are*

ideas. . . . The world in consequence gorges itself with intellectual food; and in order to swallow the more bolts it.[10]

Reading this, one becomes aware of important complexities in the argument in Chapter II of *On Liberty,* "Of the Liberty of Thought and Discussion." The basis of Mill's case for liberty is not at all a complacent faith in the marketplace of ideas; it is a worry — a surprisingly resonant worry for us — that the public forum has already been corrupted by an atmosphere in which attention spans are cut short and no one will risk taking any idea seriously, as something worth bringing thoughtfully into critical relation with the truth. "Nothing is now read slowly or twice over."[11]

Commentators were tempted to adopt the market analogy by passages in *On Liberty* such as the following: "Truth, in the great practical concerns of life, is so much a question of the reconciling and combining of opposites, that very few have minds sufficiently capacious and impartial to make the adjustment with an approach to correctness, and it has to be made by the rough process of a struggle between combatants fighting under hostile banners" (p. 114). That *sounds* marketlike; it appears to invoke something like a Hayekian process, opposed to the idea of any one person (or a central authority) taking responsibility for bringing the rival views into dialectical relation with one another in a single place through the activity of a single mind.[12] It looks for truth as emergent from struggle, rather than truth as arrived at by synthesis. But Mill doubted very much whether this adversarial ideal could be approximated by actual social conditions in England. It was not enough for the state to withdraw from the fray. Unless society changed its complexion, the phenomena of mass timidity and collective mediocrity would ensure that nothing but the blandest platitudes were manufactured in the lukewarm ambience of the contemporary marketplace.

Changing Culture and Limiting Liberty

I intend the three examples I have just given — Mill on human sociability, on the generation of preferences, and on the "marketplace of ideas" — to illustrate the point that if we read *On Liberty* alert to concerns about culture rather than concerns about state and law, we will find in it a valuable contribution to the critique of modern society, a critique much more interesting than the rather sophomoric view of the essay that sees Mill simply as a theorist of limited government. At the same time, the approach that I am suggesting not only deepens and enriches our understanding of *On Liberty*.

It also transforms our sense of the problem that Mill has set himself in the essay.

Mill is concerned, we know, with liberty of opinion and lifestyle. But if we read him as a critic of culture, then we have to understand that his book is also a critique of contemporary opinion and lifestyle. It is opinions and lifestyles of a certain sort — moralistic and "improving" opinions and lifestyles — that he is trying to combat, against which he is trying to raise a "barrier of moral conviction" (p. 84). This means Mill is faced with two difficulties, one practical and one moral, which theories of limited government never have to face or which are much less formidable in something which is merely a theory of limited government.

As a practical matter, how do you go about limiting public opinion? Effecting social change is a much more difficult business than effecting legal change. Certainly legal change is much easier to get under way. Although they may require popular support, legislative or constitutional changes can be initiated by a few people — like John Stuart Mill himself — strategically placed in the politics of the day. But "society" is not under direct political control, and initiating social change involves immense collective action problems. Not only does one have to convince people of the value of individuality — "to see that it is good there should be differences, even though not for the better, even though, as it may appear to them, some should be for the worse" (p. 137) — one also has to persuade people to take the risk of acting on that conviction. This may be costly for each individual considered on her own. And the benefits for individuality are not always easy to see. It is hard for any one person to know what contribution her action or inaction may make to the tyranny of public opinion, and easy for her to suppose there is little she can do to ease the informal plight of liberty or individuality in mass society. Since this may be true of every member of the mass, it is conceivable that even if all could be convinced of Mill's concern, still nothing might happen to ameliorate the situation.

I think Mill is well aware of this difficulty. Certainly it would be wrong to attribute to him the mindless faith in normative argument that disfigures twentieth-century political philosophy.[13] Mill was heavily influenced by de Tocqueville's account of the limits of normative argument in the face of social movement, and his own comments at the beginning of one of his major reforming works — *The Subjection of Women* — provide a masterly analysis of the difficulties that face a purely normative or argumentative campaign.[14] To the extent that his work is normative, we should see Mill not as announcing (in the tones of an American law professor) "Here's what I would do if I ruled the world." We should read him instead as attempting —

with some pessimism and trepidation ("Can this be done? Have things not gone too far?") — to evoke a new mood and to awaken new concerns in the society he was addressing.

The second difficulty, as I have said, was moral rather than practical. It arises as follows. Insofar as Mill is seeking to weaken social coercion (in certain areas), he necessarily has to try to impose limits on what people do in their ordinary social lives. For the "engines of moral repression" (p. 83) and "the influences hostile to individuality" (p. 137) are not alien forces: they are *nothing but* the upshot of people's actions and inclinations in a social context. They comprise things that people want to do, things they feel like doing, things whose doing is "energetically supported by some of the best . . . feelings incident to human nature" (p. 84).[15] Placing limits on people's ability to act on these feelings and inclinations may itself give rise to an issue of liberty. People may have a right — or it may for other reasons be desirable for them to have the freedom — to do the things which, at least when taken en masse, constitute the social coercion which Mill is attempting to stop. Coercion by society consists, presumably, of a mass of actions, $a_1, a_2, \ldots a_n$ (where n is quite large), directed, say, at ostracizing some small circle of ethical or religious deviants. But any one of these actions, a_i, may be something which a person has a right to perform.

If I say for example, that Oscar Wilde may not be ostracized for his homosexuality and for his extravagant opinions on art and ethics, I imply that people like the Marquis of Queensberry must not exclude Wilde from their circle of friends.[16] But if I stop Queensberry from excluding Wilde from his circle of friends, I may be protecting Wilde's liberty from social ostracism, but I am also and necessarily attacking Queensberry's liberty to associate with whomever he likes. If I say to Queensberry, you must not ignore Wilde or cut him in the street when you meet him, then for the sake of protecting Wilde, I am forcing Queensberry to engage in social interactions that he doesn't want to engage in. Queensberry may say, with some justice, that he has a right to withdraw himself from the company of those (like Wilde) whom he despises. Or even if this is not a right, it is surely, Queensberry will say, a fundamental constituent of his liberty. It seems then that liberty is at risk on both sides of Mill's equation. It is at risk, he argues, from social pressure. But it is at risk, too, if we try to limit or eliminate social pressure.

Indeed, the problem may be even tighter than this. Queensberry's ability to choose the people with whom he associates is not just something he wants to be free to do; it is itself one of the bases on which he establishes his own distinctive moral identity. "We have a right . . . to act upon our unfavorable opinion of any one, not to the oppression of his individuality, *but in the exercise of ours.* We are not bound, for example, to seek his society; we have a right to avoid it (though not to parade the avoidance), for we have a right to choose the society most acceptable to us" (p. 141; my emphasis). To place limits on Queensberry's doing this because masses of such actions may amount to social coercion against Wilde may mean that we are having to interfere with liberty — now in exactly the sense in which Mill values it — in our effort to protect such liberty (from social coercion).

Nothing like this difficulty arises on the traditional interpretation. On the legalistic reading of the essay, Mill is trying to alter the behavior of legislators. Although legislators are often quite heavily invested in their campaigns, it would be silly to reproach Mill with trying to interfere with their individual freedom by limiting their ability to legislate. (To the extent that he can be accused of trying to interfere with the lifestyle of a moralistic legislator, that lifestyle just is a life devoted to restricting the liberty of others.) If Mill is right about the freedom that we — the legislator's subjects — are entitled to, then there is simply no problem with his intruding upon the "freedom" of the legislator. There can be no legitimate complaint about any limits we impose on the liberty of the legislators as such. Mill's limitation of the legislator's freedom is (in Kantian terms) coercion of the coercer, the negation of the negation of liberty.[17] However, if we are attempting to restrict society itself, rather than what Mill calls its "political functionaries" (p. 76), then we are in an altogether different ballgame. Now we are trying to restrict what private people do with their lives and the way they interact with others. And that is as much an affront to the liberty of the individual — indeed, of huge masses of individuals — as any other form of interference.

The problem here is similar to — though not quite the same as — a difficulty that arises from Mill's concession, in Chapter IV of *On Liberty,* that we "owe to each other help to distinguish the better from the worse, and encouragement to choose the former and avoid the latter" (p. 140). As I have noted, Mill does not want *On Liberty* to be read as a doctrine of "selfish indifference" (p. 140); he does not want to be seen as ruling out salutary moral interaction, persuasion, exhortation, and so on. So even in cases in which he thinks social pressure illegitimate, he still wants to leave room for argument. If Wilde is living in a way that Queensberry thinks is corrupt, unhealthy, or depraved, then although it is wrong for Queensberry to force Wilde (even by merely social pressure) to mend his ways, surely it is all right for Queensberry to argue with him or at least submit his point of view for Wilde's consideration.[18] Mill particularly needs this distinction between persuasion and coercion. To insulate individual liberty entirely from argument and contradiction, to deny, in effect, that moral persuasion was ever permissible, would undermine the whole basis of the argument in Chapter II about the importance of complacent believers' being confronted with moral and intellectual opposition (p. 103). If, in the interest, say, of Wilde's individuality, we rule out persuasion and argument as an appropriate response by Queensberry to Wilde's lifestyle, then (according to the argument of Chapter II) we make it less likely that anyone on either side of the interaction will take their own views seriously. Without vigorous argument, which may be disturbing to both parties, the position on each side "will be held in the manner of a prejudice" rather than a living truth (p. 118). Mill's overall case depends on the existence of vigorous argumentative interaction. So because he thinks some forms of social interaction are coercive, it is incumbent on him to find some way of distinguishing the argumentative from the coercive. But that distinction — all very well when persuasion is being contrasted with the violent means characteristic of the state — is much harder to draw when argument is being contrasted with the imperceptible pressure of public opinion. In that context, it is much more difficult to say when vigorous debate leaves off and inappropriate social pressure begins. This is especially so because Mill believes not only that we should engage in debate with other people and bring various considerations to their attention, but that we should if necessary "obtrude" our opinion on them — thrusting it forward even when they make it clear that it is not welcome (p. 140).[19] Mill seems to believe that it is perfectly all right for your neighbors to express in a way that is "telling and powerful" (p. 118) what they think of your eccentric lifestyle and your peculiar beliefs. How, then, is that offensive and obtrusive persuasion to be distinguished from what Mill wants to condemn, social pressure?

That is a delicate assignment. But even if Mill did not need that distinction between obtrusive moral persuasion (good) and social pressure (bad), he would still face the moral difficulty that I have identified. Limiting social pressure limits the liberty of those who exercise it. Protecting the individuality of people like Wilde seems to mean restricting the individuality of people like Queensberry.

At least one commentator has despaired of Mill's argument at this point, and suggested that we should scuttle back to the comparative straightforwardness of the legalistic account. The English political philosopher D. D. Raphael acknowledges that "when Mill talked of the scope of authority, he was not thinking simply of the law and the state. He was thinking of social pressure as well." But, he continues: "It is difficult enough to suggest a principle for limiting the authority of law, which consists for the most part of a definite series of rules. It is really impossible to suggest a practicable principle for limiting the exercise of social pressure which is manifested not only in action but also in words, looks, tone of voice, cast of countenance, all sorts of little things often not deliberate at all." Raphael thinks that Mill is attempting the impossible by trying to suggest "one simple principle" to govern the exercise of social pressure. So he says, in effect, "Let us adopt the legalistic interpretation, which makes the problem easier. Let us look at Mill's principle as though it had nothing to do with social pressure at all."[20] We, however, with our determination to read *On Liberty* as an essay on culture, should not allow ourselves to be infected with this philosophical pusillanimity. Or before we do, we should at least look at the way Mill proposed to deal with the difficulty, for he was, I think, acutely aware of the challenge it posed to his enterprise.

Untangling the Conundrum

How did John Stuart Mill answer the charge that a limit on social pressure is itself a limit on the liberty of those who make up the social mass? The problem is one that has to be approached from both sides — from the side of the person who is arguably implicated in the constitution of public opinion (in our example, the Marquis of Queensberry), and also from the side of the person who is vulnerable to public opinion (Oscar Wilde). From Queensberry's side, we must ask what sort of activities (in respect of people like Wilde) Queensberry needs to be able to perform if his (Queensberry's) liberty and individuality are not to be stifled. From Wilde's side, we have to ask what sort of activities (by Queensberry and others) Wilde needs to be protected from if his individuality and liberty are not to be crushed. If either distinction is unclear, the problem remains unsolved. And it remains unsolved, too, if the distinctions on the two sides do not match up. (That is, it remains unsolved if the actions that Queensberry needs to be able to perform are actions that Wilde needs to be protected from.)

Let us begin with Wilde. What sort of limit on Queensberry's actions does Wilde need to protect his individuality? One point that Mill makes involves concern about an individual's vulnerability to economic coercion: a person whose "pecuniary circumstances" leave him dependent on "the good will of other people" is likely to be intimidated out of the pursuit and expression of his own individual lifestyle if others condition their employment of him or their assistance to him on his ethical or religious conformity

(p. 100). Of course, absent any special circumstances, Wilde has no entitlement to Queensberry's support, and so Queensberry may "may give others a preference over him in optional good offices" (p. 141). But Mill suggests that things may be different if Queensberry goes out of his way to ensure that Wilde is denied employment or assistance. At that stage, Wilde would be the victim of a conscious effort to attach a conformity-condition to his economic vulnerability; and Mill certainly does want to raise a barrier against that. The same seems to be true of Wilde's vulnerability to ostracism. I have noted that as a social being, Wilde is vulnerable to being treated as an outcast. To avoid this predicament, Wilde does not need anyone to include him in any particular social circle, provided that no concerted effort is made to cast him out of society altogether. This, I think, is why Mill says that even if we have a right to avoid Wilde's company, we do not have a right "to parade the avoidance" (p. 141).[21] But the line is a delicate one, for Mill does not want to deny Queensberry the right to caution others against Wilde if he thinks "his example or conversation likely to have a pernicious effect on those with whom he associates" (p. 141). And its being permissible for Queensberry to warn others away from Wilde is perilously close to Queensberry's regarding it as permissible to orchestrate boycott and ostracism.

Mill tries to save the position by insisting that a distinction must be drawn between Queensberry's punishing Wilde and Wilde's experiencing social penalties "only in so far as they are the natural, and, as it were, the spontaneous consequences of the faults themselves" (p. 141). We can look at this purported distinction (between natural consequences and those that are artificially imposed by others as punishment) from a number of different angles: we can ask whether it makes any difference from Wilde's point of view; and we can ask too whether it captures anything significant so far as Queensberry's sense of his own rights are concerned.

Mill's view seems to be that the distinction ought to matter to Wilde. Wilde cannot reasonably expect, Mill says, that he will not suffer some disadvantage in regard to his own poor conduct, even if it is purely self-regarding. If he acts imprudently, for example, he must expect to suffer the disadvantages that imprudence connotes. In a case like financial misman-agement, the line between natural and artificial consequences is pretty straightforward: "We shall reflect that he already bears, or will bear, the whole penalty of his error; if he spoils his life by mismanagement, we shall not, for that reason, desire to spoil it still further" (p. 143). Wilde can hardly ask to be protected from the financial consequences of bad investments, say, simply to vindicate his "originality" as a businessman!

The difficulty lies in cases where it is arguable that the natural consequences of the conduct include the moralistic reaction of others. Mill says (of someone like Wilde): "A person who shows rashness, obstinacy, self-conceit — who cannot live within moderate means — who cannot restrain himself from hurtful indulgences — who pursues animal pleasures at the expense of those of feeling and intellect — must expect to be lowered in the opinion of others and to have a less share of their favorable sentiments" (pp. 141–42). Wilde has no right to complain of this, Mill suggests, for it is something he should have taken into account in deciding upon his action.

I don't think this will do. Mill's way of putting it makes it sound as though Wilde has chosen to incur social obloquy: by making a bad choice, he chose to put up with the consequences of others' "natural" response to its badness. But the lowering of a person in the opinion of others described in this passage is not necessarily a consequence of the badness of that person's choices. It is a consequence of the unpopularity of his choices, and it would attach to them even if they were noble and generous in themselves, provided only that they were contemptible in the eyes of the crowd. If Mill wants to sustain this sort of "What did you expect?" point, he has to be willing to say it of anyone who has courted the majority's disfavor, whether that person's actions are good or bad, noble or ignoble. And if he is willing to do that, he might as well give up the whole argument.

I think Mill wants to say that Wilde has a right to be protected only against actions that are intended punitively — that is, "purposely inflicted on him for the sake of punishment" (p. 141).[22] We will consider in a moment whether sense can be made of this distinction from Queensberry's point of view. Before we get to that, however, we may wonder whether this distinction really matters to Wilde. If the effect of a social response is the same, why should the intention make a difference? As Mill's great Victorian critic James Fitzjames Stephen observed, "It is like telling a rose that it ought to smell sweet only for the purpose of affording pleasure to the owner of the ground in which it grows. People form and express their opinions on each other, which, collectively, form public opinion, for a thousand reasons; to amuse themselves; for the sake of something to talk about; to gratify this or that momentary feeling; but the effect of such opinions, when formed, is quite independent of the grounds of their formation."[23] Mill is trying to make us solicitous of individuality, trying to teach us to care about it, in cases where we might otherwise be careless. So it would not be enough for Queensberry to say, "I didn't intend to punish Wilde," if his response to Wilde's lifestyle nevertheless contributes recklessly to making the social environment more stifling. In other words, whether our reasons for shunning a person or avoiding his company are punitive or nonpunitive, the effect may be the same. It is the effect, not the intention, that Mill cares about (at least so far as his arguments for liberty are concerned). Remember, too, that we are not just talking about Queensberry's individual response, considered in isolation: we are talking about Queensberry's response as part of a mass response to people like Wilde. From that perspective, probably too much has been given away already in Mill's argument, in his concession of pity and dislike. The expression of other people's pity and dislike, especially when they are mass expressions — expressions of the majority's pity and dislike — are already sufficiently powerful social sanctions to lead to all the bad consequences that Mill predicted if the individual were not sheltered from the pressure of those around him. In its effect social pressure is social pressure no matter what its motivation. And because it is the effect of social pressure that Mill is concerned about — its effect on the mental life of individuals, its effect on the pursuit of truth, its effect on progress, and its effect on the overall social atmosphere — I do not think that this distinction between intentionally punitive and nonpunitive pressure will do the work that Mill wants it to do.

There is a general point to be made here about conceptions of toleration and neutrality. Political philosophers often ask whether those concepts are to be understood as concerned with intentions or consequences. Is a law, for example, neutral if it does not have the purpose of disadvantaging a particular religion, or is it neutral only if its impact turns out to be neutral (whatever the purpose might have been)? Some philosophers think that this is something you can read off from the concept of neutrality.[24] But this is a mistake. Neutrality is a concept of which there are many conceptions, and which conception one chooses depends on the character of one's argument.[25] If one makes an argument like that of John Locke in the *Letter Concerning Toleration,* the conception will be intentionalist, because Locke is arguing that the enterprise of using coercion to change belief is necessarily irrational, and this argument has no grip on action which does not have this as its aim.[26] But if one's argument is consequentialist, as Mill's undoubtedly is, then one is not free to simply adopt an intentionalist conception.[27] One must follow one's values where they lead, and in Mill's case, they lead us in direction of concern about the effect of social pressure on Wilde's individuality, whether that effect is intended by anyone or not.

Let us look at the matter now from Queensberry's side. Queensberry claims a right to act upon an unfavorable opinion of Wilde, not to the oppression of Wilde's individuality but in the exercise of his own. Mill reckons that Queensberry has to be allowed to have and express distaste for Wilde's values: as he puts it, "a person could not have the opposite qualities

in due strength without entertaining these feelings" (p. 141). And Queensberry is entitled also to act on his distaste. He is not bound, Mill suggests, to
seek Wilde's society; he has a right to avoid it, for he has a right to choose
the society most acceptable to his own values (p. 141). So much Mill
concedes.

He insists, however, that Queensberry does not need and may not claim
the right to punish or penalize Wilde. Thus Wilde may be to Queensberry
"an object of pity, perhaps of dislike, but not of anger or resentment" (p.
143). He has no right to try to penalize Wilde, for this is not something, Mill
suggests, that is required for the integrity of Queensberry's own moral
position. Even if the penalty is purely social, Queensberry has no need and
no right to inflict it or to orchestrate or participate in its infliction.

I wonder whether this is really well thought through. There is, first, the
sheer difficulty of actually drawing the distinction. A. D. Bain suggested in
1880 that Mill "might have gone further and drawn up a sliding scale or
graduated table of modes of behaviour, from the most intense individual
preference at the one end to the severest reprobation at the other. At least
fifteen or twenty perceptible distinctions could be made; and a place found
for every degree of merit and demerit. Because a person does not stand high
in our esteem, it does not follow that we are punishing or persecuting him;
the point where punishment in any proper sense could be said to begin
would be about the middle of the scale."[28] Once we start thinking along
these lines, it is obviously going to be very difficult to establish a consensus
as to the point at which disapproval leaves off and punishment begins. In
itself, that may be a smaller difficulty for Mill, because he is not proposing
to use this distinction as the basis of any sort of legislated test. And anyway,
the prospect of dissensus does not by itself establish that the distinction is in
principle misconceived.

But there is a larger difficulty. In moral philosophy, Mill actually takes
the position that there is no distinction at all to be drawn between the
judgment that something is wrong and the view that a punitive approach is
appropriate. "We do not call anything wrong, unless we mean to imply that
a person ought to be punished in some way or other for doing it; if not by
law, by the opinion of his fellow-creatures; if not by opinion, by the re-
proaches of his own conscience. . . . It is a part of the notion of Duty in every
one of its forms, that a person may rightfully be compelled to fulfil it."[29] If
we insist that Queensberry may not respond punitively to Wilde, we are, on
Mill's analysis, limiting the kind of judgment he can make. And that in turn
threatens to deprive Queensberry of any way of expressing his own values
and his own ethical commitments. The only way Mill can untangle this is to

deny that it is ever necessary or appropriate for someone like Queensberry to use the language of right and wrong in relation to self-regarding ethics, or to ever speak of another failing in a duty that he owes primarily to himself. Apparently Mill is willing to flirt with this position, for he says, in Chapter IV of *On Liberty:* "What are called duties to ourselves are not socially obligatory, unless circumstances render them at the same time duties to others. The term duty to oneself, when it means anything more than prudence, means self-respect or self-development" (p. 142). But I am not sure how far Mill is willing to take this, or how far he understands that the logical upshot of this would be not just a critique of culture but a thoroughgoing critique of existing moral vocabulary (to purge it of all its implicitly punitive elements, so far as self-regarding conduct is concerned).

A Barrier of Moral Conviction

How much of the difficulty we have been examining stems from the impression that Mill is trying to put a stop to certain attitudes and activities that Queensberry might want to express and pursue in his dealings with Wilde? We are worried about the impact that a defense of Wilde's liberty will have on Queensberry's liberty. But is Mill really proposing something that would affect Queensberry's liberty at all? Maybe we have lost sight of the point that Mill is not proposing to legislate against social pressure. Social pressure (not law) is indeed his main target, but social pressure (not law) is also his instrument. He is proposing only to try and raise "a strong barrier of *moral* conviction" (p. 84; my emphasis) against the way people express their moralistic opinions. He wants the harm principle to be accepted, but he is not proposing to have it imposed by force.

Now this won't quite do. For if Mill is right in the thesis we began with — that social pressure is as every bit as oppressive as legal coercion — then social pressure imposed for the sake of individuality is presumably at least as consequential as its legislative imposition would be. To put it crudely, Mill wants to enlist the intelligent members of the public to pressure people like Queensberry not to pressure people like Wilde. But if such people are acting (with others) in a way that amounts to social coercion of Queensberry, then the problem is not avoided after all. We still have the same symmetry: either there will be social pressure exerted against Wilde's ethical individuality by Queensberry (and his crowd) or there will be social pressure exerted against Queensberry's ethical individuality by the high-mindedly tolerant crowd.

Perhaps there is a way out of the difficulty — a way that brings us back to the theme of Mill as a critic of contemporary culture. At the end of Chapter III of *On Liberty,* Mill suggests that he will have succeeded in raising the moral barrier that he wants to raise against the moralistic impositions of public opinion if only "the intelligent part of the public" can be made to see and feel the value of individuality and the value of free and open interaction between opinions and lifestyles (p. 137). The intelligent part of the public must be made "to see that it is good there should be differences, even though not for the better, even though, as it may appear to them, some should be for the worse" (p. 137). If the intelligent part of the public can be made to see the value of diversity, then Mill suggests we may be able to influence public opinion in a more liberal direction so that the morality of the masses becomes in some sense at least partly a liberal morality.[30] This is not a matter of imposing anything on them, or or limiting their liberty, even by social means. It is a matter rather of conveying the importance of some value to them, in a way that can subsequently factor into their own thought about their exercise of liberty. Any right, we know, can be exercised better or worse.[31] *On Liberty* is written in order to convey to people — something that may not have occurred to them — that there are ways of exercising their associational and other rights better or worse, so far as individuality and progress are concerned.

The issue, then, that has been troubling us may be posed not as: "Is Mill's case in *On Liberty* an unacceptable restriction on people's right to associate with whomever they choose, and express their own values as they choose?" but rather "Is it a reasonable request to make of them that they bear Mill's case in mind as they exercise their rights of expression and association?" Queensberry is not having his rights trampled on or denied. Instead, he is being asked to exercise them more considerately, rather in the way in which we ask someone to vote for the right candidate, or exercise his property rights philanthropically. Once we see the question in those terms, it is far from clear that the "barrier" Mill is trying to raise is unreasonable or that it would defeat the purpose of having associational or other similar rights in the first place.

I admit that this way of looking at the matter is not a panacea for all the difficulties we have been examining. If Queensberry takes seriously Mill's urging to be more considerate in his response to Wilde, Queensberry still has to find a way to make that considerateness compatible with the expressive integrity of his own values and convictions. And that conundrum is as difficult as we have found it to be. But it is not now an issue of liberty. It is to be seen more as a matter of liberal ethics: the perennial problem the liberal faces of being true to his own values and yet tolerant of the values of others.

Earlier I alluded to Mill's practical problem. How can one person hope to change a whole culture? What good can any individual do, what good does any single reader of *On Liberty* think that he can do, against a whole atmosphere of mental slavery in society? I have said that the difficulty seemed to have the shape of a collective action problem: why should I play my part in the battle to support individuality — and what, indeed, can I do — if I am not sure that others will play theirs? I want to conclude by suggesting — optimistically — that maybe this puts the matter exactly the wrong way around.

The threat to liberty and individuality comes from the collective action of the public, inadvertently but lethally embodied in a concerted public opinion and a monolithic social atmosphere. "Formerly, different ranks, different neighborhoods, different trades and professions, lived in what might be called different worlds" (p. 137). But in our time even more than in Mill's, with an increase in mobility, an increase in commerce and manufacture, an increase in the scope of the media, and an increase in common education, people are terribly vulnerable to mass public opinion. People "now read the same things, go to the same places, have their hopes and fears directed to the same objects," and so on (p. 137). There is no need, really, for partisans of individuality to concoct an equally concerted campaign to oppose that, because, on Mill's account, liberty will have a chance of flourishing whenever the social environment is *dis*concerted, whenever it is *not* collectively organized. This is one of those wonderful instances where the term "collective action problem" actually means what it says — it is collective action that is the problem, and there is no need for collective action in order to secure a solution. Any form of chaos, any lack of coordination, in individual views and lifestyles will help (though of course, the more the better).

This doesn't mean that the problem is easy: just that it does not partake of the particular difficulty associated with concerted campaigns. To repeat — the problem for Mill is that people "like in crowds." The solution is the encouragement of just about any form of "liking" — any kind of preference, or opinion formation — that breaks up that monolith. People do not need to be assured, as they take the first steps in Mill's campaign, that they will be working in close coordination with all others who follow them in responding to his call. Simply by starting to assert their own individuality in a way that does not involve this desperate taking of cues from and emulation of others, they will be doing all that may reasonably be expected of them, and all it takes, for their part, to clog up "the engines of moral repression."

NOTES

1. By the way, it is worth noting Mill's observation that popularization of the phrase "the tyranny of the majority" was one of the few deplorable effects of Alexis de Tocqueville's work *Democracy in America.* John Stuart Mill, "M. de Tocqueville on Democracy in America" (1840), in Mill, *Dissertations and Discussions: Political, Philosophical, and Historical* (New York, 1882), 2: 81.

2. For example: Alexis de Tocqueville, *Democracy in America,* 2 vols. (New York, 1994); Karl Marx, *Grundrisse* (Harmondsworth, 1973); Friedrich Engels, *The Condition of the Working Class in England* (Oxford, 1971); Emile Durkheim, *The Division of Labor in Society* (Glencoe, Ill., 1949); Max Weber, *The Protestant Ethic and the Spirit of Capitalism* (New York, 1930).

3. As Mill put it in his *Autobiography* (New York, 1957), p. 162, the fear was that "the inevitable growth of social equality . . . should impose on mankind an oppressive yoke of uniformity in opinion and practice."

4. For the image of China as a "stationary society," see John Stuart Mill, "Guizot's Essays and Lectures on History" (1845), in *Dissertations and Discussions* (New York, 1882), 2: 317–18, where this fate is predicted for the United States. See also *On Liberty,* pp. 135–36.

5. John Stuart Mill, *Utilitarianism,* ed. George Sher (Indianapolis, 1979), pp. 30, 31, 33.

6. However, he does say something to this effect in an earlier essay. See John Stuart Mill, "Civilization" (1836), in *Dissertations and Discussions,* 1: 206–7: "Compared with former times, there is in the more opulent classes of modern civilized communities much more of the amiable and humane, and much less of the heroic. The heroic essentially consists in being ready, for a worthy object, to do and to suffer, but especially to do, what is painful and disagreeable; and whoever does not early learn to be capable of this will never be a great character. There has crept over the refined classes, over the whole class of gentlemen in England, a moral effeminacy, an inaptitude for every kind of struggle. They . . . cannot brook ridicule, they cannot brave evil tongues: they have not hardihood to say an unpleasant thing to anyone whom they are in the habit of seeing, or to face,

even with a nation at their back, the coldness of some little coterie which surrounds them."

7. Consider also this comment on the role of newspapers: "The real political unions of England are the newspapers. It is these which tell every person what all other persons are feeling, and in what manner they are ready to act: it is by these that the people learn, it may truly be said, their own wishes, and through these that they declare them." "M. de Tocqueville," *Dissertations and Discussions,* 2: 96–97.

8. See the discussion in Elizabeth S. Anderson, "John Stuart Mill and Experiments in Living," *Ethics,* 102 (1991): 4–26, and Michael S. McPherson, "Mill's Moral Theory and the Problem of Preference Change," *Ethics,* 92 (1982): 252–73.

9. That is a phrase which was never his, and I think would never have occurred to him. I believe it was first used in the dissent of Justice Holmes in *Abrams v. United States* 250 U.S. 616 (1919).

10. "Civilization," 1: 211–12.

11. Ibid., 1: 212.

12. Cf. F. A. Hayek, *The Constitution of Liberty* (London, 1960), pp. 22–25.

13. See Jeremy Waldron, "What Plato Would Allow," in *Nomos XXXVII: Theory and Practice,* ed. Ian Shapiro and Judith Wagner DeCew (New York, 1995). See also Richard Posner, *The Problematics of Moral and Legal Theory* (Cambridge, 1999), pp. 3–90.

14. See the discussion in Mill, "M. de Tocqueville," pp. 84–85. See also Tocqueville, *Democracy in America,* 1: 3–16 (Author's Introduction). John Stuart Mill, *The Subjection of Women,* in *On Liberty and Other Essays,* ed. John Gray (Oxford, 1991), pp. 471–77.

15. In his *Autobiography,* pp. 161–62, Mill notes that he himself was inclined in this direction (before he fell under the influence of Harriet Taylor): "There was a moment in my mental progress when I might easily have fallen into a tendency towards over-government, both social and political; as there was also a moment when, by reaction from a contrary excess, I might have become a less thorough radical and democrat than I am. In both these points, as in many others, she benefited me as much by keeping me right where I was right, as by leading me to new truths, and ridding me of errors."

16. I use these historical names, instead of the usual algebra ("Suppose X does A to Y"), just to make the argument more vivid. The Marquis of Queensberry was the father of Lord Alfred Douglas, a friend and intimate of Oscar Wilde's at the height of Wilde's notoriety. Infuriated by the asso-

ciation, Queensberry brought about Wilde's ruin by publicly accusing him of being a sodomite, leading Wilde to commence an ill-fated lawsuit for defamation.

17. Immanuel Kant, *The Metaphysics of Morals,* trans. Mary Gregor (Cambridge, 1996), pp. 25–26.

18. As Mill puts it at the beginning of the essay, although a person's own good or his own self-regarding virtue are never good reasons for compelling him — whether the means of compulsion are legal or social — they "are good reasons for remonstrating with him, or reasoning with him, or persuading him, or entreating him, but not for compelling him, or visiting him with any evil, in case he do otherwise" (p. 80).

19. See Mill's criticisms of received notions of temperate or moderate discussion, pp. 118–20. See also his comments on the relation between character, virtue, and passion, pp. 124–25, and the discussion in Peter Berkowitz, "Mill: Liberty, Virtue, and the Discipline of Individuality," in Eisenbach, *Mill and the Moral Character of Liberalism* (University Park, Pa., 1999), p. 32.

20. D. D. Raphael, "Liberty and Authority," in A. Phillips Griffiths, ed., *Of Liberty: The 15th Royal Institute Of Philosophy Lecture Series* (Cambridge, 1983), p. 5. "Still, let us look at Mill's principle as if it were a proposal for the limits of law. It has been used like that in recent controversy about the scope of the criminal law."

21. Cf. Alan Ryan, *The Philosophy of John Stuart Mill,* 2d ed. (Atlantic Highlands, N.J., 1990), p. 237: "It seems coercion is involved where harm is *organized* to deter someone from an action."

22. The element of punitive intention seems to be crucial also to Alan Ryan's interpretation, in *The Philosophy of John Stuart Mill,* p. 238: "The crucial point about ill-consequences which are contrived and organized is that they are inflicted on the individual *because* he has done whatever it is, and not simply as a causal consequence of the action." Unfortunately, however, Ryan spends too much time establishing the reality of this distinction, and not enough time to establishing its importance.

23. James Fitzjames Stephen, *Liberty, Equality, Fraternity* (1873) in Gerald Dworkin, ed. *Mill's On Liberty: Critical Essays* (Lanham, Md., 1997), p. 175.

24. See Robert Nozick, *Anarchy, State, and Utopia* (Oxford, 1974), pp. 271–73, and Joseph Raz, *The Morality of Freedom* (Oxford, 1986), p. 113.

25. See Jeremy Waldron, "Legislation and Moral Neutrality," in *Liberal Rights: Collected Papers, 1981–1991* (Cambridge, 1993), pp. 151–53.

26. John Locke, *A Letter Concerning Toleration,* ed. Patrick Romanell

(Upper Saddle River, N.J., 1950), pp. 18–19, 34. See also Jeremy Waldron, "Locke, Toleration, and the Rationality of Persecution," in *Liberal Rights,* pp. 103–7.

27. See Waldron, *Liberal Rights,* pp. 106, 151.

28. A. Bain, "John Stuart Mill," *Mind,* 5 (1880): 89.

29. *Utilitarianism,* p. 47.

30. This, by the way, is a intriguing example of Mill's so-called elitism — hoping to turn public opinion around and raise moral barriers in popular consciousness against social repression, by appealing in the first instance to an educated and intelligent elite. Of course, if you take the legalistic interpretation of *On Liberty,* then it is obvious that one appeals to the elite, because they are (or, on Mill's theory of representation, they ought to be) the ones with the most control over legislative decision making. See John Stuart Mill, *Considerations on Representative Government* (Buffalo, N.Y., 1991), p. 335. But in *On Liberty* Mill proposes to appeal to the elite in a much less straightforward role — in their capacity as leaders of popular opinion and molders of popular consciousness. His feeling seems to be that if the educated and intelligent cannot be convinced of the danger of social repression, there is no hope at all of influencing popular opinion at large.

31. See the discussion in Jeremy Waldron, "A Right to Do Wrong," *Ethics,* 92 (1981): 21 (rpt. in Waldron, *Liberal Rights,* p. 63).

Bibliography

The indispensable resource for a student of Mill is the thirty-one-volume *Collected Works of John Stuart Mill,* published by the University of Toronto Press and Routledge and Kegan Paul, under the general editorship of J. M. Robson (Toronto and London, 1963–91). Below is a selection from a wide and valuable scholarly literature, dealing first with *On Liberty* itself, and second more generally with the life, thought, and milieu of John Stuart Mill. We include a few collections of articles by several hands, as well as critical editions of *On Liberty* that reprint essays of some interest.

Writings About *On Liberty*

Berger, Fred R. *Happiness, Justice, and Freedom.* Berkeley, 1984.

Cowling, Maurice. *Mill and Liberalism.* Cambridge, 1963.

Donner, Wendy. *The Liberal Self.* Ithaca, N.Y., 1991.

Dworkin, Gerald, ed. *Mill's On Liberty: Critical Essays.* Lanham, N.Y., 1997.

Eisenach, Eldon J., ed. *Mill and the Moral Character of Liberalism.* University Park, Pa., 1998.

Friedrich, Carl J., ed. *Liberty,* NOMOS 4. New York, 1962.

Gray, John. *Mill on Liberty: A Defence.* London, 1983.

Gray, John, and G. W. Smith, eds. *J. S. Mill: On Liberty in Focus.* Cambridge, 1983.

Griffiths, A. Phillips, ed. *Of Liberty.* Cambridge, 1983.

Hamburger, Joseph. *John Stuart Mill on Liberty and Control.* Princeton, 1999.

Himmelfarb, Gertrude. *On Liberty and Liberalism: The Case of John Stuart Mill.* New York, 1974.

McCloskey, H. J. *John Stuart Mill: A Critical Study.* London, 1971.

Pyle, Andrew, ed. *Liberty: Contemporary Responses to John Stuart Mill.* New York, 1954.

Radcliff, Peter, ed. *Limits of Liberty: Studies of Mill's On Liberty.* Belmont, Calif., 1966.

Rees, John C. *John Stuart Mill's On Liberty*. Oxford, 1985.

Riley, Jonathan. *Mill on Liberty*. London, 1998.

Robson, John A. *The Improvement of Mankind: The Social and Political Thought of John Stuart Mill*. Toronto, 1968.

Ryan, Alan. *John Stuart Mill*. New York, 1970.

———, ed. *Mill*. Norton critical edition. New York, 1997.

Skorupski, John, ed. *The Cambridge Companion to Mill*. Cambridge, 1998.

Spitz, David, ed. *On Liberty*. Norton critical edition. New York, 1975.

Stephen, James Fitzjames. *Liberty, Equality, Fraternity*. Cambridge, 1965.

Ten, C. L. *Mill on Liberty*. Oxford, 1980.

Villa, Dana. *Socratic Citizenship*. Princeton, 2001.

Writings About Mill's Life and Thought

Bain, Alexander. *James Mill: A Biography*. London, 1882.

———. *John Stuart Mill: A Criticism*. London, 1882.

Berlin, Isaiah. *Four Essays on Liberty*. London, 1969.

Burrow, J. W. *The Crisis of Reason: European Thought, 1848–1918*. New Haven, 2000.

———. *Whigs and Liberals: Continuity and Change in English Political Thought*. Oxford, 1988.

Carlisle, Janice. *John Stuart Mill and the Writing of Character*. Athens, Ga., 1991.

Collini, Stefan. *Public Moralists: Political Thought and Intellectual Life in Britain, 1850–1930*. Oxford, 1991.

Courtney, W. L. *The Life of John Stuart Mill*. London, 1889.

Dicey, A. V. *Law and Public Opinion in England During the Nineteenth Century*. London, 1952.

Halévy, Elie. *The Growth of Philosophic Radicalism*. Boston, 1955.

Hayek, F. A. *John Stuart Mill and Harriet Taylor*. London, 1951.

Lecky, W. E. H. *Democracy and Liberty*. London, 1896.

Letwin, Shirley. *The Pursuit of Certainty*. Cambridge, 1965.

Oakeshott, Michael. *Morality and Politics in Modern Europe*. Cambridge, Mass., 1993.

Packe, Michael St. John. *The Life of John Stuart Mill*. London, 1954.

Pankhurst, Richard. *The Saint-Simonians, Mill, and Carlyle: A Preface to Modern Thought*. London, 1957.

Ruggiero, Guido de. *The History of European Liberalism*. Oxford, 1927.

Ryan, Alan. *J. S. Mill*. London, 1974.

Semmel, Bernard. *John Stuart Mill and the Pursuit of Virtue*. New Haven, 1984.

Stephen, Leslie. *The English Utilitarians*. London, 1900.

Trevelyan, G. M. *British History in the Nineteenth Century and After, 1782–1919*. London, 1947.

Turner, Frank Miller. *Between Science and Religion: The Reaction to Scientific Naturalism in Late Victorian England*. New Haven, 1974.

Rethinking the Western Tradition